A DOCTOR IN PARLIAMENT

DONALD McI. JOHNSON

A

DOCTOR

IN

PARLIAMENT

CHRISTOPHER JOHNSON

LONDON

CHRISTOPHER JOHNSON © 1958

First published 1958

SET IN 11/12 PT. TIMES AND PRINTED AND MADE IN
GREAT BRITAIN BY PAGE BROS. (NORWICH) LTD. FOR
CHRISTOPHER JOHNSON PUBLISHERS LTD.,
11/14 STANHOPE MEWS WEST, LONDON, S.W.7

CONTENTS

This book is dedicated

to

Betty

and to
those several others who either
do not figure prominently in this
book, or do not figure in it
at all, but without whose
help and support it could
never have been written

AUTHOR'S PREFACE

Frequently, while seeking self-expression, one finds that the words for which one gropes are already said far better than one could hope to do so oneself.

So, with this Preface, I am able to quote Lord Hailsham in his speech to the Northern Home Counties Area Conservative Association on 22nd April, 1958.

"Being a Conservative," said Lord Hailsham, "does not mean rigid acceptance of every item of policy of a Conservative Government. We encourage differences of opinion to be honestly aired."

My forthcoming pages will not invariably reveal signs of that encouragement of which Lord Hailsham speaks. None the less, it is in this spirit that this book has been written and it is hoped that the thoughts and impressions of a single Conservative backbencher, a recruit from the Liberal Party, concerning the crucial and interesting years of the second post-War Conservative Government, will be of value and interest in solving the problems that face us.

Over and beyond this I have also endeavoured to tell a further instalment of my personal story, in particular the further denouement of that curious aspect of it which I dealt with in *A Doctor Returns*.

I am grateful to the *Spectator* and the *Twentieth Century* for permission to reproduce articles and extracts; and also to all those who indirectly have become contributors to these pages.

DONALD JOHNSON

A NEW BOY IN AN OLD SCHOOL

A *Doctor Regrets*, *A Doctor Returns* have been my previous books. And now *A Doctor Resigns*? How liltingly the alliteration trips off the tongue. Resignation after all, has been in the air on my side of the House of Commons and why not I? None the less, I am still here. ("Don't resign. Wait until they throw you out" is an adage that has tended to be neglected by all too many of my colleagues.) I am still here, maintaining my precarious prospects with my majority of 370, narrow enough, but good enough to grant me a length of term in Parliament such as better men with larger majorities have not always been granted. So, as I am still here, a Doctor in Parliament and, as my book essentially centres on the activities of a Doctor in Parliament, so be it. Let it be entitled *A Doctor in Parliament*.

One of the problems of that special subject of mental health, concerning which this book has something to say, is that of institutionalization. "Don't let our lunatics loose" yells the *Daily Express* in its editorial of 3rd July, 1957. But neither the *Daily Express*, nor its anxious readers, need greatly worry. The locked doors of our mental hospitals are opened through the modern, progressive change of policy, but far from escaping, the patients do not wish to go—they wander across the green fields, or round the suburban streets and that is all—they are too dependent on the institution and are unable to thrive without it.

Thus, arguing in the reverse fashion to usual, from the ridiculous to the sublime, the same principles apply to that most august of all institutions to which I belong. That formidably

underlined document—the Party Whip—appears in Friday
morning's post. "Divisions will take place and your attendance
throughout the sitting is particularly requested." Then, with
Monday afternoon, the treadmill starts for another week.

Yet even the harshest of régimes has its elements of re-
laxation. Perhaps there is only the uncertain message that
"divisions may take place"; perhaps unexpectedly "the whipping
is relaxed"; perhaps there is a Second Reading debate and no
division summons until 9.30 p.m. Yet we, the inmates, are loth
to leave and stay about haunting our place of detention.

So, the prey of centripetal force on one hand and centrifugal
force on the other, I pursue an evening stroll along the Embankment, roaming as far as Charing Cross Bridge, before being
overcome by the feeling that I may be wanted, that there may be
a 'Count', or that I must talk to So-and-so if he is about, or that
I must book the tickets for my next journey to Carlisle, or that I
have forgotten to get a copy of the recently issued Report of
the Inter-Departmental Committee on The Teaching of Botany
in Girls' Schools as a Causative Factor of Prostitution; and I
am drawn backwards once again.

I return along the Embankment, that same path along which
I would walk in my medical student days, when, well over
thirty years ago, the first overwhelming desire to enter Parliament seized me and changed the course of my life. I have told
in my first autobiography, *A Doctor Regrets* . . ., how this
happened and also, in my subsequent book *Bars and Barricades*,
how the barque of my political fortunes was tossed about on
the stormy sea of unending political disaster. But the goal had
stayed with me throughout; and here I am.

During all these gloomy years there had loomed in front of
me the Fata Morgana, the vision of the Promised Land. It is
natural enough that this vision should, for one born into the
circumstances of a provincial professional home as I was, take

the shape of the parliamentary era of my boyhood, the era of the great Liberal politicians: natural enough too that this idealized Parliament should remain, as it were, as an archetype of thought in my mind, even though I lacked any direct knowledge that might relate it to actual fact. Indeed, at my first impact with facts, I found them disappointing; for I have described my feelings of deflation when, as a medical student, I obtained a spectator's ticket, only to find myself listening to the Clydeside members, those reforming zealots of the nineteen twenties, devoting parliamentary time to the discussion of the need for installing separate ladies' and gentlemen's lavatories in the Scottish expresses.

(Now, suddenly, thirty years later, travelling northwards on my constituency ticket as Member for Carlisle, I am unexpectedly reminded of that distant debate when, about to enter the train lavatory, I find the door marked LADIES and, as a consequence of this, I have to walk back along the length of the coach to the lavatory at the other end before I can accommodate myself. Who says that progress does not take place in this static country of ours?)

Yes, here I am and I no longer have to walk up and down outside the railings, as I did those many years ago. But I stride through to the end of that mysterious underground passage beneath Parliament Street, whither, despite the fact that it is entirely public, I had never hitherto ventured prior to my election to Parliament, along the cloistered pavement and across to the Members' entrance, exchanging signs of recognition with our habitual Cerberus, P.C. A 234.

How thoughtful of them, it occurs to me in passing (and you will note that, as an M.P., one still thinks of *them*), to put the most cheerful policeman of the lot on to our Members' entrance! Though all our policemen at the House are, of course, wonderful. ("Who says we are not a Police State?" remarks my son Christopher with the irreverence of youth, as the cries of "DEE—VEE—ZHUN" echo through the Westminster corridors, rounding up straying members for the vote, and interrupting our cosy chat in the downstairs bar.) But the cheerful greeting of P.C. A 234, as we enter our slightly sombre premises, has often seemed one of the brightest features of the parliamentary day.

"See you in school."

So runs the routine valedictory greeting between parliamentary colleagues who have met during the Recess.

For me, at least, this remark has more than a facetious significance. As I walk up the inner cloister to the swing doors leading to the Members' Cloakroom, this is not only like school: it IS school. This Victorian Gothic architecture of the 1840 period, the mock buttresses and the crenellated decoration on the exterior, the stone staircase, the alcoved lattice windows inside, are identical with those of Cheltenham College, built at just this same period and, one almost suspects, by the same architect. Once again, I am the lonely boy, the boy whom nobody talked to, the boy who walked to College by himself while others linked in two's and three's, the outsider long before the days of Mr. Colin Wilson's 'Outsider'—the reason for this being (and I do not record it without some sense of amusement) that, though today in my years of maturity I may fill a substantial part of a parliamentary bench with my seventeen stones in weight and six feet two and three-quarters in height, in those days I was 'a physical wreck', a designation in large part arising from my inability to co-ordinate in dealing with any ball, of whatever size or shape. Moreover, I compounded this offence by being a Scholar also! Thus incurring a dual stigma, a double untouchability that put one quite beyond redemption in the Public School ethos of my day.

Indeed "A New Boy in an Old School" is, I find, the title of my first article which I contributed as a Member of Parliament to my local paper, the *Cumberland News:* and this is what I say:

This is a new school that I am in. It is, of course, the oldest of old schools of parliamentary democracy. It is merely I who am 'the new boy'.

I am back 40 years ago in my first term at Cheltenham College looking anxiously round to see that there is no prefect in sight ready to tell me that I am not allowed to put my hand in my trouser's pocket; I am in my first few days at Cambridge speculating (after the restrictions of school life) if it is all right to visit the sweetshops of the town; I am watching my first operation at hospital, wondering if I am going to faint from the sight of blood; I am in my first day of Army life when my C.O. tells me I must not go out without wearing a hat.

Yes, entering the Houses of Parliament as a new Member, with its centuries-old traditions and customs, its long rambling passages, its senior members who have assimilated themselves to the place over 20 to 30 years, is all these.

I must not give the impression that this is an unkindly place. It is not. Everyone whom you talk to is kindness itself. Everyone is most helpful—when asked. The last two words of the previous sentence are the operative ones. For, if you want to find anything out, you have to ask—otherwise you are left to find your way about this labyrinth for yourself.

Awe-inspiring is perhaps the proper word for the House. After a few days, one can understand how wild men have entered belching forth fire and smoke and, in a year or so, have become tamed so that they eventually graduate into the mellowed and benevolent elderly statesmen such as here and there we see on the benches opposite.

One can understand how the tycoons of big business or even the luminaries of the law have from time to time entered the House only to become immediate and sometimes unexpected 'flops'; one can understand how the much publicized heroes of contentious by-elections have been absorbed into the mould and disappeared from sight.

* * *

The possession of a modicum of brains, though not by itself
the passport to success, is a characteristic that is not quite at the
discount that it once was in the generation in which I have
lived. Yet it is no breach of privilege to remark that there is a
powerful atmosphere of conformism about this place. There
are thus other reasons now why I am not always the first
person to be engaged in conversation amongst public gatherings
of my colleagues; why I do not invariably get the 'Big Hello'
from those on their way up, those who are maybe waiting for
the glittering prize of the next vacant parliamentary private
secretaryship. But I must not anticipate my story.

From all this it might be thought that, at the end of thirty
years of aspiration to enter Parliament, of twenty years of
direct endeavour, I have arrived at a different type of place to
that which I had imagined. Sometimes I think so myself.
Indeed I ask myself whether the Parliament I had thought to
enter was the hallucination of a youthful imagination: or is
it perhaps that Parliament itself has changed in the intervening
thirty years since I first formulated my ambitions? Is it the
consolidation of the two large Party machines, established by
the long and (disagree as you may with its ultimate directive)
successful Patronage Secretaryship of Captain Margesson on
the one side, and by the rigid disciplinarianism of the Labour
Party on the other, that has moulded Parliament into the form
that it is today?

I do not know. I do not know. Nor do I intend to pursue
this speculation here. For, powerful as are the Party machines,
there is, for anyone who has been in but a little time, a consciousness of something transcending even them—a tradition of
Parliament descending through the centuries, that existed before
the Party Machines were thought of in their present shape, and
will maybe still be continuing when, in their present shape,
they have been forgotten—a tradition that, whether by written
enactment or by unspoken custom, guarantees the individual
member his rights, his freedoms and even his privileges, for the

protection, when necessary and proper, of the rights of the humblest of his fellow men. It is to this that I am grateful in that it has enabled me to have been of such use as I am during my first term in Parliament: it is this that has enabled me to further the cause which I have had at heart, in the face of what has frequently seemed an overpowerful and contemptuous executive, which unless checked and counterbalanced at every point, will use the present tight-knit system to exert its power, regardless of consideration for the individual.

*   *   *

It will perhaps be concluded by this time that I am a Party rebel.

But that is not so. Or, at least, it is only so to a limited extent.

Let me make it clear. I believe in the Party system. Such taste as I may have had for political anarchy was exorcised by my sojourn in the jungle of Independence of wartime politics, populated as it was by political birds of paradise of every strange hue. Power can only be sought and exercised wisely by the restraints that arise out of common endeavour and the mutual forbearance which that involves: which again is impossible without Party organization and a modicum of Party discipline.

None the less, though I am a member of a Party and have good reason to owe loyalty to the Party to which I belong, the course of events has tended to disacculturate me from the workings of the Party system. Most important in this connection, perhaps, have been the many years of delay before I got into Parliament, during which my development was inevitably that of a publisher and an autobiographer—years spent in acquiring the more solitary disciplines and the sense of detachment associated with these attainments, rather than the collective virtues that are the essential *vade mecum* of the Party politician.

Luck is the most important perquisite of the politician. I owe it to luck that in May 1955 I acquired the extra 370 votes that gave me victory in Carlisle in a poll of over 40,000 electors. I may have done this, that, and the other to win this seat. But I won it mainly because I got breaks. By the same token, during the previous twenty years, I did not have the breaks. I did not have the breaks when in 1935 I joined the Liberal Party and the War with the Party Truce came shortly afterwards, and thus stultified the progress which that Party was then making. I did not have them when I broke away, a true rebel, and fought the Chippenham by-election of August 1943 as an Independent, losing to David Eccles by only 195 votes. I did not have them when I joined the Conservative Party in 1947 to find nearly all available constituencies filled with new candidates and, in respect of the remainder, Conservative Associations exasperated by the failure of attempts at reciprocal arrangements with the Liberals, so that, in the face of whatever recommendation one might produce, they delighted to turn down anyone who had been associated with the Liberal Party.

While I had been waiting outside, my more fortunate contemporaries had founded great careers. I do not complain. I merely state cause and effect. The final outcome for me was that I entered Parliament at the age of 52 with no other particular distinction to my name. I entered at an age at which, for a new Member, the prospects of a top rank career cannot fairly be regarded as a serious possibility; an age at which to grow new roots in a different soil to that in which one has been politically nurtured is not an easy matter. Entering in an era of U and non-U, when U receives nearly all the first prizes and non-U a sprinkling of the second prizes, I am neither 'U' nor am I particularly 'non-U', neither Trinity nor Balliol on the one hand, nor 'Red Brick' on the other. At a time when even the most modest distinctions that the Party has to offer are put in the way of young men in 'an age of youth', I am out all round. On the face of things, here am I, merely lobby fodder for a few years, before my final relegation to the knacker's yard.

It is pardonable, I hope, if I have found it difficult to forgo the detachment of the autobiographer, as I have viewed what has sometimes seemed a transient phase of my existence; if, while I retain the precarious tenure of my marginal seat, I have used this to make some review of my association with our important national institutions during such time as notice may be taken of my words.

I formulate no particularly original conclusion when I say that the most prominent feature of Parliament today is its domination by the Party system in the form of the two strongly-entrenched Parties, ensconced as the fountains of all power, all honour and patronage which stems from this. It is unlikely to be otherwise as long as the Parties retain their capacity to adjust themselves to changes in public sentiment and the course of social evolution. None the less, it is not an immutable law of the universe that it should be so and circumstances inevitably arise in which the two-Party system endangers itself by its failure in adjustment and adaptation. There can be little doubt that one such crisis is now: and to make some diagnosis of this is the theme of this book that underlies my personal story.

The problem, as I see it, is this. On the one hand we have the Party system with its fixed loyalties evolved in the days of comparatively simple issues, capable of interpretation in the form of broad principles. On the other there is the challenge of the vast extension in the scope of Government in the first half of the twentieth century and the accompanying increase in the sphere of its administration. The reaction of the Party machines to this has been to become more rather than less rigid. Yet it must be obvious that, with the complexity of Government, there must be certain commonsense restrictions to the Party's claims to complete loyalty, even if only to save these latter from falling into obloquy or ridicule, or even both together—which is the risk in the present situation.

If I am to give one example, I would instance matters of scientific fact, which so often come within the purlieu of Government decision. To be in the House of Commons at such

B

times as matters of scientific fact become the interplay of Party feeling, is to see the House at its worst; just as it is to see it at its best on the rare occasions when debates are on a non-Party basis. It is a worthy tradition perhaps that an administrative decision made within his Department must be defended by the Minister with his own reputation, supported loyally by his Party. But what if the decision is a professional or scientific one, in which a lay Minister cannot possibly have more than indirect responsibility?

As a Doctor in Parliament, the affair of the Salk Vaccine of the summer of 1957 springs to my mind. It will be remembered that, during the first part of 1957, in the face of outbreaks of poliomyelitis of epidemic proportions and delay in our own vaccine production, the Ministry of Health resisted the rising popular agitation to import the Salk vaccine from the United States of America.

"When drawing up our scheme, we decided," said Mr. Dennis Vosper, the Minister, on 15th May, "that the vaccine to be used in this country should have a composition different in certain respects from that of American vaccine which is made from strains of virus including the virulent Mahoney strain. That advice still stands."

As the summer session of Parliament came to its close, the agitation rose to a height. The resistance stiffened.

"I have nothing to add to that statement of policy," announced Mr. John Vaughan Morgan, answering an adjournment debate on the part of Mr. Cronin (Labour) on 31st July.

This was the time for all good men to come to the aid of the Party!

In the meantime, M.P.s, particularly medical M.P.s, were being canvassed vigorously by pressure groups, headed by those specialist experts who, with apparently good reason, extolled the harmlessness of the Salk vaccine, despite its Mahoney strain.

Yet, even as one staked one's professional reputation defending the Minister's decision ("Whitehall MUST know best" one thought, when advised by the Medical Research Council!), rumours started to emerge that a Ministry team was visiting America. What they discovered in America that was not already known to my own medical friends and colleagues in this country who had been insisting all along that the Salk vaccine was safe, I cannot say. But one was no sooner ready to go to the stake for Mr. John Vaughan Morgan, Government and Party than, lo and behold, in mid-September, the scientific ideology had changed and, by contradictory decision, the Salk vaccine, including its "virulent Mahoney strain" was proclaimed as safe for British children.

Pity the poor medical Member of Parliament, caught up in the most violent politico-scientific *volte-face* since the discrediting of the Lysenko theory of biology in Stalin's Russia. In those societies where the doctrine of dialectical materialism holds sway, it is a natural state of affairs that a change in advice should mean a change in Party line, or even vice versa. It is natural that, from it being ideologically correct to declare that Salk vaccine is a danger and a menace unfit to be supplied, it should suddenly overnight become ideologically correct to say that it is safe for use.

But surely, in a liberal society, the question as to whether or not it is safe for Salk vaccine, containing the Mahoney strain of virus, to be injected into British children is exclusively a medical and scientific one, and should not be one to be capable of being translated in any way into political ideology.

Another proper ground for the restraint of Party influence and Party feeling are, so it seems to me, matters of moral right as they concern the individual—by which I mean the individual case, rather than that meaningless abstraction concerning whom we hear talk in political manifestos. But I must restrain myself! I can see that, despite my protests, I must already be accounted, by some of my readers, still as a Party rebel. At least, however, I shall hope to show during the course of this book, that I am not "a rebel without a cause".

QUESTION TIME

I HAVE described how I entered the House of Commons with a feeling of 'difference'.

There was one further difference, however, that I felt within myself as, during my early months in Parliament, I passed through the Members' entrance.

I was a former certified mental patient.

There is little need at this juncture other than to state this fact baldly, starkly perhaps. Have I not already written some four books round various aspects of my experience? Have I not already, through the medium of these and thanks to the news value of an M.P., had it blazoned throughout all the principal newspapers in the country?

THE FANTASTIC STORY OF THE TORY M.P. AND A MENTAL HOME: I WAS DRUGGED, HELD 6 WEEKS.

Pity my long-suffering lady Chairman being rung up by our local reporters and asked if she knew that her Conservative Member was making such headlines in the Co-op paper *Reynold's News*.

DOCTOR M.P. TELLS AN AMAZING STORY: "I WAS DRUGGED AND KEPT IN A MENTAL HOME." THEY LOCKED ME UP AS A LUNATIC—M.P.: IT TOOK HIM SIX WEEKS TO GET FREE AGAIN. M.P. IN THE MADHOUSE. CERTIFIED INSANE WHEN DRUGGED, AN M.P. CLAIMS. M.P. WHO WAS CERTIFIED: "NOT INSANITY BUT DOPE." AMEND LAW, HE SAYS. M.P. SAYS: I WAS DRUGGED—THEN CERTIFIED INSANE.

These are the headlines that leap at me from the pages of my scrapbook.

Pity me perhaps? When no less than three Ministers of Health, of varying political hue, one Socialist and two Conservative, have offered me their sympathy.

("The expressions of meaningless sympathy which I received in lieu of help and proper enquiry were the most terrifying part of my whole experience," writes one of my intelligent ex-certificatee correspondents.)

Defer your pity, however, for the moment.

It can by no stretch of the imagination be accounted a blessing to be manhandled and to be put and kept behind locked doors for some weeks at a critical time in one's affairs.

At the time—and indeed for long afterwards—it was far from so.

Even now, an eerie feeling of discomfort overcomes me as, looking back, I appreciate how close I have been to the brink of the abyss of total destruction—only to be rescued when it seemed that I must inevitably fall. An uncomfortable exercise in brinkmanship!

It would, therefore, be grotesque to allege that this has been the most fortunate thing that has ever happened to me.

None the less—but for this experience you would probably not have heard either of me or of this book.

Fame is the reward, the sole reward of the aspiring politician. A politician without at least a measure of fame is as a woman without beauty. And such measure of fame as I possess I owe entirely to this incident. For my experience imbued me with a natural curiosity as to the mysterious mechanism of our mental health system: and so endowed me in turn with the absorbing interest that has arisen therefrom and that has been the mainspring of so large a part of my activities in Parliament.

I am, as I have said, in school. But this school, conformist as it may be in so much, gives ample and variegated opportunity for the mischievous boy. This opportunity comes *par excellence* at Question Time.

Thus we find that Hansard of 13th February, 1958, contains the following entry:

Mr. Nabarro asked the Chancellor of the Exchequer whether he is aware that, in view of the fact that a nutcracker is liable to purchase tax at 15 per cent, whereas a door-knocker over 5 inches in length is free of tax, there is an increasing practice of supplying nutcrackers with screwholes so that they could theoretically be used as door knockers, with the result that with such modification these nutcrackers become free of tax; and what instructions have been issued to Customs and Excise staff with regard to this matter.

"Why," asked Mr. Nabarro in his supplementary question, "is there this invidious distinction between doorknocking nutcrackers and nutcracking doorknockers?"

In Hansard of 25th March, 1958, we find again:

Mr. Nabarro asked the Chancellor of the Exchequer whether he is aware that a pottery piggy bank is subject to 30 per cent Purchase Tax, but if painted with the words 'Razor Blades', is subject to 15 per cent Purchase Tax, the former as a toy and the latter as a salvage receptacle; why this discriminatory fiscal treatment is accorded to piggy banks; and whether he will free piggy banks of tax, as being conducive to small savers on the one hand and to proper salvage of steel from used razor blades on the other hand.

These two extracts are from the famous series of 100 Questions on Purchase Tax asked by Mr. Gerald Nabarro, the *enfant terrible* of our Conservative benches.

Question Time, the most stimulating hour of the parliamentary day, starts (with only the intervention of a few formalities) immediately after Prayers when the House opens at 2.30 p.m. and as soon as the cry goes through the lobbies "Speaker in the Chair": and it continues until the commencement of the proper business of the House at 3.30. It is a feature with rules and customs of its own. Each in turn, by a fixed roster, on the four full days a week on which the House sits, Ministers are called upon to answer for the omissions or faults of their Departments, by virtue of the questions which private members put upon the Parliamentary Order Paper.

It is a time of infinite fascination to the curious, of inestimable value to those seeking information. Here, by the cunning supplementary, a case can be made that will expose abuses; by a properly-worded request for information—always supplied accurately if available—the secrets of Government Departments can be laid bare. To the more sombre-minded political philosopher of today, it might seem that the last vestige of our traditional liberties remains at this free-for-all in which Members of both Parties, Government and Opposition, join. It is natural that the Opposition questioners should predominate: and though as loyal a Government supporter as you might wish to find in all major issues, on one score—that of our out-of-date mental health legislation—I have opposed. How can it be otherwise? An experience such as mine (which originally occurred, incidentally, under a socialist government) is not a matter of either whim or fancy that can go this way when the Labour Party are in power, and this other way when it is the Conservative Party. It is a matter of principle, of individual liberty, of the strongest personal feeling, of reputation, of faith in the civilization in which one is living—strong and deep things—stronger and deeper even than Party loyalty.

Inevitably, therefore, I am allured by Question Time. As I sit on the Terrace enjoying the first interchanges of talk with my younger parliamentary contemporaries—apart from perhaps half a dozen, the average entry age of new Conservative Members into the 1955 Parliament was not much over 35—I am not concentrating heavily on the conversation. I am thinking of my first Question to the Minister of Health.

It is generally known that it is a custom of the House that the parliamentary newcomer should not take part in its business until he has crossed the watershed represented by his Maiden Speech. Question Time is, however, not regarded as formal

business and it is therefore in order for him to start questioning
Ministers even before he has made his début. Indeed, it is
recommended technique that the new parliamentarian should
accustom himself in this way to the atmosphere, the acoustics
of the Chamber and so on, prior to taking his main plunge.

Much has been said, and is rightly said, of the terrors to the
parliamentary neophyte of his Maiden Speech—it is his first
test. It is the first time—and perhaps the last—that he commands
an audience, in as much as his fellow Members, expert listeners,
troop from all parts of the House to hear him, before dispersing
again to assess him and his performance in the Smoking Room
and other places. Great as are the terrors of this occasion, they
pale, however, before the sheer horror (felt even by the most
hardened questioner) of getting up in a crowded House at
Question Time and asking what must appear to be a spontaneous supplementary question. It is small wonder that there
are only a minority of M.P.s who indulge in this form of
parliamentary exercise.

Since not only my first assays, but also my main parliamentary
endeavours in the three years since, have been centred in the
asking of Questions, I will endeavour to explain its procedures,
its functions, and also its limitations. For, as Mr. Speaker,
bewigged and robed, rises in his chair to call the sponsor of
question Number One immediately Prayers are over, few
spectators have a clear idea of the mechanics that lie behind this
hour of business, which is no 'free-for-all' as it might seem, but
a carefully-governed, and carefully-regulated procedure.

For instance, it is by no means every subject that can be
brought up at Question Time: certain fixed rules limit the
nature of Questions. The Question must either ask for information not otherwise available: or it must ask the Minister
to do something: or both. It must be within the Minister's
powers or within the scope of his Department. As Mr. Speaker
remarked of a recent unsuccessful question, "The Minister is
not responsible for the conduct of Sir Bernard Docker."

Questions, in order to appear on the parliamentary order paper, are handed in at the Table, which means, in effect, the Table Office in the corridor behind the Speaker's Chair. It is the invidious task of the Table to shape them, prune them or suggest alterations to them so that they fit in with the rules of the House according to that highest of authorities, Erskine May. In this 'The Table' is invariably helpful. Any suggestion that 'The Table' is obstructive in some peculiar way and, so to speak, in league with 'The Establishment' to prevent awkward matters being raised, is utterly erroneous. The ethos of the Table is one of complete impartiality and of anxiety to be of assistance to any Member striving after the truth. They are bound by the rules of the House, such as I have described, but these, with the possible exception of questions relating to Chief Constables and nationalized industries, are not unreasonable.

Let me illustrate what I say by giving a short account of the occasion when, only some few months after my entry to the House, I owed to the advice offered by the Table my first, and certainly my easiest, piece of major publicity.

I am inclined to take an even dimmer view than does the average citizen at any over-close association of the police with the criminal elements of the country. It was therefore more or less automatic that I should gravitate to the Table Office when I read in the *Daily Telegraph* of 11th November, 1955, of a well-publicized publication party of a book by a certain Mr. Billy Hill (subsequently of 'telephone-tapping' fame) at which "among Mr. Hill's guests were former C.I.D. officers and well-known leaders of London's underworld. They included 'Johnny Up The Spout', 'Three Pints Rapid' and 'The Monkey' ".

It was neither 'Johnny Up The Spout', 'Three Pints Rapid' nor 'The Monkey' who interested me, as much as did the presence of former C.I.D. officers. But a Question to the Home Secretary was out of order—he had no control over private

parties at which no crime was committed: or over the move-
ments of retired Police Officers. None the less (I was advised) a
Private Member's motion would be in order, if I would care to
put it on the Order Paper. Hesitant as I was, I have seldom been
daunted by the prospect of independent action.

The next day, therefore, the following motion appeared on the
Order Paper in my name solo:

CONDUCT OF FORMER POLICE OFFICERS: That
this House views with concern the attendance of former
officers of the Criminal Investigation Department as guests
at a much publicized party given by the self-styled Boss of
Britain's Underworld and urges Her Majesty's Government
to suggest to Metropolitan police officers on their retirement
that they should refrain, in any of their activities, from assistance in the glamourizing of crime and violence.

From a publicity point of view this took the jackpot. It
produced no less than 25 cuttings of various shapes and sizes
from the main national and provincial papers, while the *Daily
Sketch* gave it the full front-page treatment—'the real McCoy'—
with bold upper and lower case heading. M.P. HITS AT
EX-YARD CHIEFS WHO GLAMOURIZE VIOLENCE.

I later paid Mr. Billy Hill the compliment of reading his book.
It is an amazing publication, well worthy of attention by the
social students of our day and age.

Question Time is rightly considered the most rewarding time
from a spectator's point of view and the demand for tickets is
competitive and subject to careful allocation to members.
Rightly also, Question Time gets as much newspaper space as
all but the most important debates even in such papers as *The
Times*, the *Daily Telegraph* and *Manchester Guardian*; while a
single well-phrased supplementary will hit the headlines in the
popular press in a manner never granted to a backbencher's
speech—probably made while the Press (and most other people
also) have deserted the House for dinner.

Once framed and shaped, the Question is printed on the Order Paper under the number and the Member's name: a Member is limited to three oral questions at a time to each Minister—though he may put down as many questions for written answer as he wishes. As the turn of each question comes in numerical order, Mr. Speaker calls the name of the appropriate Member, who rises in his seat and replies with the number of his Question. The Minister reads out his Department's reply from the despatch box. To this the Member may then ask a Supplementary Question, to which the Minister must answer 'off the cuff'. 'Supplementaries' are expected to appear spontaneous. But, as often as not, they are conspicuous examples of careful forethought.

Certainly my own first supplementary question had been a matter for careful thought.

For, at last, some two months after entering Parliament, on 18th July, 1955, I rise in my parliamentary seat for the first time as Mr. Speaker calls Question number 28. My Question is to the Minister of Health and it is to ask him how many people in England and Wales were certified under Section 16 of the Lunacy Act (as amended) and admitted to involuntary detention in mental hospitals in the years 1952 and 1953; what proportion were admitted direct and what proportion after an intermediary period in the observation wards of general hospitals. I am told 20,297 and 20,579 respectively and the percentage that go through observation wards of general hospitals is respectively 16.92 and 15.69 per cent: and, as I have said, I have my carefully prepared supplementary ready. I am anxious to get as much in as possible—regardless of the fact that I still have some years in which to ask Ministers of Health supplementary questions. (I am told later by an old parliamentary hand that I have at least ten supplementaries in what I say.) And as my mind is apt to go blank in times of stress, I have had it all typed out on a nice piece of white paper, from which I start to refresh my memory.

I am, however, just about half-way through. I am just at the point where I am starting to ask the Minister whether he was aware of the statement made by a number of prominent psychiatrists that, in spite of the warning of the Royal Commission of 1926, the certification of people suffering from temporary delirium and their consequent detention in mental hospitals was still taking place (DOCTOR M.P. AND 'UN-HEEDED WARNING', *The Star*), when I am conscious of a murmuring about the place. The murmuring is over on the opposite side of the House and I do not at first appreciate what is amiss. However, as the murmur gathers to a roaring crescendo, there is clearly something wrong—it is the Opposition going into action—and I sit down, leaving out the second part of my sentence.

The cry was, of course, the now familiar one (but one then new to me) of 'Reading'. Supplementary questions must be spoken and not read. That is the rigid custom of the House. They must have at least the appearance of spontaneity, however premeditated, and however deadly the trap laid for an un-suspecting Minister. To appear, above all, with a piece of white paper, which stands out against the green of the Order Paper even from across the floor of the House, is to give the game away completely.

Also, a supplementary question must be short and to the point—the object is to get through 50 Questions in as many minutes, and consequently the other barracking cry at Question Time is that of 'Speech'. For the habit of turning Questions into speeches, so familiar at public meetings, is one from which even our august assembly is not immune. I have in my early days been barracked on this score too, but, as far as the Hon. Members of His Majesty's present Opposition are concerned, any protest of this kind is surely an outstanding example of the pot calling the kettle black.

Thus one learns the hard way—and it has been my lot in life to learn the hard way. I learnt as a parliamentary neophyte that I must not read supplementary questions, that I must not turn supplementary questions into speeches. I did not learn at once, but only after numerous unsuccessful attempts at subterfuges, first by trying to hide my typed piece of white paper in the folds of the green Order Paper, then by writing notes on the green Order Paper itself. Devices that have proved all too often of no avail, so that finally I have had to take my courage into my hands and forego written aids to memory entirely.

However, to return to the 10th July, 1955, the immediate row has subsided and I am left with my answer that there are some 20,000 people annually certified as 'of unsound mind', removed against their will and detained in mental hospitals throughout the country—a formidable number of people, the population of a fair size town.

I am, in the light of this, more than a little dismayed to find on the following day that the heading for my Question in the Hansard Report in its first editions (and until I corrected it for the permanent edition) is "Mental Defectives", when, of course, my question had nothing to do with mental defect at all, this being, as will emerge later on, quite a different facet of a large issue. The mistake of the editor of Hansard was a natural mistake, it being a mistake made by many people who are unfamiliar with the subject. (Indeed I can quote an instance where one esteemed, and by no means ill-disposed, commentator even referred to me as having been certified as a mental defective! Such are the vagaries of fame, when it comes one's way!) But the confusion between mental illness and mental defect is a mistake that can be made only through unfamiliarity with the subject. I am wondering how long previous to this it has been that the subject of these 20,000 people had appeared at Question Time.

However, these forgotten people have come to light at last, and here they are, the principal, though by no means the only, *dramatis personae* of this book. And, since they will be appearing again, let us examine their position, as I pursued it through my first series of Questions.

31st October, 1955, Question 10. (This time properly headed "Mental Illness (Involuntary Patients)") Dr. D. Johnson asked the Minister of Health in how many cases in England and Wales during 1952 it has been necessary to summon police assistance for the purpose of removing persons as involuntary patients to mental hospitals under summary reception order.

Mr. Iain Macleod: I regret that the information is not available.

"Does not my Right Hon. Friend"—I find my supplementary carefully typed on a blank sheet of green paper stuck to the green Order Paper—"share my regret at this fact, in view of the interference with individual liberty which is caused by such police action and action of his officers, and does he not consider that this summoning of policemen is an unfortunate manner of initiating the treatment of the mentally sick? Will he not consider the establishment of an emergency psychiatric service so that patients will have the benefit of special advice before being deprived of their liberty?"

Mr. Macleod: I think that as this matter is before the Royal Commission we should be well advised to see what it has to recommend.

(Subsequently one of the principal recommendations of the Royal Commission has been to make just the recommendation that I suggested in this question.)

28th November, 1955: Question 62. Dr. Donald Johnson asked the Minister of Health when he expects to receive the Report of the Royal Commission on the Law Relating to Mental Illness and Mental Deficiency.

Mr. Macleod: I am not at present able to say when the Royal Commission will be reporting but expect it will be some time next year.

(The Royal Commission did not, of course, report until June 1957.)

19th December, 1955: Question 26. (Our Report paragraph headings are now getting shaped up under "Mental Hospitals (Involuntary Patients)".) Dr. D. Johnson asked the Minister of Health if he will enumerate the persons or official bodies to whom an involuntary patient in a mental hospital is allowed to address unopened and unsupervised correspondence.

Mr. Iain Macleod: These are set out in Section 41 (1) of the Lunacy Act 1890 and I am sending my Hon. Friend a copy.

Dr. Johnson: May I ask my Right Hon. Friend if the detained person's Member of Parliament is on that list?

Mr. Macleod: No he is not, but it has always been the custom that letters to Members of Parliament should be forwarded.

Dr. Johnson: Will my Right Hon. Friend make such an inclusion in the list?

Mr. Macleod: There is no immediate prospect of legislation in that field and I am not sure that it would be suitable for legislation, but when the Royal Commission report this is a matter that might well be considered.

(Two years later I am no longer the only M.P. pressing for this very justifiable inclusion.)

But here we must leave ourselves on the fringe of this peculiar subject of mine to which I was originally brought by disastrous experience, yet to which, by strange paradox, I owe such prominence as I have achieved during my time in Parliament: and, for the time being, pass to other matters.

DOCTOR IN PARLIAMENT

I HAVE, in my last chapter, introduced myself, in effect, as a patient in Parliament.

But I am a doctor in Parliament too. I have written in my first book *A Doctor Regrets*—indeed it is the theme of the book—of my feelings of maladjustment as a medical student and, after that, as a young doctor; of my arguments with my father and his worldly, but unpalatable advice, as a consequence of which, somewhat resentfully, I continued my medical career.

"Whatever you do in later life," I can still, over the years, hear my father's voice, as he spoke these words—in rather didactic fashion, as I thought at the time, for he liked to lay down the law, "your medical degree and medical experience are going to be useful to you."

And, of course, my father was right, in the same way as fathers have been before and doubtless will be again.

Such use as I have been in Parliament, I owe to my being a doctor, which enables me to bring my measure of special knowledge and years of experience to those problems of health which are the responsibility of Parliament. It is said that 'medicine is a jealous mistress': and it is a corollary to this that beneath every doctor, however professionally imposing his exterior, there commonly lies an escapist. But it has been a compensating advantage to the various disadvantages I have retailed of being a 'late entry' into Parliament that medical escapism also has passed me by. Twelve years as a hotel keeper, three years in a Ministry Regional office, two years as a

32

University demonstrator, ten years as a book publisher (these activities frequently being run in double harness with each other) have given me my fill of escapism. As a prodigal son I have been ready to return to the professional fold and devote myself to it, if not exclusively, then for the main part of my time.

*   *   *

However, before I am a Doctor in Parliament, I am a Government backbencher in Parliament, one of those patient oxen who uphold the burden of the day, who save the State, not occasionally but sometimes many times a day, at the expense of late nights, of interrupted and consequently cold dinners, of neglected business affairs cheered only by the thought of a hard-earned knighthood perhaps at the end of the road—though scarcely one for me, starting, as I do, on this long trail at the age of 52.

"A Most important Division will take place and your attendance by 9.30 is essential." "Divisions may take place and your attendance is particularly requested until the business is concluded, which may be at a late hour." "Pairing is stopped for tonight and tomorrow night." "You are appointed to Standing Committee A and your presence is requested for 10.30 a.m. prompt for the Committee Stage of the Registration of Caponized Chickens Bill."

Such are the standing refrains—the 'pop' records—of the Government backbencher's life. Not for him, the joys, the irresponsibility, the opportunities for individual action of being in Opposition. The kudos to be acquired from delaying legislation and harassing unfortunate Ministers, the reputation to be gained by filibustering, are not for him. That speech is silvern, but silence is golden is his motto. One must not

c

embarrass the Minister. The Government time-table must be kept. The Minister must get his Bill. These are the adages for every Government backbencher—whatever his Party may be, whether it be in the House itself or in Committee.

It is all fundamentally reasonable, inevitable indeed under the parliamentary system, but none the less trying—trying when the legislation concerns matters in which one has no possible interest—yet even more trying perhaps, when it concerns a matter of deep interest in which the dynamism of democratic institutions appears to have gone into reverse and to run as a one-way current from above down, rather than from below up; so that Parliament would appear to have lost its role of active legislation and been reduced to a machine of registration and occasional protest, sometimes effective, but at other times ineffective.

"What was once the 'Best Club in the World', resembles a factory on shift," writes Violet, Lady Hardy, a lady of the *ancien régime* in her memoirs. Violet, Lady Hardy, not otherwise known as a political commentator, comes close to the mark. But 'shift work', alas, without piece-time rates!

The 'Best Club in Europe', constructed, as we have already noted, in the eighteen-forties, can comfortably accommodate about 100 people, which is probably about the number who were in those days regular attenders of debates. With that number of Members around the Members' quarters, as on quiet evenings or on Fridays, there is a pleasant, leisurely and roomy atmosphere. More than that makes a crowd. With 200 the overcrowding becomes noticeable to anyone who is of claustrophobic tendencies or who is allergic in any way to concourses of his fellow men. While, on those many days when there are 400 energetic, frustrated people roaming the place, in attendance for votes on Committee-stage debates, three-line Whips, major debates, the atmosphere can be one of pandemonium. In such circumstances it is not easy to settle. It is not even easy to settle sufficiently to write this book.

Those whose minds are concerned with institutional over-crowding, can well ponder on the effect of actual physical over-crowding to this extent on the greatest institution of our country.

For the newcomer, accustomed to more ordinary workaday hours, the parliamentary time-table too is an exotic one. 2.30 p.m. to 3.30 p.m. is, as I have said, Question Time. At the end of this hour of Questions comes the peak hour of business. On two or more days a week the Prime Minister enters to answer Question 45 and any subsequent Questions addressed to him. This leads on at 3.30 to the proper Opening of the Business of the House, commencing, when occasion necessitates it, with statements by the Prime Minister and the other Ministers of State. Following this, on the days of big debates, come the speeches of the leading protagonists of Government and Opposition, taking up maybe forty-five minutes to an hour each. This brings us to 5.30, after which the debate starts its gradual decline through the medium, first of Privy Councillors, then, as the ordinary backbencher gets his opportunity while other and less interested parties drift out to dinner, the attendance dwindles until the mass of Members return for the winding-up speeches at 9 p.m. and the final votes at 10 p.m. onwards. Doubtless over the years conformity with this programme becomes second nature, but for anyone accustomed to evenings at home, visits to the cinema, the peace and remoteness of domestic suburban life, it requires major adjustments.

This arrangement of the day's business, so acutely inconvenient to anyone who does not live within a mile or two of the House of Commons, sometimes seems a relic of the aristocratic and plutocratic era, when attendance at the House could be fitted in to the pleasant round of dinner at home or club, and maybe a late afternoon or early evening Reception: of that era too when parliamentary sessions were short and attendance was fairly optional anyway. But maybe it is I who am hope-lessly suburbanized and see things in this respect with a jaundiced eye.

Certainly, the business of the main parliamentary day is
designed for that mythical individual, the part-time parliamentarian. But the part-time parliamentarian is increasingly a
figment of the past. This is particularly so when the four full
weekly sessions (plus, on occasions, the Friday session from 11
to 4 when Government business is taken on that day) are
supplemented by attendance at two mornings of Standing
Committees each week, for the purpose of considering
those Bills which have been 'sent upstairs' to the Committee
Rooms on the first floor of the House for detailed consideration.

There is no better view of the River Thames, anywhere, than
from the broad windows of the First Floor Committee Rooms
of the House of Commons. But, as a Government backbencher
in Committee I do not see the view. What I do see, as I sit
along the benches with my back to the window, are the Opposition rows of earnest, fanatical people, who believe it their
mission to condemn, obstruct and harrass, by every means in
their power, the devilish devices of what to them is unredeemed
Toryism. Since the days are gone when hearts can be melted
by eloquence from either side across the floor of the House of
Commons, the only effect of this is to create an atmosphere of
monotony and irritation, intensified by the uncomfortable
feeling that one may have pressing business elsewhere.

My own first experience of Standing Committee membership
was on the Sugar Bill. Other than in my consumer capacity, I
had not the remotest connecting link with any single one of the
provisions of the Sugar Bill. None the less, here was I, set up to
'consider' it. Little wonder it provoked me to the following
article in the *Spectator* of 18th May, 1956:

How well I remember when, a young and enthusiastic
parliamentary candidate, I taxed the doyen of my political
acquaintances on what seemed to be the political inertness of
the inter-war governments. "Ah," said he mysteriously. "You

don't see everything. You have little idea of the work that goes on in Committee."

There was no need for any mystery. The proceedings of Standing Committee 'A' in its consideration of the Sugar Bill have just been published, in bound form, by the Stationery Office.

See us sitting in Committee, therefore—I make no revelations: we are an entirely public spectacle—drawn up in serried ranks, facing each other like the opposing armies at Blenheim or Malplaquet. Three benches of Government supporters, two only of Opposition members; the Minister must get his Bill.

The Minister must get his Bill! Any intervention from a Government supporter will only delay this process. Thus it is that, out of the 744 columns of Hansard, representing sixteen twice-weekly sessions or forty hours of debate, there are only some twenty-five interventions from Government supporters— many of these being only a single sentence, or even a single word. For the rest, there are the Minister, and his Parliamentary Secretary, faced by a spate of Opposition eloquence.

Here is the 'drama' of Standing Committee 'A' on the Sugar Bill, from the viewpoint of the Government backbencher:

FIRST DAY. *11.15 a.m.*

Mr. Michael Stewart (Opposition): If I may judge from the silence on the other side of the Committee, that faith does not burn very strongly in the breast of any hon. Members except that of the right honourable gentleman and of his Joint Parliamentary Secretary.

Mr. Dudley Williams: Our silence is a token of our boredom with the honourable gentleman's views.

11.45 a.m.

Mr. A. G. Bottomley (Opposition): I hope that we do not allow the discussion to end without a further statement from the Government side of the Committee. One hon. gentleman opposite was obviously about to enter the discussion but I imagine that he got a black look from the Whip, and from then on not one hon. Member opposite has taken part.

12.20 p.m.

Mr. Dye (Opposition): . . . because the Government burned their fingers so badly, the Minister's hands must now be tied behind his back. . . .

A few minutes later

Mr. Dye (Opposition): . . . It seems to me that we are placing the Minister in the position in which, instead of having a sweet after his lunch, he is made to eat humble pie. That is an invidious position for any Minister.

THIRD SITTING. *10.35 a.m.*

Chairman: Order. I must call the attention of the hon. Member for —— to the fact that the reading of newspapers in Standing Committee is not allowed.

FOURTH SITTING. *At opening*

Mr. A. G. Bottomley (Opposition)—in the middle of a nine-column speech: . . . like the Minister, I am a man of few words. . . .

A few minutes later

Mr. A. G. Bottomley: We have no idea what their back-benchers think about it, as they have said nothing. We do not know whether they are in favour of or against the Government's proposals. They have just blindly raised their hands as lobby fodder when required to do so.

Half an hour later

Mr. Dudley Williams: The hon. Member for Sunderland North should not take our silence as showing that we are completely uninterested in the Bill. We on this side of the Committee are completely united behind the Minister.

SIXTH SITTING. *12.40 p.m.*

Mr. John C. Bidgood: I should not like the hon. Members opposite to go to their homes suffering from the delusion that hon. Members on this side of the Committee are bored. I have listened to such a wealth of oratory that I have been rendered temporarily speechless.

TENTH SITTING. *12.40 p.m.*

Mr. Godfrey Lagden (consequent on an altercation between Mr. Jeger and Mr. Dye): Would it not be as well, Sir Austin, for the two hon. Members opposite to wash their dirty beet in private?

Before the Committee has reached its conclusion on the sixteenth day, I am the object of a special mention:

Mr. A. G. Bottomley: I have a great deal of sympathy with the hon. Member for Carlisle (Dr. D. Johnson), who said that he had waited for twenty years to get into Parliament and who has served on the Committee which has been sitting for many weeks and has never opened his mouth. I imagine that he must be wondering why he came into Parliament at all.

Naturally I, too, am behind the Minister, though my unitedness is tinctured with an escapism that allows my thoughts to stray.

A genius would maybe have produced a second *Iolanthe* from this situation. For me only, however, the more simple speculations. Is parliamentary democracy starting—ever so little—to fray at the edges? Will it in due course go the way of the feudal system, so that (after the manner of 'scutage' payments) busy, restless people elected to Parliament would perhaps pay 'votage'? Instead of M.P.s, substitutes would be paid to say 'Yes' and 'No' at the proper time, and rows of elderly crones would sit and knit happily, while patiently listening to the provocative loquacity of a latter-day Mr. Bottomley, or the turgid metaphors of a Mr. Dye?

The Minister, with the aid of eighteen stalwart and prominent figures of public life, got his Bill. But after all he could equally as well have got his Bill with the aid of eighteen old age pensioners, or eighteen 'ten-shilling widows', or even eighteen 'doctors on the dole'; and simultaneously helped to solve one of the more intractable of our social problems.

*   *   *

Since my article in the *Spectator* appeared, I have—*post hoc*, I like to think, rather than *propter hoc*—been appointed to serve on morning Standing Committees almost continuously throughout the past two years. Indeed, with the Sugar Bill, the Rent Bill, and the Local Government Bill to my credit, I can lay claim to a record in this respect, unrivalled by almost any other Government backbencher. Likewise, for the information of Mr. Bottomley and others, I have even indulged myself to the extent of two three-minute speeches. But there is, alas, no sign of my 'votage' system being adopted.

In the circumstances, therefore, it has been no bad thing to have had my own special interest and my professional experience in the sphere of the National Health Service (even before it was called a National Health Service) as hospital doctor and general practitioner.

It will not surprise my readers—even those who do not already know—to hear that in this sphere too, I have been a critic. My first book, *A Doctor Regrets*, was written on the theme of my decision not to enter the Health Service in 1948—even though this theme was perhaps rather more of a 'gimmick' than the genuine occasion of the book. For my decision to leave the full-time practice of medicine had already been taken some ten years previously when I sold my practice in the suburb of Thornton Heath and bought my Woodstock hotel. Then, after the war, I started my publishing firm which, some twelve years later, is now publishing this book: meanwhile I returned to general practice temporarily and on a part-time basis between 1951 and entered Parliament in 1955.

Thus the immediate post-war years found me with a measure of freedom, in the context of which I assisted the British Medical Association to campaign the country to explain the profession's objection to the proposals for the comprehensive medical service in the form they were put forward by the Socialist Government, and in the form in which, of course, they have manifested themselves subsequently in legislation and still are today.

Newport (Monmouthshire), Bradford, Grantham, Chelms-
ford, were some of my stands on which I endeavoured to explain the ethics of the doctor—patient relationship in general
practice and the necessity of these being retained on an individualist and private contractual basis, from the patient's point
of view, to ensure the best kind of medical attention. To do this
in 1946 and 1947 was, however, merely to play Mrs. Partington
trying to sweep back the Atlantic Ocean of collectivist sentiment
which was inundating the country. Any attempt to convince
audiences that one was representing the patient's best interests,
rather than some nefarious design of the grasping doctors, was
foredoomed to failure; as was, equally so, any attempt to
impress that medical attention was not something that devolved
as of right, but rather something which in one way or the other
had to be paid for.

"But doctors are not villains," I can remember pleading to
an East End audience.

"Oh, yus, they are," came the yell from the back.

"But how?" I asked.

"My little girl was ill last night. I called my doctor out to
see her and he charged me seven shillings," came the answer.

A small girl was ill and the price to make her well again was
not worth two packets of cigarettes. This was what that man said.

A people get the doctors they deserve just as they get the
Government they deserve: in 1948 the doctors' resistance broke
suddenly and the age of bureaucratic medicine and doctoring
started. On 'The Appointed Day', 5th July, 1948, all doctors
became employees of a single employer, the State. The centre
of power in the medical world shifted overnight from those
famous and historic bodies, the Royal College of Physicians
and the Royal College of Surgeons, to that *parvenu* institution,
the Ministry of Health. (How many of the signatories of the
famous letter of compromise in *The Times* from the leaders of
the Royal Colleges appreciated this when they signed their
letter, I wonder?)

For the medical profession as a whole, the Appointed Day was The Day of No Return. On 5th July, 1948, you were either in, tempted by the carrot and goaded by the stick; or you were out.

The carrot was in the form of the Report of the Committee that had been set up under the chairmanship of Sir Will Spens, with the following terms of reference:

"To consider, after obtaining whatever information and evidence it thinks fit, what ought to be the range of total professional income of a registered medical practitioner in any publicly organized service of general medical practice; to consider this with due regard to what have been the normal financial expectations of general medical practice in the past, and to the desirability of maintaining in the future the proper social and economic status of general medical practice and its power to attract a suitable type of recruit to the profession; and to make recommendations."

Concerning this Report, the Minister had written to the British Medical Association on 26th July, 1946, in the following terms:

"The Minister desires to make his attitude to the Spens Report quite clear. He fully accepts the substance of the recommendations upon the general scope and range of remuneration which general practitioners should enjoy in a public service."

This was of particular importance to the profession in the light of paragraph 6 of the report which read:

"We leave to others the problem of the necessary adjustment to present conditions, but we would observe in this connection that such adjustment should have direct regard not only to estimates of the changes in the value of money but to the increases which have, in fact, taken place since 1939 in incomes in other professions."

In the light of the categorical statement of the B.M.A. that it was on the basis of the Minister's assurance that the general practitioners agreed to enter the National Health Service, this has formed the basis of a controversy that still continues.

Thus, on 5th July, 1948, the majority of the medical profession, tempted by the specious promise implicit in the Spens Report, goaded by the threat of the total loss of their National Insurance patients, were in. I, on the other hand, was out. So also was Dr. Michael Johnn, who many years later wrote for me that well-known book *Doctor on the Dole*, describing how, at the age of 52, he was unable to find a place in general practice in this country despite a lifetime of clinical experience.

In the course of a busy five years of Socialist Government legislation, medicine was nationalized together with the coal mines, the electrical and gas undertakings, the railways and road transport, and the iron and steel industry. Then, in 1951, came the great victory of Conservatism promoted by those who wished to put nationalization into reverse. However, it would appear that the forces of Conservatism, the guardians of the British liberal inheritance, after half a century of compromise and accommodation and surrender, had by now forgotten how to advance to any degree. On the contrary, in the perpetual retreat through the wintry snows of adverse circumstances, one facet of the liberal way of life after the other has had to be thrown from the sleigh to appease the wolves of socialism. One of the principal sacrifices in the years from 1951 onwards has been the medical profession. For, though a restored Conservative Government has had Conservative plans for steel and Conservative plans for housing, it has had no Conservative plans in regard to the Health Service. The Welfare State, as set up by the Socialists between 1945 and 1949, has become as much a touchstone of Conservative political faith as it had previously been of Socialist faith: and the National Health Service, far from being regarded as the hasty device that it was and so subject to modification and adjustment, has become a sacrosanct thing, a golden calf, an idol to be worshipped and to whom obeisance can only be denied at electoral peril.

Let me give an example. It was an integral part of Conservative policy at the 1950 election that since everyone contributed alike to the National Health Service, therefore all
contributors were entitled equally to all or part of its benefits,
and accordingly we find in *The Right Road for Britain* the
following pledge: "We shall, therefore, allow private patients to
obtain free of charge, drugs prescribed by their doctors on a
parity with people in the State scheme." This promise, having
met 'administrative difficulties', still waits to be redeemed. It
is still, in fact, in those realms of aspiration inhabited by
backbenchers' private bills, with, as far as can be seen, not the
remotest prospect of becoming law. In the sphere of the
Health Service it would seem that the accusation that a Conservative Government is merely executing a holding action,
ready to hand back the Service intact to the next Socialist
Government, is a true one.

In the meantime, the National Health Service is a parliamentary responsibility and, a doctor in Parliament, I have been
able to take only too clear a view of the development of those
trends which I feared would develop when I spoke on plat-
forms in the 'forties, such as the gradual monopolization of
practices, the lack of independence of those who work for a
single joint employer, the overcrowding of hospital out-
patients, the overlapping efforts of the different branches of
the Service, set in more rigid mould even than hitherto, the
stifling of the liberal and humanitarian outlook by bureaucratic
regulation.

STATE PUBS

IT will have been gathered that I have my full share of that part of the lot of man, which is "to be born to trouble, as the sparks fly upwards".

Over and above all this, I have found myself the Member of Parliament for Carlisle, the city of State pubs. In any country in which the spoils system of politics operates to any degree, it would have an aspect of incredibility that a Conservative Member, elected on a programme of private enterprise, to support a re-elected Government on the same programme, should represent a community in which all premises licensed for the sale of alcohol, save only three, which were excepted from the scheme at its inception, are part of a monopoly run by the State. Indeed, it might well seem to be a slur on the efficacy of the City's representation, that this should be so.

Since, however, Carlisle and its State pubs are a microcosm of the problems that run throughout this book, they are perhaps worth a chapter in amplification of these remarks.

For myself, my Election Address at the General Election 1955 contained a special paragraph which read as follows:

"It appears to be the peculiar affliction of the City of Carlisle to be the victim of socialistic experimentation. It is now almost forty years since the initiation of the so-called 'Carlisle experiment' of State-managed public houses. It is clear to me that the State Management Scheme has ceased to fulfil its original purpose. It is my intention, if elected, to press for a review of the Scheme."

Here is the text of the article which I wrote for the *Spectator* of 23rd March, 1956, which can perhaps form the most useful background explanation of the State pub situation:

The social history of bureaucracies is in its infancy. A step forward was undoubtedly taken in an article in *The Economist* by the discovery of 'Parkinson's Law', postulating an inevitable rate of increase in any bureaucratic establishment. But there can be exceptions to this rule. Toynbee, following his study of twenty-one civilizations he had divided into two categories, found that he had yet another category to consider: "We shall find examples of civilizations which have not been abortive, yet have not developed either, but have been arrested at birth."

Just as we have arrested civilizations, so do we have arrested bureaucracies: and it is of one such that I have to write. The Esquimaux, Nomads, Osmanlis and Spartans whom Toynbee quotes as making the adjustment to their surroundings which characterizes an arrested civilization, are paralleled by the State Management Scheme for the ownership and control of public houses and licensed premises which—still known as the 'Carlisle Experiment'—remains in occupation of the city of Carlisle.

The 'Carlisle Experiment' came into being as a consequence of the impetus of the radical teetotalism which pervaded the Liberal Party of the early twentieth century. It survives today— like some prehistoric monster of the deep—a sole memorial to that once great movement. The circumstances of its gestation were the war of 1914–18. "Drink," declared Mr. David Lloyd George, "is a greater enemy of this country than Germany or Austria"; and the Central Control Board (Liquor Traffic) was established. On 17th April, 1916, Mr. Gretton asked the Minister of Munitions if the Central Control Board (Liquor Traffic) proposed to acquire all licences for the sale of intoxicating liquor in Carlisle. "Carlisle has great importance from a munitions standpoint, and the question of the control and sale and

supply of intoxicating liquor there is under special consideration," replied Dr. Addison, for the Minister. In reply to further
questioning Dr. Addison later added that "the purchase referred
to and the question of the price to be paid are fully covered
by the Defence of the Realm (Amendment No. 3) Act". Suitably
enough, DORA, of the old-time cartoonists, was the original
sponsor of the experiment.

Later in the year Major Astor, speaking for the Government,
put the matter in perspective. "The Board did not say 'let us go
in for a great social experiment in the nationalization of drink'.
Little by little, step by step, circumstances compelled the Board
to take action." Further steps, however, were clearly envisaged,
as we find such places as Bedford, Sheffield and Leeds mentioned in debates.

Eventually, after parliamentary protests at lack of responsibility for its activities, the Board consolidated itself in Carlisle
and district (including Gretna—where the munition workers
were—and Annan across the border), Enfield Lock (adjacent
to the munition factories) and the Cromarty Firth area (adjacent
to the naval base at Invergordon). In Carlisle the initial dynamic
of the Scheme was considerable. Out of 150 houses taken over,
30 were eliminated—their relics can still be seen about Carlisle.
Others were reconstructed. "They have opened in Carlisle,"
said a Prohibitionist M.P. somewhat querulously, "in the old
Post Office, a sort of model public house. They have got a most
beautiful room and furnished it admirably. They have music
and various attractions and they have made a very attractive
restaurant. I believe they are having large numbers of visitors
there."

The policy of the Board was 'disinterested management'.
"As soon as you have disinterested management you have no in-
ducement to sell alcohol," stated Major Astor. By the Licensing
Act of 1921 the properties vested in the Board were transferred
to the Home Secretary and the Secretary for Scotland, and put
under the State Management Scheme—though by then the

Enfield Lock area had been released from the Scheme (it had proved a poor investment). Meanwhile, however, those familiar friends of the Toynbee fans enter: 'Yin and Yang'—'Challenge and Response'. The response to the challenge of the 'Carlisle Experiment' was not further experiments in Bedford, Sheffield or elsewhere, but an improvement in the standard of pubs throughout the country on the part of the brewing industry. The bright, sparkling saloon bars that we know, the sausage rolls and ham sandwiches, are the outcome of the stimulus of this challenge. So when the Southborough Committee reviewed the question in 1925, its conclusion was that it was not necessary to extend the experiment to any other part of the country.

The determined reaction, however, of private interests to circumscribe the Scheme has only been equalled by the tenacity with which the Scheme has held fast to its tenure of the pubs in Carlisle; and here it is in Carlisle thirty years later, stuck fast, clinging to its rock face (to paraphrase Toynbee), unable to surmount the beetling projections on the cliff face which it is attempting to climb. The only major event in the career of the Scheme in the meantime has been an abortive attempt to cash in on the socialist dynamic by extending its suzerainty to the New Towns—an attempt rapidly slapped down by the Conservative legislation accompanying the Licensing Act, 1953.

But Carlisle was sold down the river in these arrangements. "Bearing in mind the avowed belief of the Conservative Party in Private Enterprise," runs the appealing resolution of the Carlisle Conservative Association passed in 1955, "and noting that the Socialist legislation for State Management Public Houses in the New Towns has been repealed, this Conference deplores the continued application of this principle to Carlisle and District and urges the Government to introduce legislation to transfer to Private Enterprise a proportion of the State Management Scheme Public Houses under conditions of fair competition with the consequent prospect of a considerable improvement in service to the customer."

"The Home Secretary understands the feelings of the Carlisle Conservative Association," replied Sir Hugh Lucas-Tooth, M.P., on behalf of a Conservative administration. "The Scheme, however, has been continued hitherto by successive administrations of differing political complexions, and it would be misleading to hold out any prospect of reopening this complex and controversial question at the present time."

What is the state of affairs at the present time? Where are these model public houses? The visitor to Carlisle has in recent years had some difficulty in recognizing them. They have not always been recognizable even by the inhabitants of Carlisle itself. "Pubs like post offices," exclaims the newly formed Carlisle Licensing Reform League, which claims that the consumer in Carlisle is getting a raw deal from 'disinterested' service. "The accent is now on brightness, cheerfulness and comfort," replies the General Manager of the Scheme, announcing a new improvement programme, "designed as a reply to those who say we have dull, unhomely houses."

The contest continues to rage between private enterprise and State-run liquor: the Chairman of the Reform League counts the comparative numbers of pre-Christmas customers outside the single private off-licence, and the several State off-licences, respectively; the General Manager of the Scheme jealously counts the customers in his own off-licence, and boasts with disinterested pride of the increased sales of his bottled beer— though, alas, the old Adam of drunkenness still shows itself on occasions even under disinterested management ("SOLDIERS FOUGHT LIKE ANIMALS—Row in pub spreads to street" ran a recent headline in the *Cumberland Evening News*).

What object have these State pubs, dull or bright, other than that of their own self-perpetuation? Can they acquire a fresh dynamic, or will they remain a peculiar institution in Carlisle and district? Carlisle is no longer 'a wide open town'. If, indeed, the object of the Scheme is law enforcement, it may well be that from time to time other districts will manifest

D

themselves as more in need of this, than is the law-abiding city which I have the honour to represent.

*   *   *

It was a modest demand that, at the end of a thirty years' interval, the Scheme, which is run in the name of the public as a whole, should again receive a review. Indeed, whatever view is taken of the scope for State Management of pubs, whether one feels it should be abolished or extended, it would be difficult to dispute the desirability of this.

Even the demands of the reformers are of a modest nature. What is the grievance against the pubs? It is epitomized in the following extract from the memorandum submitted in 1955 to the Home Secretary by Mr. J. L. M. North, Chairman of the Carlisle Licensing Reform League, and myself.

"There is the general feeling in Carlisle that the monopoly created by the State Management Scheme is failing to give satisfaction to the customers of the establishments. There is an undoubted dullness and sameness about the Scheme's public houses, which militate against any benefit which the average person bent on recreation or enjoyment might obtain from entering them. This acts as a deterrent to potential tourists and business visitors to the city, which thereby suffers a considerable loss. It should be added that little attention appears to be paid to customers' complaints."

It is acknowledged that the State Scheme is here to stay, but a demand for the stimulus of private enterprise competition is not an unreasonable one to make. This, however, has been resisted with all the obstinacy and tenacity of which the Party machine—the Conservative Party machine, existing to further private enterprise, let it be noted—is capable. Letters and protests have been blanketed. Resolutions at Party Conferences have been at the end of the agenda. The objectors to the Carlisle State Scheme, who are naturally a minority interest, have failed on these occasions, even after repeated attempts, to obtain discussion.

It is only at Question Time in the House of Commons that the State pubs and their problems have gained a hearing. The first of all nationalized commercial ventures (other than the Post Office), the State Management Scheme, was brought into being before the conception of the Nationalized Industry Board, free in its day-to-day working from the inquiries of troublesome and persistent M.P.s, was thought of.

"The Home Secretary is answerable to Parliament for every glass of beer, or lemonade, or cup of tea that is sold and for accommodation and meals, provided in the public houses and hotels vested in his Department. What surprised me when I was Home Secretary," writes Mr. Herbert Morrison in his book *Government and Parliament*, "was the fewness of parliamentary questions put to me about this interesting experiment."

I have endeavoured to compensate for this oversight on the part of my predecessors. In the lack of stimulus by competition, I have thought, at least, to apply stimulus by parliamentary question by way of representing the consumer interest of Carlisle, not only of Carlisle itself, but of visitors also, who can form so important an asset to the city's welfare, in view of its location on the highway between England and Scotland, and its proximity to so many places of tourist interest.

There is nothing livens up the House of Commons more than a good contentious question on the Carlisle State pubs. The approval that such a question meets from my Conservative colleagues is proof indeed that zeal for private enterprise is not dead amongst the backbenchers of the Party, even if it has smouldered dimly in the breasts of members of the Government.

Here are the principal milestones in my series of questions on the Scheme. My first question was on 21st July, 1955, within two months of my election.

It was occasioned by the following complaint in the *Cumberland News:*

"I have just returned from a happy holiday in my native city of Carlisle. My brother and his wife who had not been in Carlisle for forty years joined me. We were delighted at the great advance the city has made in buildings and the wonderful housing estates which we visited, all at reasonable rents and much better than anything I have seen in the South.

"But one thing disgusted us, the fact that we entered the Citadel Tavern in Lowther Arcade and were refused a drink because my sister-in-law was in our company. Why cannot a respectable woman with her husband and brother be served? We afterwards found this applied to many licensed houses in Carlisle.

"If this is State control, it is time the citizens of Carlisle swept it away."

This is my Question:

20. Dr. D. Johnson asked the Secretary of State for the Home Department the number of licensed premises in Carlisle at which ladies can be refused service in one department or other; and the names of any such premises where there are no alternative arrangements for ladies to be served with drinks, other than restaurant arrangements, even though they are accompanied by husbands and relatives.

Major Lloyd George: In all the fifty-eight licensed houses under State management in the city of Carlisle, the public bars, in accordance with local custom, are for men only. In two of those—the Citadel Tavern and the Friars Tavern —there is no provision for ladies.

Dr. Johnson: Will my right hon. and gallant Friend review these arrangements in general, and those at the Citadel Tavern in particular, so that ladies who are visitors to the city do not suffer the embarrassment of entering the wrong part of these premises?

Major Lloyd George: I understand that the two premises mentioned are only a few minutes away from places where ladies can be admitted. The practice is not a result of State management but is, I gather, an old Carlisle custom.

In this, I subsequently found that the Home Secretary was right. It was an old custom throughout the North to have 'Men Only' bars. None the less, times change.

Here, however, is my next Question, carefully guarded ammunition kept until the Christmas season, and asked on 8th December, 1955:

3. Dr. D. Johnson asked the Secretary of State for the Home Department if he will state the number of off-licence establishments owned by the State Management Scheme in the city of Carlisle.

Major Lloyd George: There are at present four off-sales shops in Carlisle under State management: a fifth will be opened as soon as practicable. In addition, off-sales facilities separate from the bars are provided in eighteen State-managed public houses in the city.

Dr. Johnson: Is my right hon. and gallant Friend aware that in the coming season of the year there is customarily a long queue outside the single private off-licence in Carlisle, while his own off-licences generally remain in a state of under-employment? Will he not agree that this indicates a demand for more facilities for private enterprise services——?

Mr. Speaker: Perhaps the hon. Member has not yet learned that it is contrary to the practice of the House to read a Supplementary Question.

The news reports "Opposition cheers, with cries of 'No' from the Government benches", as the Home Secretary announces the off-licence. It will be gathered, however, from the long dash in the Report that my Question once again ended in uproar, as the outcome of which I was checked up on by Mr. Speaker for still using adventitious aids to memory at Question Time.

For my next two questions, dealing with minor points of service, I retire into the comparative security of Questions for

Written Answer. The following were asked on 2nd February and 9th February, 1956, respectively:

87. Dr. D. Johnson asked the Secretary of State for the Home Department if he will issue instructions that matches be readily available for sale at all times during licensed hours in all the redecorated and reconstructed premises of his State Management Scheme in the city of Carlisle.

Major Lloyd George: My information is that matches are available in those public houses in the State Management district of Carlisle where there is any demand for them but I am making inquiries to see whether there is any need to improve the existing arrangements.

88. Dr. D. Johnson asked the Secretary of State for the Home Department if he will issue instructions that potato crisps be readily available for sale at all times during licensed hours in all the redecorated and reconstructed premises of his State Management Scheme in the city of Carlisle.

Major Lloyd George: I am informed that potato crisps are available in all the State Management public houses in Carlisle where there is any demand for them and I do not think that any action is called for on my part.

The question of Spirit Sales (Small Quantities) was, however, worthy of better things and, with it on 16th February, 1956, I resumed my Questions for Oral Answer.

50. Dr. D. Johnson asked the Secretary of State for the Home Department whether he is aware that small quantities, of less than a full bottle, of spirits are unobtainable at his State Management Scheme off-licences in the city of Carlisle, thus inflicting hardship on old age pensioners and other people of limited means; and if he will make a statement.

Mr. Deedes: I would refer my hon. Friend to the answer given to his Question of 9th February.

Dr. Johnson: May I thank my right hon. and gallant Friend for the full answer he gave last week, which removed the misunderstandings that had appeared on this subject;

will my hon. Friend ensure that these small bottles of spirits will be obtainable at his public houses at all times; and, in view of the enthusiasm for small, independent private enterprises that has been shown in recent days on both sides of the House, will he transfer a number of these off-licences into private hands to allow competition?

Mr. Deedes: The first point raised by my hon. Friend was fully covered in the reply given by my right hon. and gallant Friend.

Later in the year there cropped up the vexed question of 'collars' on pints of beer. The collar on a pint of beer is the name given to the froth on the top of draught beer: and you can have a 'high' collar or a 'low' collar on a pint of beer according to the manner in which it is drawn. The advantage of a 'high' collar, from a proprietorship point of view, is that it is possible thereby, by putting sufficient froth on the top of a glass, to make twelve pints into thirteen. It was the accusation of the managers of the State Scheme, at loggerheads with the administration, that such had been their instructions in the pressure for producing profits and percentages.

This, as might be expected, immediately became a national issue with banner headlines in the *Sunday Express*.

Amidst Opposition cries of "Withdraw", I raised it in the House. The evidence was, however, sufficiently substantial for a private inquiry by Mr. C. S. S. Burt, Q.C., to be appointed.

Notwithstanding all this, I am still, two years after entering Parliament, tilting at the State Monopoly, as evidenced by the following question asked on 21st November, 1957.

17. Dr. D. Johnson asked the Secretary of State for the Home Department if he will give the reasons for his refusal of the application for an off-licence for the sale of beer, wine and spirits made by Mrs. Margaret Cheetham, of 9 Blackwell Road, Carlisle.

Mr. R. A. Butler: After careful consideration of Mrs. Cheetham's application, in consultation with the Local

Advisory Committee and the State Management Districts
Council, I did not feel justified in making an exception in this
instance from the established policy that the sale of liquor in
Carlisle should, in general, be confined to the State Management Scheme.

Dr. Johnson: Is my right hon. Friend aware that there is
room in the city of Carlisle for private off-licences of this
nature to supplement the service given under the State
Management Scheme? Will he consider seriously the
possibility of modifying the Scheme?

Mr. Butler: There is power for the Secretary of State to
authorize the sale of liquor by persons other than through
the State Management Scheme in Carlisle, and we did make
an exception for Carrow House, a country hotel. Mrs.
Cheetham's application was on behalf of the inhabitants of
Currock, and even had we granted the application the
inhabitants of Currock would have had to take a considerable
journey in order to obtain the facilities which they desired at
Mrs. Cheetham's establishment. We therefore thought it
right not to accede to it.

Am I, at the end of this, any nearer my Review? I am afraid
not.

I have, however, got brighter pubs.

I cannot do better than quote from the Report of the State
Management Scheme for the year ending 31st March, 1957,
issued as I write this letter:

The alterations and improvements to the Gretna Hall, to
which reference was also made in our last report, were
completed in May, 1956. The re-opening of the hall occasioned
considerable interest, so much so that 160 functions of
varying character were held in the year under review. Future
bookings are most satisfactory and inquiries are continually
being received. There is little doubt that the re-opening of
the hall has met a long-felt need in Carlisle.

Further improvements have been carried out at the Central Hotel, Carlisle, where the main dining room has been completely redecorated and refurnished and the old writing room converted into an attractive mixed lounge. A new reception office has been constructed and the main corridor and stairway to the first floor, including the reception foyer, have been completely redecorated and recarpeted. In the gentlemen's smoking room an attractive new bar counter and back fittings have been constructed, incorporating a service bar and separate doorway for the service of drinks to other parts of the hotel. All these and other improvements have greatly enhanced the appearance of the hotel and increased its popularity.

Far be it from me to extol the virtues of the Central Hotel, Carlisle, in comparison with those excellent privately owned establishments, the County Hotel and the Crown and Mitre Hotel, in both of which I have received hospitality. None the less, I often think that my name may be remembered in Carlisle by the improvements wrought to this hotel, when all other reasons for this are forgotten.

THE ESTABLISHMENT

I HAVE hitherto in this tale of my parliamentary experience dealt only with Question Time—spectacular, essential to the working of parliamentary democracy, just as vitally interesting to the M.P. as to any outside spectator, in as much as there rises to the surface all current grievances—as witness the fact that not only are the Spectators' galleries fullest at Question Time, but the Members' benches also.

However, Question Time is not the real business of the House. It is only the advance scouting and the light skirmishing. This statement does not imply that important battles are not, on occasions, won and lost at Question Time: but by and large Question Time is but a prelude to business, whether it be actually in time sequence on the same day, or whether it be through the introduction of urgent matters that can be transferred to the main business of the House on a later day.

The real business of the House—apart from its big debates on questions of major policy—is that of legislation, the making of laws that effect the physical and economic well-being of the millions of our fellow-countrymen and form the framework of society in which they live their lives.

To have the power to make laws is to possess the ultimate power and it is to this end that the immense struggle of the General Election takes place at its periodic intervals. The Party that wins the General Election inherits the power to make and frame the law.

Paradoxically, few people had less influence in this way in the Parliament in which I found myself than the Government backbencher. Though probably there is none left so politically naïve as to believe that an ordinary Government M.P. elected to govern, has any active part to play in the Government. By long standing democratic custom, the power to govern is passed over without reserve to the Prime Minister and his chosen Cabinet of Senior Ministers—these score or so of people, with their dependent juniors to the number of some fifty or sixty, chosen from the majority parliamentary Party, form the Executive. This being done, the sole remaining function of the Party, whether the parliamentary Party or the Party Organization throughout the country, is to 'wither away' into a mere mechanical supporting force.

The system of Cabinet Government and the doctrine of the personal responsibility of Ministers for their Departments of State that accompanies it, has been a serviceable one for some two hundred years down to the present day—so serviceable, in fact, that not until recently has it come under the strain that reminds us that it is the survival of a previous era, when the functions of Government were less complex, when parliamentary parties were less rigid than they are today.

The admonitory slogan of 'Let our Ministers Govern', the tradition of complete loyalty to every dot and every comma of the personal ministerial ukase, are tenable propositions, if a Government Member can be satisfied that each and all of these emanate solely from the innate fund of wisdom of each individual Minister. Clearly, however, this is not so. Clearly, with the complexity of modern government, it cannot be so. It is not to be expected that busy and harassed Ministers, engaged in a multitude of decisions, in a round of prestige and social functions, in political speech-making, in answering for their Departments in the House of Commons, should at the same time enjoy the necessary leisure and the appropriate sense of detachment to find continual fresh inspiration on wide horizons of detailed policy. This must be true enough for a Minister specialized in his subject and wedded to his Department for a long stretch: how much more so when our Ministers undergo the kaleidoscopic changes to which we are accustomed, when each and all are apt to find themselves unexpectedly translated to unfamiliar work, only a few months later to be moved elsewhere, or to resign, or even to fall ill.

No man, not even a Minister of State—however often his title appears in his latest Act—is to himself an island. Even in the stratospheric heights to which he has ascended by his translation to ministerial responsibilities, he must inevitably have his advisers.

Thus, in abhorrence of the vacuum created by the renunciation of his political Party, there must step in some other factor. In the realms of British government, this other factor is supplied by the civil servants of his Department. As Ministers come and go, the permanent advisers carry on, gathering to themselves the threads of power, prestige and responsibility.

This is inevitable in regard to the process of administration—how indeed can it be otherwise?

It is natural too that, with the separation of members of the Government from the original sources of their power, the bureaucracy—this vast apparatus of secret power—should be unable to resist the temptation to make policy on its own account as well as administer it: and 'departmental policy' has already over many years become an accepted political conception.

There is nothing new about this. A series of books, from *The New Despotism* by the late Lord Hewart onwards to that more recent publication *The Passing of Parliament* by Professor G. W. Keeton, have enlightened the serious-minded student of politics on the powers of Government Departments by means of delegated legislation through orders and regulations executed in the name of the Minister, supported, if need be, by his obedient parliamentary majority. It is to these books that one must refer any reader who may still thirst for detailed knowledge on this recondite subject. This book of mine concerns only life as an M.P. and these measures, as a rule, come only within the cognizance of the Member of Parliament as the consequence of the Opposition 'Prayers' moved to annul them. Departmental orders and regulations have to be 'laid on the table' of the House for a period before becoming effective and can only be dealt with by a negative motion for annulment—which occurs at the end of the day's business.

Opposition Prayer to annul the Acute Rheumatism (Amendment) Regulations, 1958 (S.I. 1958 No. 17) (EXEMPTED BUSINESS).

Divisions will take place and your attendance at 9.30 p.m.

and until the Prayer is concluded is particularly requested

unless you have obtained a pair.

Such is the glad message on the Party Whip which causes a sinking feeling in the breast of any pair-less Government backbencher; required, even if the prospects of a division are remote, to stay on to a late hour 'to keep a house' for the Government, which must always be ready to have 100 members on the premises to carry on its business.

How many M.P.s have been left virtually sleeping on the Embankment, having missed their suburban trains back home, as a consequence of these late-at-night Prayers being debated, and perhaps ineffectively voted against, until the early hours of the morning? What an ideal method is presented by such Prayers, of harrowing a Government with a narrow majority! Fortunately, by the Parliament of 1955, it had been agreed by the two Parties, as an elementary measure of mutual protection, that the maximum time of debate allowed for a Prayer is one hour and a half, so that there is, at least, in these days a chance of it being over well before midnight.

To return, however, to our main theme—that of legislative and executive power. With the slipping away of power from Parliament itself, it has naturally become a subject of popular speculation as to what has happened to this power. Where has it gone? Where is the ultimate seat of power in our country? From these questions arose the conception of The Establishment, which was delineated in a series of articles by Mr. Henry Fairlie in the *Spectator* in 1953.

The impression of The Establishment left by Mr. Henry Fairlie was of a sort of Loch Ness Monster: a mysterious force in the deep waters which, in sinister fashion, is there all the time, but which only displays itself on rare occasions for the amazement and edification of the public. The average citizen, indeed, questioned as to his idea of The Establishment might easily describe it as a conspiracy of irresponsible power shared by the Archbishop of Canterbury, the Editor of *The Times*, the Director-General of the B.B.C. and Lady Violet Bonham-Carter. This line of speculation, of course, became so profitless that Mr. Henry Fairlie finally had to attempt the infanticide of his own brain child. His attempt was, however, unsuccessful, as the idea of The Establishment still persists.

What, then, are these mysterious forces who are said to enjoy power without responsibility and, under the façade of ministerial responsibility, to form the governing element of the country and to be the mainspring of its legislation?

Does The Establishment exist? And can we say who composes it?

The answer is that it does exist, and that we can, if we wish, identify and pinpoint its members.

As we approach our appointed task, we can soon see that the issue has been over-simplified.

We can start with Government Departments. But The Establishment is obviously not comprised only of civil servants. For, as administrators, they are incapable of creation. For this purpose they call in their willing auxiliaries—those from the university common rooms, from the aristocratic strata of society, from professional and business associations, from the senior ranks of social workers, who have hurried to ally themselves with the new locus of power, and who form the membership of the intertwining system of Committees, Working Parties, Study Groups and Royal Commissions which are the feature of our national life. It is amongst this numerous throng that we find the origins of so much of our social policy. Extending to many, many hundreds in number, with the common bond of being appointees of authority rather than elected representatives, despite their variegated tasks in connection with variegated departments, these people acquire a common bond that separates them off from their more ordinary 'un-established' fellow men.

Out of this general conception of The Establishment, there arises its more particular manifestations in connection with each of the Departments of State. It is obvious in this connection that The Establishment in say Defence, or Education, is an entirely different thing from The Establishment in the National Health Service.

Since, as a doctor in Parliament, my only useful contribution to this problem can be to speak of what I know, I have made it my mission to explore this latter: and since, owing to the comprehensive nature of the National Health Service, this is a particularly prolific example, I am hoping that my exploration will be some contribution to the study of this intricate problem.

Thus, having already elicited the information from the Minister that there were no less than eleven Working Parties and Committees due to report on various aspects of the National Health Service, I asked him to give the names of the members of these in the Official Report.

Here, then, in Columns 32 and 34 of Written Answers of the Parliamentary Report of the 4th June, 1956, which I have reprinted in Appendix I of this book, in the 130 or more names of those who man the Mileage Committee, the Committee of Inquiry on the Rehabilitation of Disabled Persons (better known as the Piercy Committee), the Working Party on the

Recruitment and Training of Health Visitors and so on, is the medical Establishment of the country—as fine a collection of fauna as were ever pinned to the board of any enthusiastic collector.

Ministers of Health come and Ministers of Health go. In his recent address to the Fellowship for Freedom in Medicine Sir Francis Walshe described the Ministry of Health as "a sort of parliamentary Didcot Junction where the hopeful aspirant to Cabinet rank waits in the chill breeze until the train arrives to carry him on to the city of his dreaming spires, his political Oxford". No less than four Ministers have occupied the office during my own short term in Parliament. But the Committees and the Working Parties go on for ever. That this last statement is no mere figure of speech may be seen from the following extract from my speech concerning the need for a Psychiatric Social Service on 19th March, 1957.

"The Macintosh Committee sat from 1948 to 1951 with the special purpose of considering social workers in the mental health service, but by the time that the Committee had reported and made its recommendations, in very similar terms to what I have been describing, a Working Party on health visitors had been set up under Sir William Jameson. That Working Party took another three years to consider the matter and apparently action had to wait until it was seen how the social workers in the mental health service would fit into the general picture of social workers.

"One cannot help pointing out that three years went by before we had exactly three paragraphs in a Report, which was the sum total that seemed to deal with mental work. By the time that Report had been issued there was a further Working Party—the Younghusband Committee on social workers, whose report we are still awaiting."

Beyond this central Establishment of the National Health Service are the provincial 'Establishments' in connection with the Regional Hospital Boards, and so virtually *ad infinitum* to

Hospital Management Committees, Local Executive Councils, Health Committees of Local Authorities and so on.

Thus there runs this gigantic proliferating chain of Committee people from top to bottom, to all corners of the country, all with common interest and common outlook—an outlook of slightly disdainful welfarism, an outlook of protective discretion as against either any expression of individualist outlook or any complaint by an individual. And of this particular feature of the National Health Establishment, I shall have something to say later.

In the meantime, it is in the Reports of these appointed and co-opted Committees and Working Parties, rather than in any policy created by the political Parties—certainly any policy created by the Conservative Party during its time in government—that there can be found the genesis of the large part of our present-day legislation.

It is the particular irritant of the Government backbencher that he does not know in advance, and is frequently not consulted in advance, about the Bill which he is expected to vote for, not only in its general principles—but comma by comma, line by line, and clause by clause, each one as a matter of confidence in the Government. The Bill appears to take its place in the legislative sausage machine: it is already tied up and enveloped— a thing of joy to its sponsors, a complete job, its integrity a touchstone of prestige to the Minister, to be carried through in all circumstances by the power of the Government vote.

A Committee set up under one Minister may report under his successor or his next successor but one, and have its recommendation implemented by yet a third or fourth Minister— even though these Ministers may be of different political Parties. There is no better instance of this than the ill-omened Shops Bill of 1957, which, sponsored under the Home Secretaryship of Major Lloyd George, appeared with the avowed purpose of the Conservative Government implementing the recommendations of the Gowers Committee set up by the

E

post-war Socialist Government. The Gowers Committee on Conditions in Non-Industrial Employment had submitted its interim report on 30th January, 1947, recommending that the Shops (Hours of Closing) Act of 1928 should be amended by the substitution of 7 o'clock for 8 o'clock as the general closing hour for shops: and also that non-shop trading should be brought within the scope of the Act. During the intervening ten years this report had lain in the Departmental pigeon-holes. Now, in the session of 1956–7, came the opportunity of the Home Department to produce their Bill and, over-night as it were, this Socialist-inspired measure, with its stifling effect on the small private enterprise of the side-street, individually-owned shop and the 'barrow-boy' trader, became the touch-stone of faith for loyal Conservatives. But even for patient oxen this was altogether too much: and it was at any rate one triumph of backbench Conservative pressure that this unhappy Bill was abandoned.

However, as I have said in other connections, there is nothing like being at the receiving end: and it is my proper intention in the next stage of my story to retail my personal encounter with this type of legislation.

A RESTRICTIVE PRACTITIONER

I N this chapter I am to be found in the unfamiliar guise which the parliamentary legislation of the summer of 1956 unexpectedly thrust upon me. Whereas I have written of myself as doctor, hotel-keeper, or Member of Parliament, this is the first chapter throughout my several books in which I have written of myself as a publisher. It is proper that a publisher should be 'a back-room boy' and should only come to the front of the stage on exceptional occasions. The legislation to which I refer is, however, an outstanding illustration of my thesis in my last chapter; it is also the only major piece of legislation in which so far I have become personally involved.

When the Restrictive Trade Practices Bill was published on 15th February, 1956, and came to its Second Reading on 2nd March, these facts had no significance to me at all. Thus, the speech of Mr. Peter Thorneycroft, then President of the Board of Trade, during the Second Reading of the Bill, of which the following is an extract, passed right over my head.

There remains only one large problem with which I have not so far dealt—the problem of resale price maintenance.

Those who favour resale price maintenance are not devoid of arguments in their support. They can produce the evidence of views expressed from time to time by many manufacturers, retailers, consumers and trade unionists. In the other scale has to be put the views of other people and two major Reports which deplore the rigidities of the system, and particularly the fact that consumers are denied the benefits which would flow from economies in retail distribution, such as the introduction or development of self-service stores and the like.

Collective enforcement by trade associations of resale prices greatly exacerbates any evils which may flow from it. I will quote from the Lloyd Jacob Report on the topic contained in paragraphs 145 and 147. That Report stated:

In this connection associations of manufacturers and distributors, whose main business is to enforce prescribed retail prices, have, in our opinion, contributed in no small measure to the rigidity which at present exists in the distributive structure and which we believe it to be desirable to prevent.

The Majority Report of the Monopolies Commission returned to the same theme. They said in paragraph 175:

We consider that these agreements sustain a more rigid and more widespread system of price maintenance than would exist if individual suppliers were responsible for their own enforcement even if enforcement in the Courts were made much easier than it is at present. Such a rigid maintenance of prices and enforcement of elaborate trading rules goes well beyond anything that can be justified as necessary for preserving a reasonably stable market for branded goods or for protecting particular retailers.

Those are the extracts of the two principal Reports upon this subject. I believe those views expressed by the Lloyd Jacob Report and the Majority Report of the Monopolies Commission to be right.

The sole immediate relevance of this extract is that here we have a Conservative President of the Board of Trade quoting with approval, and indeed with concurrence, first from the Report of a Committee, the Lloyd Jacob Committee on Resale Price Maintenance, set up by the Labour Government in August 1947 and reporting during the lifetime of the same

Government two years later, and then from the Report of the
Monopolies Commission set up under the Monopoly and
Restrictive Practices (Inquiry and Control) Act 1948—again
a Socialist measure. The latter Commission had produced its
Report on Collective Discrimination in June 1955 and there
had been a debate on 13th July, 1955, to 'Welcome the Report'.
Then now, six months or so later, came the legislation.

But what have I to do with all this? Very little you might
think. For that is precisely what I thought myself at the time—
and also for many months afterwards. I was blissfully oblivious
both of the implications of the Report and of the preliminary
Debate from which I have quoted the relevant words which were
in due course to give me several headaches.

Most people, in thinking of monopolies, think of large
concerns, of the mammoths of industry: and so do I. But it was
not until the announcement of the Restrictive Trade Practices
Bill that (together with large numbers of others of my kind) I
comprehended that it was not the oil companies, the tied petrol
stations, the system of collusive tendering, the usual facets of
economic life that are associated in the mind of the ordinary
person with monopolies, against whom this new legislation was
directed, but that it was against ME. It was I, a small and
struggling publisher, making do in stern and intensive com
petition with my rival publishers, who stood condemned as a
monopolist and a restrictive practitioner. This was strange but
true: and it was, of course, by virtue of my signature, as a
member of the Publishers' Association, of the Net Book Agreement, the 'sheet anchor' of the book trade, which, in as much
as it contained provisions for the maintaining of book prices by
collective action, such as the stopping of supplies by all signatory
publishers as a penalty for a bookseller's breach of a price
agreement, now stood condemned as an undesirable trade
practice.

This was a shock to me—as it was also, no doubt, a shock to a
good many other small publishers and booksellers eking out a

living, not to mention other retailers such as chemists, grocers and motor distributors. But now, at this eleventh hour, we became aware that, while (as was pointed out from time to time during the subsequent debates) certain obviously monopolistic activities on the part of large concerns had been excluded, while other restrictive practices were perhaps of a venial nature and could be put before the Restrictive Practices Court (provided for in Part I of the Bill) for approval, yet there was one thing that incited the ire of the Monopolies Commission, not to mention the Lloyd Baker Committee, beyond measure, and that was the system of collective retail price maintenance to which we subscribed. Others of a more old-fashioned frame of mind might think that, just as the worker is legally entitled to combine in a trade union to defend his wages, so it is fair enough for the 'small man', the owner of the retail shop, to combine with his fellows in a trade association and agree in their company to take action, if necessary, to defend his prices—always providing that this was done in the context of fair and open competition otherwise. But with the purists of progress (such as the members of the Monopolies Commission) this was not the line of thought at all.

There was no small measure of consternation throughout the Book Trade at this belated discovery, as can be evidenced by the columns of the contemporary issues of our trade periodical, *The Bookseller*.

The last thing that I had ever expected when, as a last refuge of the individualist, I had started my small publishing firm, was that I should be plunged through it into the hurly-burly of contentious politics. But here was I at the epicentre of the cyclone which by the time the Committee stage of the Restrictive Trade Practices Bill had started in early May had worked up to some degree of fury.

I quote from the first speech which I made on the Committee stage of the Bill—that stage, as I have said, in which it is considered for amendment, clause by clause, line by line, and which in a Bill of this importance is taken on the floor of the House. In this I endeavour to explain how the Bill affects our trade:

Dr. Donald Johnson (Carlisle): I rise to resist the Amendment. I speak as a restrictive practitioner. As a book publisher, I should like, in particular, to thank the hon. Member for Itchen (Dr. King) for his sponsorship of the small bookseller. I have also to thank the hon. Member for Stechford (Mr. Roy Jenkins) for the few crumbs of comfort which he offers the book trade.

I assure the hon. Member for Stechford that we are very closely affected by the Bill, and as he seems to be somewhat vague as to the manner in which we are affected, I hope in my remarks to put him right. It is an assumption which has been held through the years that books are always the same price. I am sure the hon. Member, as an author, likes to see his books in different shops always at the same price, and not 15*s*. in one, 9*s*. 6*d*. in another and perhaps even 2*s*. 6*d*. in another. That arrangement depends essentially on the agreement we have in our trade, which is known as the 'net book agreement'. That arrangement was started at the beginning of the century subsequent to a price-cutting war in the book industry in the last years of the nineteenth century. It was finally fixed in 1899 and has continued since as the sheet anchor of the book trade. That is an agreement to maintain prices.

On our side, as publishers, we agree to maintain the price of a book—in the case of a fiction book, for two years and, in the case of a general book, for three years—unless we give special notification in our trade magazine to the booksellers and give credit accordingly.

The purpose of our price arrangements is to enable the bookseller to buy the slow-moving stock which is the essential of our trade. The bookshop of any standing has a varied stock, some items of which may take two or three years to dispose of. It is not quick sales stuff, which sells in a week, a fortnight or a month or two. It is essential for the book-seller to have confidence that he will be able to maintain his prices. The advantage to the public is that this stock is the culture of our country.

That is the advantage which this price maintaining arrange-ment in the book trade has for the public. It is equally true that great knowledge and skill is essential in the book trade in the acquiring of this stock.

Mr. Roy Jenkins: I am trying to follow the argument of the hon. Member carefully. I gathered from what he said that I was right in saying that it is individual resale price main-tenance in which the book trade is interested today. It is not a system of common prices. There is nothing to prevent one publisher, if he wishes, bringing out a novel for 9*s.* 6*d.*, whereas another charges 15*s.*? It is not an attempt to get common prices, but the retention of individual resale price maintenance, although clearly the means by which that can be effected is a matter for argument. Will the hon. Member tell us exactly what it is the book trade wants to maintain?

Dr. Johnson: Essentially we want to maintain the price structure of the book trade so that, for instance, a book written by the hon. Member is not sold for 15*s.* in one shop and for 12*s.* 6*d.* in the next. I do not think I can use simpler words than those. It is only by an agreement of some kind that we can do that.

Dr. King: This is a point of importance to the Committee. I understand that what the hon. Member is asking for is not the maintenance of common prices between the wholesaler and the publisher, but the maintenance of a specific price for a specific book, whereas between publishers there are com-petitive prices.

Dr. Johnson: If I publish a book I can fix the price at any price I like. That is the case now. I am sorry I did not make that clear. I have complete freedom to fix what price I like for my own books in competition with other publishers.

There is no restriction on competition whatever as between individual publishers.

I wish to go on from there to assure the hon. and learned Member for Leicester, North-East (Sir L. Ungoed-Thomas) that profit is not the only motive force in the book trade. On both sides of the trade—publishers and booksellers—there are a great many people who are struggling on a very narrow margin of profit because they think they are doing something which is very much worthwhile in other ways. That is, the promoting of ideas that come to them to retail as booksellers and create what we consider to be the culture of the country.

It is clear from the interruptions which came from Members on the other side of the House and which I have recorded, that there had been no distinction in the thinking on this matter between arrangements whereby prices are fixed by individual producers and maintained by collective action and prices which are fixed collectively and maintained collectively, though a little reflection will show that there is all the difference in the world between these two, when it comes to the question of exploiting the public by monopolistic practices.

This difference had not, however, been recognized by the Lloyd Jacobs Committee; or the Monopolies Commission; or by the President of the Board of Trade in his Bill. Small publishers and the small booksellers, as practitioners of collective resale price maintenance by way of the sanction to enforce our Net Book Agreement, were the villains of the piece. For in Part II of the Bill, collective resale price maintenance as a sanction to enforce a trade agreement was 'out', without compunction and without exception.

What is the case for collective resale price maintenance in the book trade? I put it in a second speech which I made on an Amendment to Clauses 19 and 20, which dealt with the prohibition of collective resale price maintenance, and the danger inherent in substituting for it the right to maintain prices by individual action of the suppliers.

Dr. Johnson: Our anxiety is that which has been already expressed concerning the small retailer and the small bookseller. Perhaps I may be excused for giving a résumé of our position. We have our Net Book Agreement, which we hope would be approved under the arrangements in Clause 16, paragraph (*b*). Next, we come to the question of enforcement of the agreement, which hitherto has been enforced by the procedure of collective price maintenance.

Under Clause 19, however, the President of the Board of Trade would take the agreement, so to speak, to the dentist, who, first, would yank out the upper teeth under subsection (1) and then the lower teeth under subsection (2). Now, we come to Clause 20, which is, so to speak, the orthodontic department. I would not be so unkind as to say that false teeth are being inserted, but what is being inserted is only an upper set and not a lower set. The supplier—in our case the publisher —has his remedy, but the bookseller or retailer is left with no remedy whatever other than the rather uncertain one of a complaint to his supplier.

The anxiety in the book trade is increased by the realization that it is not necessarily in the immediate interests of a publisher to maintain his prices. There might be either the large rogue publisher, who can defy anyone and do as he likes within the trade; or, on the other hand, there is the danger of the small publisher with a heavy depreciating stock—and nothing depreciates more quickly than a book after publication—who is in a desperate financial position.

Both of those people have a temptation not to maintain their prices but, on the other hand, to let their prices go, with the large publisher selling the best-seller as a loss-leader and the small publisher selling off stocks of what might be quite attractive and good books and which could very well be picked up by a department store for its book department and sold in a similar manner to the loss-leader. That is the main fear of the trade.

Books as a loss-leader are a particularly suitable commodity for the large department store. The type of book which is suitable for the loss-leader—the best seller, of course, such as *The Cruel Sea*, and books of that character—is just the thing which under the modern conditions of trade is essentially the small bookseller's bread and butter. He relies upon them to keep him afloat and to maintain his slow-moving stock and to enable him to give to the public the service that is expected of him.

It is a fallacy to think that if this system of loss-leaders, and so on, develops, books will be cheaper in the long run. The danger that faces the trade, if this develops, is that with the loss of that type of business the small retailer will go out of business. There would be a closing down of markets and the publisher, in turn, would have a narrower market and smaller editions for his books. As a consequence, the price of books would not go down, but would definitely go up.

For the benefit of hon. Members opposite, I should like to read a quotation from *The New Statesman and Nation* of 14th April this year, giving conclusions concerning the book trade:

"Under price-cutting conditions best-sellers might sell even better than at present, but if the general level of sales in Britain of the 250,000 titles in print were depressed, it would have an immediate effect on book sales abroad. These are running at about £17 million a year. Falling home sales would involve higher prices for books, and as books are Britain's biggest cultural export, the loss of price stability might have far wider repercussions than purely commercial ones."

I have said that our market hitherto has been kept up by the operation of collective price maintenance. I agree with my hon. Friend the Member for Heston and Isleworth (Mr. R. Harris), who regretted that no exceptions are possible to the prohibition under the Bill. We come, however, to the question of individual enforcement. Obviously, in the circumstances as we visualize them in the book trade, this will be a capricious matter. On the one hand, these conditions may work; on the other hand, they may not work—we do not know. If they do not work, it will be the small retailer and the small publisher who suffers in consequence.

Looking at the position of the small retailer—looking for the moment at a wider sphere than book publishing and considering, say, motor traders, chemists, and so on—there is only one remedy for the small retailer under the Bill in its present form. That is under Clause 19 (3), under which he or several other small retailers may get together and form an interconnected body corporate and so protect themselves in this way. In other words, they would be forming a trust or monopoly.

We have surely to remind ourselves that this is an anti-monopoly Bill. I am sure that it is not the intention either of my right hon. Friend the President of the Board of Trade or of hon. Members, on either side, that small retailers should go out of business or even that fresh monopolies should be born, the effect of which obviously would not be to lower prices, but eventually to close down on the consumer and to raise prices.

This speech was made to a general amendment moved by Mr. J. E. Simon: and which was 'by leave withdrawn'.

Prior to this, however, I had had my own amendment on the parliamentary paper, in which I had endeavoured to express the alarm shared by so many.

I have explained how legislation springs, like Athena from the head of Jove, fully matured, clothed and armed from the Government Department that gives it life, leaving so often little time for those who feel themselves affected by it, to protest. Certainly, the two months that intervened between the first publication of the Restrictive Trade Practices Bill in March and its Committee stage in May, were but a short time for those who,

like I, suddenly realized that they were affected by its provisions to mobilize either themselves, or public opinion in their
own support. (As a sidelight to this, one might mention that
M.P.s were still receiving memoranda from outraged and
protesting local Booksellers' Associations even after the Bill
had been passed.)

At least, however, I could put down an amendment and
my amendment to Clause 21, subsection V, of the Bill appeared
on the Order paper accordingly in the following terms:

"That any trade may be exempt from the provisions of this
Part of the Act where, in the opinion of the President of the
Board of Trade, price maintenance is in the national interest
for cultural and educational reasons."

(The Part of the Act referred to was, of course, Part II
dealing with the prohibition of collective resale price
maintenance.)

"It is difficult to see," stated the Editor of *The Bookseller* in
his columns, "how this amendment can be resisted by responsible persons."

He spoke for the small bookseller up and down the country—
as also did Dr. Horace King, Labour Member for the Itchen
Division of Southampton, in the following words in his speech
during the Committee stage:

"May I say that I have no interest to declare. I am a bookish
man, who has spent more time in booksellers' shops and
libraries than perhaps I ought to have done, but I have been
asked by the little booksellers—my friends up and down the
country—to put their case. Their case, it seems to me so far,
can only be dealt with in this subsection.

"I want to say a few words about the bookseller himself. He
is not merely a seller of books; he has to carry an enormous
stock, he has to act as adviser, counsellor and friend to those who
buy from him, and he thinks that he will be seriously jeopardized
if the abolition of net sales price agreements by the whole-
salers concerned were to make it possible for his customers,

who use the free library service which he provides to take
advantage of getting to know new books by handling them in his
shop, were then to turn to some of the multiple stores and obtain
these very books at cut prices. If some subsection to safeguard
him is not included in the Bill, then indeed the little bookseller
of England fears that his position may be jeopardized.

"I think it goes deeper than that. I think the bookseller and
the small town bookshop provide one of the instruments in the
country which preserves the British book culture when it is
being challenged more and more today by cheap commercial
culture and that the disappearance of the little bookman from
the towns of England would be a great loss to British life. On the
other hand, the case of the bookseller is that the publisher
himself is keenly competitive. This is not monopoly that I am
defending. The Macmillans, the Pitmans, the Murrays and the
rest of them fight each other in the world of buying authors and
books and fixing competitive prices against each other. Their
prices, between themselves, are competitive, so much so indeed
that publishers are not interested in the Amendment which the
hon. Member for Carlisle (Dr. D. Johnson) placed on the Order
Paper earlier."

These sentiments found echo also in such distinguished
quarters as *The Times* in their leader columns of 12th May:

"Dr. Johnson, the Member for Carlisle, told the House of
Commons on Tuesday, in plain English, as befits his name,
that he feared the President of the Board of Trade would 'yank
out the upper teeth' of collective price maintenance in book-
selling under one subsection of the Restrictive Trade Practices
Bill and, then, the lower teeth under another subsection. It is
under the shadow of such fears that the Booksellers' Association
began yesterday its annual conference and discussed the Bill, as
well as other troubles of the trade, with evident anxiety. All
concerned with the marketing of books are worried and con-
fused by the possible consequences of applying the proposed
restraints on monopoly to their trade.

"The sympathy expressed by the President of the Board of Trade has by no means dispelled the obscurity about the future which is worrying publishers and their allies and which is a matter of general public interest. We do not want books to become, as to a considerable extent they have in America, mere counters in a competitive struggle to tempt customers to buy other goods. A bookshop which carries on its shelves all kinds of books and not merely best-sellers is a necessity of civilized life. This is a fact that must be recognized, just as the special claims of serious drama are recognized for purposes of taxation, those of the sale and purchase of works of art are recognized in trade and currency regulations and in general cultural values confer some exemption from pure economic tests. The social vitality of the nation could be impoverished if booksellers, who have a hard struggle as it is, were swept into a net spread for other fish."

"It is difficult to see," I repeat the words of that hard-fighting personality, Edmond Segrave, in his capacity of Editor of *The Bookseller*, "how this amendment can be resisted by responsible persons."

The responsible persons amongst my parliamentary colleagues who supported me by putting their name to it, were, however, few in number. They were, I find, Mr. Robert Chichester-Clark, Mr. James Lindsay, Mr. Robert Crouch and Captain Henry Kerby.

On the other hand there was the Minister anxious to get his Bill. The President of the Board of Trade was very determined to get his Bill.

Part I of the Bill concerned the intricacies of the setting up of the Restrictive Trade Practices Court and, on this, the lawyers of the House 'went to Town' in no uncertain fashion through days and days of Committee debate. However, as the time for debate on Part II and consequently on my own amendment, approached, it was soon clear that a lawyer's paradise could simultaneously be a small publisher's nightmare. My amendment, which was not entirely without its appeal (indeed, I was informed at a later date that it had worried the Government as much as any other amendment on the paper), had received not only the support of my five responsible persons in the House, but also of the Booksellers' Association—while the enthusiasm of *The Bookseller* was already conferring on me an almost embarrassing degree of prominence.

Now, it is to some degree natural that the organization of the book trade should be a twofold one, with the Booksellers' Association representing the retailers on one side and the Publishers' Association representing the publishers on the other side: and that these two organizations should represent the different, and sometimes divergent, interests of the two sides of the Trade. It might have been thought, however, that faced with the common threat to their joint welfare, these two would have made it their primary purpose to speak with a single voice. This, however, was not to be. On the contrary, an unnatural obsession with divergent interests bedevilled this situation which I entered, to such an extent as to preclude joint discussions between these two Associations during those vital months of April and May 1956.

Thus it was that, while I marched out boldly into the open at the head of my small, but heroic band, I became conscious of another and considerably weightier army manœuvring in the woods and thickets surrounding my advance. This was the heavy armour of the Publishers' Association, of which I am, of course, a member, but which is naturally dominated by the large publishers whose representatives almost exclusively form its Council.

The fate of amendments to Government bills is not as a rule a happy one. Indeed, it is not too much to say that, except by the grace and favour of the Minister in charge of the Bill, they are stillborn from the start. If, for instance, they are Opposition amendments, they are defeated by the steam roller of the Government majority; if, on the other hand, they are amendments sponsored by Government supporters, they are, under pressure of Party loyalty, 'by leave withdrawn' before a vote is taken. On rare occasions, however, a third course develops; this is when an amendment proposed by Government supporters is called for a vote by the Opposition—it cannot then be withdrawn, but a vote has to take place. Many a Government supporter has, in these circumstances, found himself faced with the invidious choice of either defying his Party Whip, or voting against his own amendment. Needless to say, his feelings for his own brain child have to be very strong indeed for him to take a major hazard with his career in this fashion.

Mr. Peter Thorneycroft, President of the Board of Trade, was in no mood for grace and favours on this Bill. At the same time, it struck me forcibly that my amendment was just perhaps the sort of amendment which the Opposition might like to call for a vote: and it is useless to deny that, as I contemplated this, my own zeal for political martyrdom did not entirely measure up to the enthusiasm I had evidently aroused amongst my out-side supporters. None the less, one's colours once run up, it is an ignoble thing to strike them as long as there is any real chance of victory.

I was, however, to be saved from a political hero's grave by the action of the Publishers' Association. For, some three or four days before the debate on Clause 20, and the possible calling of my amendment, was due, the following statement was put out by the Publishers' Association and circulated amongst M.P.s:

Obviously the Book Trade would like to retain its present simple, effective and economical methods of maintaining prices and it is earnestly hoped that its case for special treatment will be recognized. (There follows in brackets a mention that my amendment "would, of course, facilitate the retention of the present Book Trade methods".)

Nevertheless, the Book Trade realizes that its present methods are collective methods and that there is powerful

F

political dislike of such methods. In these circumstances the Book Trade seeks the right to have some organization which can assist publishers individually to maintain their resale prices and conditions.

In other words, the Publishers' Association, relying evidently on various assurances given in circumstances of which I had been unaware, had decided to withdraw its opposition to Part II of the Bill; and accept the system of individual resale price maintenance proposed in Clause 21.

Despite the sop to my amendment in the middle of this communication, I was left high and dry. Obviously I could no longer talk for the Book Trade with any degree of authority, when a substantial part of the Trade, such as the Publishers' Association, had no wish to be talked for. To avoid a fiasco—and indeed to make some sort of protest—there was only one thing to do and that was to withdraw my amendment.

*   *   *

The Restrictive Trade Practices Bill went through virtually unamended, to become the Act that it is today. I have already quoted the expression of my own fears that the Bill—in its prohibition of collective resale price maintenance—was a pro-monopoly Bill rather than an anti-monopoly Bill. It might seem that, in so doing, I am merely setting down a biased point of view. I cannot therefore do better than quote from the concluding speech of Mr. Donald Wade who, as representing the Liberal Party, a body that *par excellence* had pressed for this type of legislation, said:

"As I listened to the debate on Part I of the Bill, I came to the conclusion that a number of the smaller fish may well be caught by the new net, but it seems highly probable that some of the larger fish will escape. Again on Part II, I came to the conclusion that it was probably the larger concerns which would derive most benefit from the new procedure." (Hansard Col. 2241, 17th May, 1956.)

The effects of the Restrictive Trade Practices Act have still to work themselves out. My own fears for the Book Trade have not as yet been given substance by subsequent developments— the customs of the Trade are too well enshrined to alter quickly or be broken lightly—but the future is none the less clouded and uncertain.

DOCTORS ON THE DOLE

THE keeping of a scrapbook is a slightly childish pastime as one is continually reminded by the decorative covers on the only cheap scrapbooks one can buy. Yet, on browsing through a meticulously kept one, it is surprising how often one stumbles upon even recent records of events, of immense importance apparently at the time, of considerable significance a year or more later, yet which have none the less escaped one's recollection. Thus, as I turn the pages of my *Boys' Own Cutting Book* with its gaudy cover pictures of aeroplanes, trains and steamships, which covers the first six months of 1956, I find, amongst mementoes of the luncheon to Sir Anthony Eden by the Parliamentary and Scientific Committee, of the Reception at Number 10 Downing Street by Lady Eden, of the inauguration of the Conservative Coffee Club in Carlisle, of the visit of Mr. John Boyd-Carpenter, Minister of Pensions, to Carlisle, of the receipt of an assurance from the Secretary for Air that appropriate technical qualifications are taken into account in the choice for promotion in the junior grades of civilian employees of the R.A.F. at out-stations, of a Question to the Chancellor of the Exchequer on the reduction of the entertainment tax chargeable on the admission fees to professional football games, that I come upon that arresting headline, DOCTORS ON THE DOLE.

I have already remarked upon how a single well-chosen phrase at Question Time can 'work the oracle' in a manner denied to perhaps forty minutes of a carefully-prepared 'There also spoke' intervention in the course of a debate. Had I doubted this, it would have been proved to me earlier in that same year of 1956 when, consequent on responsible constituency representations being made to me on the embarrassing effect of the suddenly-applied credit squeeze on many small business men and individual traders, I decided to intervene with a Question to the Chancellor of the Exchequer. My Question which I asked on 14th February, 1956, and its subsequent supplementary was as follows:

Dr. D. Johnson asked the Chancellor of the Exchequer if he is aware that the credit squeeze is pressing with particular severity on the small independent businessman; and what action he will take to mitigate this.

Sir E. Boyle: My right hon. Friend is aware that small traders, like other members of the community, are finding it more difficult to get credit. But he does not think that the limitation of credit is affecting them so severely that he ought to ask the banks to discriminate in their favour.

Dr. Johnson: Is my hon. Friend aware that the banks appear to be working on the principle of "the smaller the man the tighter the squeeze"? Will he ask them to tackle their larger customers with the same ferocity as they sometimes use towards their smaller ones?

Sir E. Boyle: If my hon. Friend has any evidence that he would like to send me in writing I shall be glad to consider it, but I would remind him that the control of credits to large businesses is operated not only by the banks but also by the Capital Issues Committee.

Nothing succeeds like success, but sometimes one can be altogether too successful. I had only got as far as the first part of my supplementary—"the smaller the man, the tighter the squeeze"—when I became aware of that familiar sound, cheer after ironical cheer from the opposite side of the House. ("Jubilant Labour cheers interrupted him," stated the *News Chronicle* report. "A Conservative critic of the credit squeeze won loud and delighted cheers from the Socialist benches," commented the *Daily Telegraph*.) And this, alas, as I stood on my feet in one of the most crowded houses I have spoken in, was mixed with other noises that sounded like, "Tut, tut, tut," and "No, no, no," from my surrounding hon. Friends.

Taken aback as I was by this unexpected and embarrassing ovation, and equally bewildered by the expressions of disapproval coming from the representatives of private enterprise, I finished my sentence and sat down.

All the same, the expression "the smaller the man, the tighter the squeeze" caught on. A fortnight later it shared the honour, in company with M. Poujade, of being the subject of a *Times* leader. What is more to the point, I was informed by my authoritative source in my constituency that the credit squeeze ceased to press on the small man with quite the same ferocity from that time onwards.

So back to our doctors on the dole. It was in the first place my friend, Dr. Michael Johnn, who directed my attention to this problem. I am best perhaps letting him explain himself, as he does in competent fashion in the Preface to his book:

I write this first chapter—says Dr. Johnn—towards the end of 1956, as a Prologue to the story of my professional life. During the past year, I have assisted several other doctors by undertaking locums for them, but I have been unable to find for myself permanent employment under the National Health Service. My professional qualifications are high, but they have not been sufficient to provide for me employment, either in my specialty as a paediatrician (children's specialist) or in general practice. It may startle many to know that a well-qualified doctor in the prime of life and in good health has no alternative but to go on the dole—I hope that it does. That is my plight and I am not alone in it.

I returned to England in November 1955. Five years in the tropics had played havoc with my wife's health so, for her sake, I came home. It was wonderful to return "to this blessed land, this pearl set in a silver sea".

It was exhilarating to walk again through the quiet English lanes, rambling between rich ploughed fields, with gentle hills against the horizon. Such a marked contrast to the vast emptiness of the Australian landscape! I felt vigorous as I strode through the Lincolnshire by-ways swinging my stick and humming a tune.

But soon I sang no more. I walked less jauntily. For I could not find a job. I contacted many colleagues, some of them famous names in the profession. I visited the agencies. I dashed hither and thither, never failing to follow up even the remotest possibility. But, wherever I went, I was told the same story:

"Wasting your time, Michael, it's a hopeless proposition."
Can anyone offer assistantship, any prospects, to graduate, British, 32 years, married, family, general practice experience and midwifery, ex-R.A.M.C. Homeless, jobless.
Doctor, age 37, married, on the dole, homeless. Accept any job.
Doctor, British, 32, single, three years hospital traineeship, tired of unemployment, invites suggestions. Anything reasonable considered, medical, non-medical, nautical.

"Where in heaven's name," you ask, "do such advertisements appear?" This is the era of full employment. The press is crowded with vacancies. Nobody need to be out of a job. "Oh! I know," you think, "they appeared during the slump of the 'thirties."

Sorry, your surmise is incorrect. They are culled from the recent issues of that illustrious publication, the *British Medical Journal.*

"But how come? Every time I visit my doctor his waiting room is crammed to capacity. I wait ages for attention and then receive perfunctory treatment. He has not time to listen to my complaints, let alone examine me. He always looks as though he could do with a long night's sleep and I thought there was a scarcity of doctors. Only the other evening in his waiting room we were talking about it."

Fair enough, but what you fail to appreciate is that when the benevolent Government introduced the National Health Service, they set the ball rolling for the establishment of monopolies in general practice.

Those doctors with maximum insured lists of three thousand five hundred patients are quite unable to cope with the demand on their services, yet many will not employ assistants because that would deplete their income.

I have applied for every general practice vacancy which has been advertised, since I returned to England. At last, being one of the fortunate chosen from the two hundred who had applied for a deceased doctor's practice, I found myself amongst seven shabby down-at-heel doctors, four of whom had held only spasmodic employment during the previous two years. They were from all parts of England and made forced conversation as we waited for our interviews.

One embittered forty-three-year-old doctor with a wife and three children said to me:

"It's quite pleasant at the Labour Exchange nowadays, almost home from home. No queuing, appointments only. I call on Mondays, very few present, I have a chat with a well-dressed official, much better clothed than I. Quite the club atmosphere. I draw my four pounds, indulge in a cup of tea at a nearby café, my one weekly extravagance, and turn up next Monday. All very agreeable," he concluded, without a smile or a spark of animation.

After an hour's wait my turn for interview arrived. Seated round a long table were assembled the twenty members of the selection committee. The chairman, a well-padded, ponderous gentleman wearing heavy-rimmed spectacles peered at me keenly. The practice was situated in West Ham.

"Why do you wish to practice in West Ham?" enquired the chairman.

I could not very well say that I had a special liking for the place as a summer resort, so I deferentially replied:

"I have had considerable experience of this kind of practice and prefer to work in an industrial area."

He peered round the room and one or two members nodded their heads in unison like wise owls. More questions were flung at me about my professional experience and then I was told to wait outside.

I was not the successful candidate, but the magnanimous bureaucracy paid my third-class rail fare, though no allowance was granted for subsistence. As I had to travel over two hundred miles to attend the interview, I was a pound out of pocket.

The only other interview for a general practice to which I have been called was for the selection of a doctor to succeed to a very small practice in Lewes. Here I met Dr. Stout, who had graduated from an underpaid assistant to a hopeful unemployed doctor and he too now dismally on the dole.

"Bloody lot of twisters these big panel G.P.s," he growled at me in introduction, as he slumped into an adjoining chair in the passage where we waited for our interview. "Don't know what you've been doing, but I've been six months on the dole. I had a good assistantship where I had been promised a partnership. Two months before I was due to go into partnership, the boss said cheerfully: 'I've arranged to take my nephew in, so in two months' time I shall not be needing you any longer.' There was nothing to say, so I had to get out with my wife and child. I couldn't get another assistantship and I've been trying to get a job or a practice for six months. I've put in a hundred and five applications and this is the first interview I've had. Couldn't live properly on this income in any case, but I suppose it is better than four pounds a week on the dole."

Just then he was called in and I after him. He silently walked away heavy-footed and expressionless as the little man in the corner was appointed. The committee selected him because he was the only one with a private income

which would enable him to exist, while he was building
up the nucleus.

"But why not open up in practice?" people ask.

Disillusion yourself. In this free democracy, in this
England for which we fought, I just can't do that. No, sir,
the great monopoly prevents me.

England is divided into three types of areas for medical
practice. First there are a number of 'designated areas'
where one is permitted to open a new practice, because there
are theoretically not enough doctors. Second are the 'inter-
mediate areas' where application to practice is frequently
withheld. Finally, there are the 'restricted areas' in which it
is forbidden to start practice.

I have had several goes at 'designated areas'.

Abandoning the pursuit of designated areas, I was sitting
disconsolately in the beautiful lounge of the British Medical
Association's magnificent building in Tavistock Square
dismally sipping a cup of the inevitable tea, when I got into
conversation with a young doctor.

"I've had it hook, line and sinker," he confessed to me.
"I've just finished my registrar's job a month ago and can't
get fixed up anywhere. I'm thirty-one and now I'm stuck, so
I'm clearing off to Australia, sailing on Friday. There's no
future for fellows like me who wish to specialize. The
profession's overcrowded and it takes years, waiting for
dead men's shoes, before you get a chance. Most of the
openings sent by the B.M.A.'s Advisory Medical Board,
are taken by the time the particulars reach you."

"I know," I responded, "I have applied for every vacancy
only to be told that the posts were already filled. In any case,
you've hit on a good idea in going to Australia. There's
plenty of work for a young enthusiast there. Good luck and a
good voyage!" I farewelled him as he hastened away to
finalize his arrangements.

The solution to the problem of general practice is a

ruthless reduction of overloaded lists down to a maximum of two thousand five hundred patients. The immediate retirement of aged doctors and the restoration of the doctor's liberty to practice anywhere. Out with the area classification.

And what about specialist appointments? When a consultant post is advertised there are often over a hundred applicants, many first-class men with several degrees. If you are over forty you have little chance. For a recent vacancy in Southern England, there were one hundred and thirty-two applicants. Seven were selected, all equally experienced and each with four post-graduate degrees. Faced with the thorny problem of selecting one of these doctors, the committee chose the nephew of the chairman of the Board. Heaven knows what they would have done but for this fortuitous relationship! Spun a coin or given the post to the winner of an egg and spoon race, perhaps.

A famous London children's specialist on whom I called, said: "You haven't a chance in spite of your Australian experience. There are over two hundred first-class men seeking paediatric posts. Now and then one is appointed. The rest continue the fruitless search. Many are leaving the country. Soon we shall lose most of our able young men."

His depressing words are emphasized in whichever direction I turn. Dr. Bacon, holding a higher surgical degree, having completed his term of office as a senior surgical registrar in a London hospital, was unable to find work as a doctor and is now engaged as a garage hand.

So far, I have applied for one hundred and thirty-eight posts advertised in the medical and lay press with negative results.

A letter from one of the leading medical agents in response to my enquiry about possible vacancies in which I offered myself for any job, assistantship, locum or industrial appointment, depressed me further:

"... *I am sorry*," he writes, "*I have absolutely nothing to*

*offer you. There are a considerable number of doctors out of
work, as no doubt you are aware. Assistantships are very
scarce and the odd locum is snapped up. I have just inserted
an advertisement in the* British Medical Journal, *but the post
was already filled before my notice appeared.*"

"But, your Association is the strongest Trade Union in
the world. Don't tell me they can't solve the problems."

The British Medical Association is not affiliated to any
union. It is a voluntary organization to which not more than
eighty per cent of doctors belong. It prides itself that it is
free and unfettered, and will not permit a member to accept
any appointment where membership of the Association is
required by the appointing authority. It advocates increased
pay for doctors established in practice and for consultants,
but does little to assist the overcrowded, underpaid assistants.
The pundits with whom I have discussed the difficulty of
getting work, always give the same complacent answer.

"Unemployables, my dear fellow, don't want to work,
won't go here, won't go there." Perhaps you remember
these stock-in-trades if you were one of the unfortunate two
million unemployed during the Depression? They ring
familiarly, don't they?

It is a strange world we live in when politicians are young
fellows at sixty-five, judges mere babies in arms at seventy-
two while, according to the British Medical Association,
unemployed doctors are too old at fifty. However, established practitioners continue in practice over seventy and
recently a doctor aged ninety was reported as still going
strong.

Outweighing all other considerations, however, there are
the interests and welfare of the patients to be taken into
account. It was for them, presumably, that the National
Health Service was established. The slipshod treatment that
they receive, inevitably, from doctors with large lists is not
conducive to a good medical service. Unless the problem

is tackled with wisdom and foresight, British medicine and the British people are going to be the sufferers.

I have spent years of hard work, acquiring experience at home and abroad, years too of endeavour in securing post-graduate degrees, yet all my efforts to obtain any type of permanent medical work have proved unavailing.

So, driven by necessity, I am on the dole. I am treated with courtesy and tact, as I make my way every Wednesday and Friday, by appointment, to a Lincolnshire Labour Exchange. Nothing is said that might possibly embarrass me; in fact, I am grateful to the officials, one suffering from asthma and the other from lumbago, who ask my professional opinion upon their complaints, just as if I was a real National Health Service doctor. The unemployment benefit is not much, but I take it, because I need it desperately.

I still smoke an occasional cigarette, but feel guilty when I do so. I keep myself clean, tidy and well-groomed, for, whatever the apologists for the present state of affairs may say, I am unemployed, but not unemployable.

"Despite all my years of experience," declared Dr. Johnn to me in his rich Irish brogue, as we had tea together in the Harcourt Room at the House, "I've tried and I've tried, and I can't get a job anywhere. The Ministry likes to say, 'Go to Wigan and try there.' Well, I've applied in Wigan and there were one hundred applicants for the job. One hundred, I tell you."

Dr. Johnn was, as he admitted, a rolling stone, and this world of Committees in which we live has no place for rolling stones.

However, Dr. Johnn did not need to tell me. I was well aware. He and I shared in common the one fact—though rich with most of a lifetime of clinical experience, we were both middle-aged men out of the National Health Service. I only differed from him in that my political career had taken a slightly more fortunate turn than his own nascent efforts in the Labour

Party. After all, I reflected as we talked, a wrong turn in my own career and I would be a Doctor on the Dole too.

I therefore did not need much persuading to set down a Question to the Minister of Pensions and National Insurance. This is the way the question went when I asked it on 26th March, 1957.

Dr. D. Johnson asked the Minister of Pensions and National Insurance how many doctors are in receipt of unemployment insurance benefit.

The Minister of Pensions and National Insurance (Mr. John Boyd-Carpenter): I understand from my right hon. Friend, the Minister of Labour and National Service, that on 19th March, 1956, there were 35 doctors registered at appointments offices in receipt of unemployment benefit.

Dr. Johnson: May I ask my right hon. Friend to confirm as far as possible and as far as he knows that these doctors are genuinely seeking work in the National Health Service and are unable to obtain it?

Mr. Boyd-Carpenter: I should like notice of that question, and I should probably like notice of it to be given to one of my right hon. Friends.

"Many people are surprised today by the statement made by the Minister of Pensions," states 'The Londoner's Diary' of the *Evening Standard* in reference to this question.

I accordingly pressed matters further with the Minister of Health three weeks later as follows:

Dr. D. Johnson asked the Minister of Health (1) whether he is aware that there were thirty-five doctors in receipt of unemployment benefit on 19th March, 1956; and what steps he is taking to find opportunities for employment for them in the National Health Service;

(2) whether he is aware of the existence of a permanent reservoir of unemployed or under-employed doctors unable to find work under the National Health Service; and if he will institute a full enquiry into these circumstances.

Miss Hornsby-Smith: It is estimated that there are 53,000 doctors in active employment in Great Britain; the proportion receiving unemployment benefit is therefore extremely small. Every effort is made to bring vacant posts to notice. My right hon. Friend the present Minister of Labour and National Service appointed a committee to enquire into future requirements for doctors and medical students.

Dr. Johnson: Does my hon. Friend appreciate that this small number of thirty-five is in fact only symptomatic of a considerably larger number, many of them young and competent doctors, who are unable to find places in the National Health Service? Is she aware that for every vacancy there are some 80 to 100 applicants?

Miss Hornsby-Smith: It was to meet these problems that the committee was appointed.

There are varying degrees of dissatisfaction with a Minister's reply, and varying methods of expressing that dissatisfaction. The dramatic way is to rise in the House 'to a point of order' and notify that it is one's intention to 'move the Question on the Adjournment'. The Adjournment Debate is the half-hour's debate which takes place at the end of each daily session, which gives the private member a further opportunity to ventilate a grievance, be it a general one or be it concerning an individual case: and to receive a reply from the Parliamentary Secretary to the appropriate Ministry.

An Adjournment Debate is an important and valuable facility for the individual member—it has the important advantage that he can get his grievance on the record of the parliamentary paper; it has the corresponding disadvantages that the Parliamentary Secretary has the last word and also that, if one desires publicity for a cause or an individual grievance, the Adjournment Debate, as often as not, takes place at an hour when the following day's papers have gone to press. It is apt, in fact, to be something of an anti-climax: it is the dramatic gesture of moving the debate at Question Time that registers!

For Government backbenchers, however, dramatic gestures at Question Time are not exactly *de rigueur:* they are, in most instances, best left unsaid. There is therefore an alternative method of moving an Adjournment Debate and that is to put a quiet note in to Mr. Speaker. This was the method which I adopted in this instance. The Debate added little to what has been said: but this is the gist of the Parliamentary Secretary's reply:

"I would like to assure the hon. Member that the number of doctors in practice is certainly not decreasing. May I give him an analysis of what has happened in the year from 1st January to 31st December, 1955? Practices which have become vacant owing to death or retirement or resignation numbered 259. One hundred and seventeen successors were appointed. Seventeen amalgamated with other small practices. That left a residue of 125 dispersed. Some of them were single-practice doctors who had died and whose practices had been given up. Against that, of the practices dispersed, 40 had no patients on their lists, so they would obviously have had no goodwill assets to pass on; 51 had under 300 patients, and perhaps the age and incapacity of the doctors had led to their practices running down in their later years; and 14 practices had lists of 700 or more, but in the majority of them certain significant factors applied, such as their being situated in a rehousing area and diminishing because of the population moving to other districts. That comprises the total of 125 dispersed.

"During the year 613 doctors were admitted to the list to practise in partnership. Of these, 297 were assistants entering into partnership in practices where they were already working. Therefore, the 613 shows a substantial balance of increase of doctors in practice against the 125 practices dispersed."

That was the position some two years ago. What is the position now? It is not greatly different. The Committee under Sir Henry Willink has reported and suggested a cut by one-tenth in the output of doctors to take place after 1961. In the meantime there were still 32 Doctors on the Dole according to the answer to my Question on 16th December, 1957, while general practitioners with full lists do busy surgeries.

To give the other side of the balance, the Minister of Health, Mr. Derek Walker-Smith, reported in the National Health Service Contribution Bill Second Reading Debate on 5th March, 1958, that 22,500 doctors were engaged in general practice in 1956 as opposed to 20,500 in 1951, thus showing an increase of 2,000 doctors absorbed into general practice in five years, almost entirely as junior partners as a further breakdown of the figures showed.

But Dr. Michael Johnn has not been amongst those so absorbed. After working for many months in a pharmaceutical firm, he has rolled on further and, in order to find a nitch in his profession, has emigrated to America where, despite being classed among the unemployables in Great Britain, he is now installed in a job at a salary of £2,500 per year. And the problem still remains whether, under the present restrictive system, this country is not losing many of her best and most enthusiastic doctors, such as those with hospital experience as registrars, who, unable to find a place at home when they have finished their hospital appointments, are also emigrating.

It was these fears that prompted me to ask an appropriate question to the Minister on the 29th July, 1957: and the interchange of question and answer went as follows:

Dr. D. Johnson asked the Minister of Health if he is aware of the number of qualified doctors who are emigrating to appointments in the Commonwealth and the United States of America owing to not being able to find employment in the National Health Service; and if he will make an enquiry into this situation.

Mr. Vaughan-Morgan: It is no new thing for some doctors from this country to take appointments overseas. Figures of the number doing so are not available, but I will willingly consider any further statistics which my hon. Friend can produce. The report of the Committee which has been enquiring into future requirements for doctors and medical students is expected shortly.

Dr. Johnson: I am not at the moment able to produce statistics, but might I none the less ask my hon. Friend to take careful note of what is undoubtedly a drift overseas, including to the United States, on the part of many of our more competent doctors? Might I inform him of at least one case of a very well trained and experienced doctor who returned from overseas, was unable to find a place in the National Health Service after searching for a year or eighteen months, and has now obtained a very excellent appointment in the United States in his specialty as a paediatrician, a post he was unable to obtain here?

Mr. Vaughan-Morgan: I note my hon. Friend's remarks.

Mr. B. Harrison: As large numbers of doctors are coming here from the Commonwealth, will my hon. Friend do absolutely nothing to stop this exchange, which is of mutual advantage?

Mr. Vaughan-Morgan: I entirely agree with my hon. Friend's remarks.

The challenge of Mr. Harrison's question led me to make further enquiries—this time of the President of the Board of Trade concerning the number of doctors and dentists entering and leaving the country by sea over a period of six years 1951-6. These figures showed two contrasting trends. On the one hand there was a balance on the influx side of emigrant doctors and dentists into the United Kingdom over the five years of 240 from South Africa and of 542 from India and Pakistan: this being counterbalanced by a loss of 138 to Australia, 231 to New Zealand and no less than 707 to Canada.

It cannot be said that the general picture is entirely a reassuring one, particularly in the light of the complaints of assistants and unestablished practitioners of the level of both their own and junior partners remuneration that fill the press at the time of writing relative to the deliberation of the Royal Commission as Doctor's Remuneration. It is certainly not a reassuring one for me personally, as, were I dependant entirely on my professional attainments for my economic survival, what would I be myself, but a Doctor on the Dole?

A DOCTOR RETURNS

SOMETIMES I felt that in my own person I epitomized the dichotomy of feeling experienced by many Conservatives during the middle 'fifties. My double position was a curious one. Here was I, on the one hand, a Member of Parliament and a pillar of society, on the other a victim of our society's harshest and most antiquated law—the law of 'certification' of mental patients against which there is no redress: a supporter of the Government on the one hand, yet with a 'personal case' grievance against the Government on the other, in that, despite the evidence submitted to them, our medical bureaucracy, speaking through the mouths of successive Ministers of Health, had barred any investigation into this evidence: while, more paradoxical still, Conservative Ministers were defending the 'official line' in regard to an incident under a Socialist Government as against one of their own kind.

I have told in *A Doctor Returns* how the *élan* imparted to me by the resolution to solve my special problem, had carried me forward from the day I was discharged from mental hospital an ex-certificatee, to that other and happier day a little over four years later on which I had stepped on to the stage of parliamentary life as the Member of Parliament for Carlisle. No part of these efforts had, however, led to the satisfactory clarification of the strange events of October 1950, when I went down to stay in the country on my legitimate business of straightening out my hotel affairs; and, while staying on my own premises of the hotel which I then owned, was, together with Betty my wife who showed identical symptoms, taken suddenly ill and

removed by a summary reception order under Section 16 of the
Lunacy Act for a six-week stay in a mental hospital, where I was
detained while my affairs were in parlous state, and were only
salvaged from utter ruin by the skill and courage of my friend,
Ivor Davies.

Neither the fact of the strange double illness of Betty and
myself, nor my own repeated assertions that we were the
victims of poison, nor the background evidence that I offered to
produce with a view to corroborating this suspicion, had
produced the least visible effect on our administration. Their
motto, be they Ministry of Health or be they County Police,
appeared to be, not so much that of eternal vigilance, but that of
"See no evil, hear no evil, speak no evil", despite even the
publication of my researches into the hallucinogenic drugs,
which could well have caused such symptoms as Betty and I had.

Thus that same sense of indignation and injury which had
been mine on my first apprehension on the street pavement of X—
outside my hotel, which had been only whetted by the continu-
ous rebuffs I had suffered at the hands of authority, was still
mine as I walked about the lobbies of the House of Commons.

It had been considerably assuaged, by my appreciation of the
confidence that had been placed in me by the Conservative
Party, both by its Central Office, and by its Carlisle Association,
in supporting me for election to Parliament, despite their full
knowledge of all circumstances. Thus, though my loyalty to
administrative government was under strain to a degree, my
loyalty to the Conservative Party was a stronger one than that
dictated by political sympathy alone.

In my anxiety to leave no stone unturned in the problem that
confronted me, I had approached an officer of the Conservative
Party Central Organization, as perhaps others in their innocence
have done before me, and wanted to know what could be done.

"You must get into Parliament," was the encouraging reply.

This conversation took place after my adoption at Carlisle
with a 3,000 Labour majority against me.

But here I was in Parliament and what did I do now? A wide range of privileges lay open. In practice, however, it would be an incorrect use of those privileges to use them blatantly for the purpose of pressing one's own personal case. There was, however, one thing that I could do with complete correctness and that was to write a book. Thanks to being chairman of my own publishing firm, I was fortunately not only able to ensure that my own book would be published, but to time the exact moment when it could be done.

Whenever things got too much for me, I could go and put them down in my book—just as I am doing now. So the book was written and it was decided to publish it for our autumn programme of 1956 under the title of *A Doctor Returns*: and *A Doctor Returns* tells the story of my irritations between the years 1950 and 1955: and also of my social and scientific researches in connection with my illness.

Thus, the writing complete and the publication date settled, my feelings of frustration were sublimated for the time being into feelings of apprehension as *A Doctor Returns*, like an unexploded time bomb with its fuse set for not later than the end of October, started on its way through the printing presses. To get my case across, to make news, to sell the book, these were the problems on which we started to exercise our ingenuity. These were my worries. Would *A Doctor Returns* misfire in the same way as my previous attempt to do just this thing, in my second autobiography *Bars and Barricades*, misfired some four years previously? Would the Press overlook me, as they had done then? A multiplicity of ingenious schemes for activities connected with its publication presented themselves to me to ensure that this should not happen again.

I need not have worried. *A Doctor Returns* exploded in my face long before any carefully laid schemes came to fruition.

A Doctor Returns was not due for publication until October, but it was the middle of July, as I was discussing its prospects, that one thing led to another—a word over the dinner-table to an introduction, the introduction to a tea conference in that most desperate plotting place of all, the public cafeteria of the House of Commons. I was given the invitation: would I like my story splashed? Would I think about it over-night and give an answer?

In many ways this was premature—many months premature from the point of view of publishing technique. But, particularly in the light of my past experience, a bird in the hand was worth two in the bush as far as newspaper publicity was concerned. Besides, as Ivor, now my publishing partner, pointed out, a few popular press headlines would be good, excellent, in fact, publicity to show the booksellers when the book was represented to trade buyers for pre-publication subscription.

I picked up our office phone and dialled.

"Go ahead," I said.

I have already, earlier in this book, referred briefly to the publicity: here is a reminder of it in a little detail:

The front page of *Reynolds News*: the starred story:

The Fantastic Story of the Tory M.P. and a Mental Home

"I WAS DRUGGED, HELD SIX WEEKS"

"Gang wanted to get rid of me"
By Kenneth Wanstall

A DOCTOR M.P. last night told the amazing story of a man who was drugged to prevent him from exposing a criminal gang, then mentally certified and held for six weeks in a mental home.

Dr. Donald Johnson, M.A., M.B., B.Ch., M.R.C.S., L.R.C.P., Conservative M.P. for Carlisle and a barrister, told the fantastic story. And he was telling it about himself.

His experience happened five years ago when he owned a luxury hotel near Oxford.

"Rumours of queer goings-on in the town reached my ears," he said.

"I decided on certain actions which I have since discovered cut across the activities of a number of desperate men.

"They set about getting me out of the way. I was given sherry in which Indian hemp mixed with certain other drugs had been added."

And so on, and so on, for a column and a half.

A Tory M.P. doped and put into a mental home!

Once sparked, the thing went exploding round the world like a cracker-jack and with the speed of that later phenomenon, the Russian sputnik. My Canadian friends tell me that the Toronto papers made a particularly good show.

More immediately at home the *Sunday Dispatch* had picked it up, virtually before the ink was dry, and had it in their later editions. Going from there, the entire Monday morning's press 'made whoopee'—as also did my telephone bell, which did not cease from 10 o'clock on Sunday morning until 11 o'clock at night. "Mention the book," I asked all enquiring Press representatives. "Have you any further statement to add, doctor?" "Yes, I'll have it all in the book. Do mention the book." Some of them did and some of them evidently forgot to, but they did me proud just the same: editorials in the *Evening Standard* ('The Lost Report') and, in addition, the *Daily Herald* ('Probe those Laws') emphasizing the need at an early date for revised legislation. I only quelled the turmoil eventually by a 'bromide' statement to the Press Association in which, believe it or not, I promised fuller and better particulars in the book when it was published. Otherwise my telephone might well be ringing yet. Content, however, with this, my Press friends went off to their next 'View Hallo'.

To get into the Sunday papers is, after all, the acme of

achievement to the aggrieved person and I cannot deny that this holocaust of publicity was satisfying to me after years of living with my problem in the shadows. For the rest I could only hope that such age-old political adages as "There is no publicity which is bad publicity", and "It doesn't matter what they say about you, as long as they say something", would pull me through.

My constituency friends, with their usual staunchness, had rallied to the cause.

"I am very glad that our Member has decided to tell the whole story," said my friend and agent, Stanley Walker, to *Reynolds News*. "In the interests of the general public these things should be exposed."

It was considered by my supporters, I am glad to say, the best thing that could have been done. For, of course, many a quiet use could have been made of the knowledge (which we knew our opponents to have) of a political antagonist's stay in a mental hospital, had this piece of information been treated in hugger-mugger fashion.

On the other hand, I have made some mention of the feelings of self-consciousness which entry to the House of Commons brings to a new member. Certainly never have I felt so self-conscious in moving amongst my parliamentary colleagues as I did the Monday afternoon when I walked into the House after being the central figure of this fiesta of week-end sensationalism. It was well perhaps that, throughout my life, I have acquired a certain immunity to the meaningful silence that can, on occasions, speak louder than words.

However, I had no need to feel myself lonely! For during the next few days, there came the most surprising phenomenon of all. This was the letters. Letters of all shapes, sizes, varieties and handwriting. Manifestly sane letters from those who were detained inmates of mental hospitals. Equally manifestly lunatic ones (including the one from the lady in Chippenham, Wilts, who complained that she was 'being electrically raped') from those who were at large and free in the community. Letters that started within twenty-four hours of my splash of news, and that have continued through the weeks, months and years from that day to this, until by now my correspondents number several hundreds of distressed people, one and all complaining of the operation of our mental health laws. Letters continued, as I have said, to reach me through devious channels. Day after day, there is a fresh pile of letters in my post at the House of Commons. I go 300 miles north to Carlisle and there is a batch of letters addressed to me there, while others come to me at home. Yet others are delivered addressed 'care of the Royal Commission on the Law Relating to Mental Health'. (The Post Office even developed the habit at one stage of sending me letters that were addressed to the Royal Commission and not to me!), or 'care of the Lord Chancellor', or even 'care of Number 10 Downing Street'! while others arrive through the medium of my parliamentary colleagues, or through the *Daily Express*, or even the august *Times* and *Observer*. Perhaps not the most numerous correspondence an M.P. has had, but certainly the most fantastic.

These summer weeks of 1956 were busy ones.

In the last chapter of *A Doctor Returns* I have told the story of Colonel Drummond. There were others who had written to me with strange stories in addition to Colonel Drummond. There was the local government officer in the East Kent town who had endeavoured to organize a petition to the Minister of Health and who had been certified as suffering from an 'obsession': the architect who, after two years incarceration in a Scottish mental hospital, had escaped to Eire and there set up forthwith in practice in his own profession: the schoolmaster in a north-east coast town; the scoutmaster in a south coast town; the retired lady living in Sussex. These people may or may not have qualified for the dire formality of 'certification' at the time it happened to them, but certainly they had no straws in their hair. They were not lunatics in the

usually accepted sense of that term, either now or, as far as one
could tell, at any time.

Then the inspiration struck me. We would have a party—a
publication party. It would be at the House of Commons.
These people would be my guests, to meet a number of my
parliamentary colleagues and the representatives of the Press.
It would not only be a publication party, but the kick-off for
our campaign to reform the law.

What a party! One of the most unusual, perhaps, that have
been held in the reception rooms of the House.

"For the life of me I can't think of a last line for this paragraph," says Rex North reporting the event in advance in the
Sunday Pictorial under the heading 'House Party'. This
sardonic note was the only occasion on which the *Mirror* papers
reported me either then or at any time subsequently during my
campaign for the mentally ill.

Did the party go? Yes, of course it went. With full marks
for my half-dozen or more ex-certified guests who came from
Eire, from the North of England, from the South Coast and from
the Midlands, to display themselves under numerical labels
with a cross-reference to the hand-out of their stories that was
circulated to the journalists, and who allowed themselves to be
interviewed in this anonymous fashion, behaving, need it be
said, as normally as any 'non-mental' person whom you would
wish to meet. Full marks too to my parliamentary colleagues,
Harry Kerby and Godfrey Lagden, on my own side, Norman
Dodds and Marcus Lipton on the Opposition side, who came
along to support me and subsequently supported my motion on
the parliamentary paper urging an early change in the mental
laws. A raspberry, however, for the enterprising 'special
reporter' who rang me three days before the party for further particulars of what was to happen, which I good-naturedly gave him:

"You will, please, mention the book, won't you?" I requested.

"Yes, of course, I'll be reviewing the book later," he assured
me.

His feature appeared the following morning—still two days before the party, so that on the day of the party all the other national Press representatives felt they had been 'scooped' by a rival. But he did not mention the book, nor did either he or his paper review it!

I could not, however, complain at my publicity. I find that I have some twenty to thirty news features on the party—even if they do not all mention the book! Then the book reviews and features go on from there, including one otherwise excellent one in the *Sunday Graphic* which, I find, has me 'leading a procession to the House of Commons'. (My post immediately started to snow with offers to join my procession! What a procession this would have been!) The *Sunday Graphic* feature was read by the pleasant young man from Radio Luxembourg and this led to Betty and I featuring together on the 'Jamboree' programme—stardom indeed! My own very first appearance on the air and a fulfilment, at least, of one of Betty's intuitions at the time of her illness.

From the more serious point of view, there were reviews and supporting features in the weeklies such as the following one from the *Spectator* by Brian Inglis, one of the Press guests at our party, for which I am particularly grateful:

"I must say that, talking to his 'cases', it was clear that the law as it stands is not only outmoded, but a positive incitement to ill-intentioned persons to put their enemies out of the way. All that is required is a doctor's signature (the signature of a J.P. is usually a formality) and you and I can be incarcerated, without benefit of *habeas corpus*, until such time as the hospital authorities agree that we are sane. Still, I feel that the more important part of Dr. Johnson's work is his campaign against the stigma of lunacy. Why people should boast about going into a hospital to have their insides carved up, but should regard it as shameful to go for mental treatment, I cannot understand—particularly as getting on for half the hospital beds in the country are occupied by the mentally sick. Experience at advanced hospitals like Warlingham Park in Surrey has shown that the old concept of lunatic asylums, walled, bolted and barred, can safely be abandoned: even the ward keys can be thrown away. I wish Dr. Johnson best of luck in his enterprise."

This paragraph alone made our party worth while.

We could, at least, claim that we had put *A Doctor Returns* on the map. With the aid of the reviews that followed during the ensuing months in provincial papers, periodicals, both lay and professional, with their curious mixture of censure and praise, encouragement in one paper, belittlement in the other—which I will not weary the reader by quoting—and thanks to the support of booksellers and librarians, it sold out the substantial proportion of its edition, despite its strongly technical medico-legal element.

Of its further repercussions, the later part of this book will speak. Perhaps, however, the *Aberdeen Press and Journal* will be allowed the final word for the moment with its comment: "But even entry to Westminster seems for him to have done little to smooth the stony path that the reformer must tread. If it had, his story would make less interesting reading."

THE SUEZ CRISIS

IT was coincident with the events described in my last chapter that President Nasser of Egypt startled the world, not to mention the Chamber and the lobbies of the House of Commons, by announcing his intention to nationalize the Suez Canal. Thus the distractions and the excitement of my personal affairs in the autumn of 1956 were equalled by the distractions and the excitement of the political atmosphere in which I was living. It was an exhausting time.

It is doubtless true that the Battle of Waterloo was won upon the playing fields of Eton; but, be that so or not, the Battle of the Suez Canal was certainly lost in the Debating Chamber and the lobbies of that particular House of Commons of which I am a member. Let it not be thought, however, that I have another Bromberger story to offer. It is merely for me to record the impressions of a public spectator of those momentous but unfortunate events. To a Conservative backbencher the Suez Canal crisis in the House of Commons was like one of those shattering nightmares which, as a dreamer, one is compelled to watch in paralysed horror, as melodrama beyond all conscious fancy relentlessly unfolds itself before one's helpless gaze.

As I look back through past Hansards reporting the months prior to the explosion of the Suez crisis, it is remarkable how sparse are mentions of the Suez Canal. Indeed, there are only two during the whole of the summer session of 1956: they are perhaps worth recording.

The first occasion was when Mr. Emmanuel Shinwell, on the 30th May, asked the Foreign Secretary whether he would now direct the attention of the United Nations Organization to the refusal of Egypt to permit vessels of any nationality free passage through the Suez Canal.

"Is it not an extraordinary situation," asked Mr. Shinwell in his supplementary Question, "when Egypt can defy the whole United Nations Organization and a decision of the Security Council? What is the use of the Security Council if Egypt, and countries of this kind, can defy those bodies?"

The second was when Major Legge-Bourke, in the discussion of the Business of the House on 14th June, asked the Leader of the House whether his attention had been drawn to the all-party Motion, embodying a tribute to Her Majesty's Armed Forces who served in Egypt?

The Motion was:

That this House, on the occasion of the final evacuation of the Suez Canal Zone by British troops, desires humbly to reaffirm its abiding appreciation of the exemplary devotion to duty shown during three-quarters of a century by all ranks of Her Majesty's Forces in upholding the honour of Great Britain and the sanctity of her covenanted word, in bringing justice, compassion and enrichment to the weak, and in boldly withstanding the assaults of dictatorial Powers; and, more especially, in renewing its homage to the blessed memory of all those of Her Majesty's subjects who have laid down their lives in defence of Egyptian sands and soil, this House earnestly prays that the mutual interests of Great Britain and Egypt may be furthered by truth and cordiality in the years to come.

"I noticed the Motion on the Order Paper," replied Mr. Butler, "embodying a tribute to Her Majesty's Forces in the Canal Zone. I am sure that I speak on behalf of my right hon. Friend the Prime Minister and my colleagues in the Government when I say that we certainly endorse the tribute given in this Motion, to the services rendered by Her Majesty's Forces, and the homage expressed to the blessed memory of those who lost their lives in the Canal Zone, and endorse the hope for good relations and cordiality between Britain and Egypt in the future."

"May I," joined in Mr. Gaitskell, "on behalf of my right hon. and hon. Friends, say that we, also, would desire to associate ourselves with the sentiments expressed in the Motion?"

*   *   *

Not until 1st August does the record give any warning of the coming storm, so shortly to break in full force. Then:

Mr. Harold Davies asks the Foreign Secretary whether he will refer the decision of Egypt to nationalize the Suez Canal to the Permanent Court of International Justice at the Hague; if he will seek the co-operation of the Soviet Government in dealing with the problem of the recent action of Egypt on the Suez Canal; if he will give the exact terms which the Egyptian Government have communicated to him regarding compensation for Suez Canal shares.

Mr. Warbey asks the Foreign Secretary what were the specific changes in Egyptian political and economic policy which took place between February and July of this year and which led the Government to withdraw its offer of financial help for the Aswan Dam project; what offer of compensation has been received from the Egyptian Government for the British Government's share in the Suez Canal Company?

Mr. Zilliacus asks the Foreign Secretary in view of the latest action of the Egyptian Government in relation to the Suez Canal, whether he will give an assurance that Her Majesty's Government are prepared to co-operate with the other permanent members of the Security Council represented at the Summit Conference in Geneva last July, in order to bring about a settlement through the United Nations of all outstanding issues in the Middle East.

These Questions, however, had already had their answer two days previously from Sir Anthony Eden.

"This much, however, I can say," pronounced Sir Anthony Eden. "No arrangements for the future of this great international waterway could be acceptable to Her Majesty's Government which would leave it in the unfettered control of a single Power which could, as recent events have shown, exploit it purely for purposes of national policy."

*   *   *

Thus the stage was set, in as imposing fashion as for any Grand Opera, for the first of the big (I cannot call them 'great') Suez Debates, which took place on 2nd August, 1956, the day that the House dispersed.

On the eve of a Recess the House of Commons is customarily forlorn and desolate: but on this occasion every seat was crowded.

"That is still our position, and it must remain so," Sir Anthony repeated his assurance given three days previously.

Many will recall to mind, as something unreal, the strange unanimity of this debate.

"In view of the uncertain situation created by the actions of the Egyptian Government, Her Majesty's Government have thought it necessary to take certain precautionary measures of a military nature." Sir Anthony developed his theme with scarcely an interruption—save those which the House has learnt to expect from Mr. Sidney Silverman, more or less as a matter of custom.

"I must make it abundantly plain that anything that the Government have done or not done in no way excuses Colonel Nasser's action in seizing the Canal," said Mr. Gaitskell. ". . . it is all very familiar. It is exactly the same that we encountered from Mussolini and Hitler in those years before the war . . . I believe we were right to react sharply to this move. While force cannot be excluded, we must be sure that the circumstances justify it and that it is, if used, consistent with our

H

belief in and our pledges to the Charter of the United Nations
and not in conflict with them."

Mr. Gaitskell stood for firmness combined with sagacity. He
spoke for England, an England anxious to strike the right
attitude—and then go off on holiday.

"Would we get our own family holiday in Austria, fixed for
the end of August?" I reflected sombrely. It would be the first
Continental holiday Betty and I had taken for ten years.
Already the Chief Whip had been on to each of his flock
personally, making the special plea that we should not fail to
let him know of our whereabouts during the coming Recess.
'An uncertain situation'—'certain precautions of a military
nature'—it did not sound too promising, as I calculated the
chances. It was a seductive thought that, as this debate of
2nd August progressed, the matter was being properly covered
for the time being. It was not without a sense of relief that I said
'good-bye' to the crowded lobbies and turned my attention to
plans for a holiday in the Tyrol, which I had never hitherto
visited. But this sense of relief? When had one felt it before?
Was it not twenty years ago when, during each crisis of the
'thirties, the sudden alarm had subsided and one could again
resume life's pleasant tenor—at least, for the time being.

But in the meantime, let us go away on holiday, ready as
loyal Government backbenchers to reassemble and support the
Government as and when we were told, ready, as a nation, to
deal with the Egyptian upstart at our convenience.

Only one jarring note had been introduced into the debate
of 2nd August.

"The problem that raises itself and which must be solved in
the next few days is the problem: who will bell the cat? Who,"
declared the speaker, Mr. Hugh Fraser, Conservative M.P. for
Stafford and Stone, "will chain the mad dog in Cairo?"

The next few days, Mr. Fraser? No! No! No! It was
August Bank Holiday.

But who would bell the cat?

Was it to be Mr. Sidney Silverman, chattering excitedly as, like the Walrus and the Carpenter, he and Mr. Zilliacus strode the lobbies together? What had Mr. Silverman been saying to Mr. Zilliacus? What had Mr. Zilliacus been saying to Mr. Silverman? I did not know. But as—at intervals during holiday arrangements—one contemplated the potentialities of their conversation, it boded no good.

Who would chain the mad dog in Cairo?

Hitler planned his coups in the nineteen-thirties on Saturdays, secure in the knowledge that the British week-end would prevent immediate action. With equal cunning perhaps Nasser siezed the Suez Canal immediately before the August holidays. It may be that he was even more clever than he knew. With Parliament dispersed, the process of formulation of public opinion passed by default elsewhere, to the editors of newspapers and periodicals whose commentaries on events assumed enhanced importance.

Who would chain the mad dog in Cairo? Not the editor of the *Manchester Guardian*. Nor the editor of *The Economist*. Nor the editor of the *Observer*.

During the succeeding weeks, as the days passed by without parliamentary recall, this became all too clear. As for our holiday, we had it all but for a single day, but, as once again an M.P. in temporary harness, I returned for the special session on 12th and 13th September, it was all too obvious that our respite had been dearly bought: and that resolution for firm action had been sapped by delay in a way that is perhaps inevitable in a democratic community.

Who then would chain the mad dog in Cairo? That was what, a full complement of M.P.s still in semi-holiday mood, crowded and gossiping in the lobbies and without the usual distractions to occupy us, we had returned to Westminster from near and far to hear.

Who would bell the cat? Who besides Mr. Hugh Fraser and the *Sunday Express*?

Sir Anthony Eden, facing the reassembled Parliament, spoke firmly in the face of the hesitations that had shown themselves.

"Of course, there are those who say that we should not be justified and are not justified in reacting vigorously unless Colonel Nasser commits some further act of aggression. That was the argument used in the nineteen-thirties to justify every concession that was made to the dictators. It has not been my experience that dictators are deflected from their purpose because others affect to ignore it. This reluctance to face reality led to the subjugation of Europe and to the Second World War. We must not help to reproduce, step by step, the history of the 'thirties. We have to prove ourselves wiser this time, and to check aggression by the pressure of international opinion if possible; but, if not, by other means before it has grown to monstrous proportions . . . the Government are not prepared to embark on a policy of abject appeasement, nor, I think, would the House—or most of the House—ask them to, because the consequences of such a policy are known to us. A stimulus is given to fresh acts of lawlessness. With the loss of resources the capacity to resist becomes steadily less, friends drop away and the will to live becomes enfeebled."

Thus spoke the wisdom of twenty years of diplomatic experience in this debate of mid-September. But as for 'belling the cat', that was not just yet—not during the next few days.

Were we proving ourselves wiser this time? Who of my own political vintage and mindful of pre-war political battles could avoid that curious feeling of *déjà vu*?

But no, it was not quite the same. For here was Mr. Richard Crossman, forgetful—except perhaps in his preliminary apologia—of the time when he, an Oxford don and up-and-coming member of the Oxford Labour Party, and I, a Liberal prospective candidate for the Bewdley Division, toured the streets of Oxford together in October 1938 in support of Professor Lindsay, champion of resistance to aggression:

forgetful, too, of that noble speech, directed against the Appeasement of Mr. Chamberlain, made from the platform of the
Oxford Town Hall, and supported by my friend, Ivor, making the
first of his many appearances as Liberal Candidate for Oxford
(momentarily, indeed, an 'ex-candidate', as he had withdrawn
in favour of Lindsay's 'Independent Progressive' candidature)
and myself sitting amongst a galaxy of Liberal and Progressive
talent. What was Mr. Richard Crossman saying now from his
place below the gangway on the Socialist benches?

"I am convinced that we have to negotiate." These were the
words of Mr. Richard Crossman on 12th September, 1956.
"It has never been made clear why we think it is worth while
risking a war to have an international civil authority in charge
there rather than Nasser's authority . . . I think that if this
country took a more reasonable view of this matter it would be
easier to negotiate a satisfactory settlement."

Not—oh, dear me—Sir Lionel Heald, speaking from our
Conservative benches, as a former Attorney-General. As I sat
in the Members' gallery upstairs where I had to find refuge
owing to every seat on the floor of the House being full, I
could not believe my ears as I heard Sir Lionel Heald saying:

"There is, I believe, a great deal of uncertainty and some
ignorance of what our international obligations are. . . . I
believe it will not be doing a disservice to the House if, very
briefly, I indicate what precisely our international obligations
are, because I myself am not prepared to support any action
which would involve a breach of our international obligations. . . . If a reasonable and proper plan, supported by 18 or
12 nations or whatever the number may be, is put forward to
the United Nations and approved there, then I personally will
be perfectly willing to support the Government in any measure
they think it necessary to carry out."

Not, in these circumstances, Mr. Gaitskell:

"I should like to ask the Foreign Secretary whether he is now
prepared to make a declaration that Her Majesty's Government

will use force only in accordance with our obligations under the United Nations' Charter?" asked Mr. Gaitskell, coming to the despatch box, immediately after Sir Lionel Heald sat down.

Who would chain the mad dog in Cairo? Would it be the United Nations, as suggested by Sir Lionel Heald—the United Nations that had already allowed itself over a period of years to be defied by Egypt over the Suez Canal, as Sir Lionel Heald must surely have known? Not a hope from the start! The United Nations, born of twentieth-century idealism, albeit a forum of world opinion, could not be anything other than an agglomeration of the individual views and interests of its constituent nations. In this respect, the system of one nation, one vote, combined with that of immediately admitting all the colonial peoples as soon as they were translated to nationhood, could not do other than to ensure that the former Imperial Powers would have a numerous block of states against them in any endeavour they made to support their rights—particularly, of course, their rights as against their former subject peoples.

I had hitherto been but a spectator of all these events. A new Member, deeply engrossed in other aspects of affairs that I have explained, it could not be expected that any attempt at intervention by me on Foreign Affairs would carry any weight. In any case, there was the Suez Group with its stalwarts, there was the Imperial tradition of the Conservative Party. Or was there? A sense of alarm started to fill me. In any case, Sir Lionel Heald was altogether too much. Particularly as it was all too clear that Sir Lionel Heald did not speak for himself alone in the Conservative Party.

As I sat on the Terrace discussing these things with Bob Crouch, we felt that some protest must be made, by us if by nobody else. This took the form of a letter to *The Times* in which we were joined by Henry Kerby. In this we state:

"During the course of our experience of listening to the debates in the House of Commons we have come to appreciate that legalism is one thing, reality sometimes another. We would like therefore to put on record an opinion that is to some extent corrective of certain aspects of such speeches as those of Sir Lionel Heald."

After a brief explanation of the mechanics of the United Nations, we go on to say:

"In these circumstances only one thing is certain—namely that aggression will succeed. It will succeed moreover, whenever it is practised, at whatever time and in whatever place.

"The first half of the twentieth century will undoubtedly be distinguished in history as a time of ineffective attempts to establish bodies of supranational authority. It may be that in the second half of the century we shall be more fortunate. In the meantime, however, we have surely to face the fact that once again, for a second time, a noble attempt is failing to measure up to the needs of a grave situation.

"We have in these circumstances to remind ourselves that Hitler was not stopped in the end by the League of Nations, but by the will of the free nations of the world, exercised individually, to resist totalitarian aggression."

The Times printed our letter three days later. But it could not be said to have exercised any influence in the course of events.

Who would chain the mad dog in Cairo?

We had met for two days in September and dispersed again with the question left unanswered, only with a deepening sense of uneasiness which accompanied us all during the ensuing weeks—not allayed by the disquieting stories that started to circulate both in the press and elsewhere.

Who would bell the cat?

Not, so it seemed, Old Etonian Mr. Anthony Nutting. Not Old Etonian Sir Edward Boyle. Not Old Etonian Mr. Nigel Nicolson. Not—who else? How can a mere backbencher either credit or discredit the rumours that still surround those critical weeks?

Where then was the support for Sir Anthony Eden when eventually he considered the time ripe for action? "Millions of inarticulate but informed people in Asia and Africa are watching us," wrote Dr. Edith Summerskill in *The Times* of 10th August. What, however, of the millions of inarticulate but informed people—the non-U people—neither intellectual-U nor social-U —of Great Britain? From my early constituency reports it was clear to me that they were solidly, almost to a man and regardless of Party allegiances otherwise, in support of resistance to the action of Colonel Nasser. They were not, however, people whose opinions counted in the pages of the *New Statesman* or *The Economist*, not the types who might be asked to the exclusive conclaves of the Suez Group.

During all these critical days their voice was not heard.

*   *   *

So the elements of the Suez tragedy assembled themselves. We had reassembled again for the final days of the Session at the end of October. It seemed as if the stalemate which now surrounded the discussion on the merits and demerits of the United Nations would last for ever, when wild rumour started to fly through the lobbies of the House of Commons. The Israelis had invaded Egypt. They were advancing swiftly. They were within a few miles of the Suez Canal. The tape machine was surrounded by such a crowd of eager Members as may be seen round it during the course of Test Matches.

Here was a break to the deadlock! Someone had belled the cat at last! Smiles of an all too premature elation were exchanged between one Tory M.P. and another.

But we can leave the crowds of M.P.s round the ticker tape. For neither the details of the military campaign, nor the various political *démarches*, nor the political moves behind the scenes, are the concern of this book. Nor, from now on, were they major factors in the situation. The Suez campaign was to be lost in open light of day in the House of Commons.

It was lost within the heart of Sir Anthony Eden as, with an increasing sense of concern, we watched him speak during the ensuing days at the despatch box.

It is difficult, on looking back, to appreciate that the series of harrowing debates that followed lasted only a week from the time when Sir Anthony Eden, interrupting the Third Reading of the Education (Scotland) Bill at 4.30 on Tuesday, 30th October, announced the address of urgent communications by the U.K. and French Governments to the Governments of Egypt and Israel, until his announcement of the 'Cease Fire' at a slightly later time on the following Tuesday. Seldom can so much drama, so intense and varying a conflict of emotion, have been packed into so short a time in the whole history of Parliament as during these day-by-day debates when, in the interlude of such more placid preoccupations as those of Agriculture (Fat Stock Payments), Hill Farming, and White Fish Authority (Levy), the fate of the old-time British Empire was finally decided. Never can it have seen such personal tragedy as that of the failing Prime Minister, hounded into ill-health and irresolution by his enemies, yet totally unaware, apparently, of the number of his friends and admirers.

For, following long hesitation (inevitable perhaps through military unpreparedness), then impulsive action, Sir Anthony's self-appointed task was now to explain—to explain—and to explain again. To convince by daily explanations those progressive and intellectual circles, to whom he had even so lately been a hero, yet who now spurned and derided him—oddly enough because he took a firm line of action in 1956, his advocacy of which twenty years earlier had first won him the support of just those people. To convince an Opposition which had neither desire nor intention to be convinced, an Opposition whose only desire and intention was to wear him down.

Day by day, the wearing down process continued. This is an example, for instance, of an interruption to his opening speech on the Debate on the Middle East (Situation) on Wednesday:

Mr. R. T. Paget: On a point of order. How can we debate

a war when the Government will not tell us whether it has started?

Mr. Speaker: The hon. and learned Member must do the best he can with the material at his disposal.

The Prime Minister: I am not in any way prepared to give the House any details (hon. Members: "Resign") of the action which will follow the statement which I clearly made yesterday, that British and French forces will intervene in whatever strength may be necessary to secure compliance.

Mr. Gaitskell: This really is a fantastic situation. It is not only hon. Members on this side of the House, but it is the whole House and the whole country that are waiting for an answer to this question.

On the following day, Thursday, 1st November, there came the expected statement about the military situation by Mr. Anthony Head who announced bombing action against Egyptian airfields. It is unfortunate, indeed, that the bellicosity that this statement aroused amongst the Opposition could not have been directed against the common enemy, rather than to the cause of political faction. For it led to Mr. Speaker, pursuant to Standing Order No. 24, suspending the sitting for half an hour at 4 p.m. 'consequent on grave disorder'.

This was Sir Anthony's statement to the House when, after the 'grave disorder' we resumed:

"I hope it is not unreasonable if I say that these questions do involve certain definitions. I am quite confident that I can give a satisfactory and reassuring answer to the House, but I would much rather do it—if the House will allow me—in the speech which I am shortly to make—because I can assure the right hon. gentleman that there are legal matters involved in this. I will give the House an account which I am sure will reassure the House on the points which the right hon. gentleman has raised.

". . . I ask the House to believe that I am not in the least attempting to dodge these questions, but I would prefer to put them in their context, in which I think that the House will much more readily understand them."

"This has been for our country a black and tragic week," announced Mr. James ('Hand-on-the-heart') Griffiths, moving that this House deplores, etc. etc. "The Government has plunged our country into an unjustifiable and wicked war . . ."

"We are in an armed conflict: that is the phrase I have used. There has been no declaration of war," maintained Sir Anthony Eden at the start of yet another long speech amongst many interruptions.

Armed conflict—NOT war. Intervention to maintain peace between belligerents. Those were the slightly unconvincing legalistic attitudes that had to be maintained as a kind of magic incantation against the fiery shower of parliamentary criticism. They were unconvincing either to those who—on the one hand—had the touching faith that justice against Colonel Nasser could be obtained through the United Nations, or those who—on the other—considered that Nasser was a Russian stooge and an incipient menace to the Western World.

This legalistic essay failed conspicuously to quell the tumult. For, as the inevitable vote at 10 p.m. took place, there were demonstrations outside the House. There were demonstrations inside the House—featuring mainly Mrs. Braddock, as the flames of a turbulent youth blazed again in this highly respectable middle-aged lady.

"Murderers!" yelled Mrs. Braddock, the inhibitions of a hundred hospital management committee meetings slipping away, as this portly dame pranced the floor of the House in this glorious moment of latter-day exhibitionism.

We had sunk to this!

*   *   *

But now, beyond and above everything, the phantom—the Frankenstein, one might almost call it—of the United Nations was stalking abroad.

On Friday Mr. Gaitskell asked the Prime Minister whether Her Majesty's Government are prepared to accept the decision of the United Nations General Assembly for a cease-fire in the Middle East.

On Friday, one minute later, Mr. Gaitskell asks: Surely the Prime Minister must have been well aware of the nature of the resolution moved by the United States delegate? Surely he must be aware by now of the issues at stake? Does he not realize that a resolution, carried by a majority of 64 to 5—an overwhelming majority—is one which Her Majesty's Government, in all honour, in our opinion, are bound to accept?

On Saturday, shortly after the opening of the special Saturday sitting, Mr. Gaitskell states that the first paragraph of the Resolution carried by 64 votes to 5 in the General Assembly of the United Nations calls upon all parties now involved in hostilities to agree to an immediate cease-fire and to halt the movement of military forces and arms into the area.

"It is unfortunately perfectly clear," Mr. Gaitskell lays down his unprecedented thesis, "that the British Government are not carrying out the recommendation of the Assembly. We are, therefore, faced with the position that our Government are defying a Resolution of the United Nations Assembly, carried by a majority which is larger, I believe, than that on any other Resolution previously carried by the Assembly. We can only say that, for our part, we regard this as utterly deplorable.

"As regards the conditions laid down by the Government, it is no part of the business of Her Majesty's Government to lay down conditions in this matter. It is their duty, as loyal members of the United Nations—if they were loyal members—to accept that majority decision."

"And sell Britain?" rejoin the Conservative benches.

But Sir Anthony Eden, worn and pale, the victim as we know of insomnia, his health under strain, answers with delaying apologetic legalistic arguments. He makes no attempt to question the good offices of the United Nations.

During all this time, every sitting place in the House is packed. Conservative Members assemble in the lobbies and the entrance to the Chamber, with the three-line whips in the offing, and gossip and chatter. Amongst them there moves a lay figure. It is the large frame of Harry Kerby.

"This can't go on. This simply can't go on," says Harry Kerby. Like all Cassandras, Harry Kerby is frequently right. He was right this time.

But need I continue? Monday afternoon's elation when Sir Anthony Eden rose to announce the surrender of Port Said turned all too soon to Tuesday's dismay when, on the first day of the new parliamentary session, he announced the acceptance of the 'cease-fire' terms by Israel and Egypt, the standstill by British and French forces when but a short way along the Suez Canal, and the acceptance of the United Nations force as guardian of the Canal.

Did I say 'elation' to describe the emotional mood for Monday afternoon's news? On the Government side, indeed, there were Conservative Members standing up and waving their Order Papers and cheering. But what on the other side of the House? At this news of an almost bloodless British victory, a victory characterized by humanity and restraint, never can there have been so many disappointed-looking people crowded together in so small a space as the Labour Members on the seats on the Opposition side of the House of Commons. For the hour or more before the session ended with the prorogation of the House, as the exciting thought of British disaster and Labour Party gain had been replaced by the shocking thought of British triumph and Labour Party discomfiture, this customarily noisy and boisterous crowd sat there, glum, punctured and disconsolate—only to revive their spirits on the following day on receipt of the fresh news that meant certain triumph for Colonel Nasser.

"Whatever controversies we have had this week, I think that the House will, at least, admit that I have tried to attend upon its debates," concluded Sir Anthony Eden at the end of his speech on the Debate on the Address when he announced the 'cease fire'.

Sir Anthony was to appear in Parliament again. But this was, in effect, his swan song. As his political obituary it might be said that, while millions of his fellow countrymen were clamouring to give him their support, he had broken his heart through not being able to convert the editor of the *Manchester Guardian* to his point of view.

Let none hold the first part of this statement in doubt. Certainly I had no doubt. The front page of the *Cumberland News* on Saturday, 3rd November, contains my own affidavit in support of Sir Anthony Eden's Suez action. My letter at the head of the correspondence column of the *Daily Telegraph* of 17th November puts on record the unanimous resolution of 500 members of our Carlisle Denton Holme Working Men's Club, giving Sir Anthony Eden support in his action—action of invading Suez, that was.

I end this letter:

"The unfortunate part of the present situation is that it allows Nasser time for recovery and, clearly, for obstruction in regard to that part of the Canal still in his possession: it also offers the Soviet Union continuing scope to bedevil the situation.

"It needs no great powers of precognition to appreciate the time may not be far distant when once again we may be placed in the quandary of whether to act or not to act. Should this arise, let us hope at least that one benefit that has been extracted from our recent difficulties is that the true feeling of our people can and will be seen in better perspective than has perhaps been possible during past weeks."

But, alas, the resolution was too late. So was my letter for any good that it might have done. Exhausted from partisan strife, paralysed from further action, our national destinies rudderless and for the time being beyond control, our House of Commons could only contemplate the ruin that had been created, without having the will to arrest the decay.

Once subordinate to the hostile majority of the United Nations—we were powerless to prevent the situation deteriorating to its eventual nadir, when the final decision was taken that British troops should evacuate Port Said.

This was endorsed in the Motion put forward by the Government for yet one final Debate on the Middle East on 5th and 6th December:

That this House supports the policy of Her Majesty's Government as outlined by the Foreign Secretary on the 3rd December, which has prevented hostilities from spreading, has resulted in a United Nations Force being introduced into the area, and has created conditions under which progress can be made towards the peaceful settlement of outstanding issues.

Stripped of its euphemistic verbiage, this meant that, as Conservative backbenchers, we were being asked to vote for a policy of withdrawal from Port Said and the Suez region without compensating guarantees of any kind; that, with only the flimsiest camouflage covering the uncomfortable fact, we were underwriting the end of British power in the Middle East; that, at the end of all this travail, we were handing the Suez Canal over to Nasser—and, of course, his allies, foremost amongst these being Soviet Russia. ("What has happened as a result of that operation," said Mr. Selwyn Lloyd in his apologia, "is that the magnitude of Soviet penetration has been revealed. It had permeated every branch of the Egyptian armed forces, and, as Egypt is a military dictatorship, that meant that the Communist influence was in a position to have a dominating effect upon events.")

To vote or not to vote for this shocking Motion, that was the question. Even backbench feet, however well-trained, do not find their way into their appropriate lobby at all times with unflinching nonchalance. As the two-day debate progressed, the doubts spread round Tory backbenchers.

Who was going to abstain?

Many agreed with Mr. Julian Amery's interjection to the Foreign Secretary on 3rd December.

"Is my right hon. and learned Friend not aware that, whatever differences there may be on Middle East policy on this side of the House, all of us wholeheartedly condemn the part played by the United States, by the Party opposite, and by a small handful of hon. Members on this side of the House in bringing us to the humiliating withdrawal which he has just announced?"

Many too with the words of Captain Waterhouse, leader of the Suez Group, on 5th December:

"When in opposition my right hon. Friends took a strong line. They objected to the holding up of the Israeli ships in the Canal. It was said that a gunboat ought to be sent to let them through. That was a fairly drastic remark. Still in opposition, they objected strenuously to the surrender of Abadan. I am not blaming my right hon. Friends for not reversing those two policies when they came back to office, because there are many actions which, to be effective, must be taken immediately. What I say is that the same tendencies which lay behind those two actions seemed to me to continue in the further handling of the Middle Eastern problem.

"Nothing was done at all when the (Suez) base was dismantled and the troops withdrawn. No strategic force was set up anywhere, as far as any of us know or can see. What is more, no real effort was seen to be made to reorganize our defence system by conventional arms.

"The fact remains that when this crisis came we had no plan, no ships, no aeroplanes, and no men in sufficient quantities to hit quickly. If we had been able to hit quickly on those first days of Nasser's aggression in seizing the Canal, we would have had a very different picture today both here and there, because, do not forget, that at that time the right hon. Gentleman, the Leader of the Opposition, was on our side."

But what a choice! Between voting for national humiliation on the one hand: and on the other allowing the Government to be defeated in a major vote and letting in the Opposition, the primary cause of our ruin. Would there be a mass abstention of Conservative backbenchers? Hardly in these circumstances. Would there be fifty abstentions? Forty? Thirty? The estimate of numbers started to dwindle. Twenty-five? That was the number given to me when, at the end of the first day's debate I was approached by a prominent member of the Suez Group: they knew my views—would I abstain with them? I viewed the number with scepticism. If they had come to approach me, I told myself, at this eleventh hour (for my views had been made known in the *Daily Telegraph* some three months previously), then they were scraping the bottom of the barrel for support. The number of abstentions would, I guessed, be about fifteen. Should I make it sixteen? I was sympathetic, but I stalled.

The final Suez vote of December 1956 is one of the historic votes of the House of Commons. The behaviour pattern of M.P.s in their votes in the lobby was described by W. S. Gilbert in *Iolanthe* these many years ago:

When in that House, M.P.s divide,
If they've a brain and cerebellum, too,
They've got to leave that brain outside,
And vote just as their leaders tell 'em to.

Generally this impression may be correct. But it is not always correct. Face to face with history, a Member of Parliament has only his own conscience and his own sense of destiny. He has not only the past to guide him, but he has also the future to consider. He must consider too whether, in abstaining from an inconvenient and embarrassing vote, he is not just 'contracting out' of an unpleasant situation and leaving his colleagues to 'carry the can'.

I have already set out the alternatives of this vote that were in my mind during the twenty-four hours before I had to make my decision. To vote for the Suez humiliation was bad—tears

I

welled up into my eyes as I thought about it. But to abstain and
to complete the triumph of Mr. Gaitskell was worse. Those were
the stark facts. To be one of 15 or 16 abstainers was perhaps
safe enough: but was it not 'contracting out'—something only
to be done if there was a positive rather than a negative purpose
to it?

But what positive purpose could there be in an abstention to
this vote? There was no Winston Churchill alas, among the
Suez Groupers to form an alternative Government: indeed, at
the crucial time, 'the moment of truth', so to speak, during the
early stages of the crisis, the Suez Groupers had, in unaccount-
able fashion, failed to give guidance to potential supporters
within the Party.

These were the thoughts that ran through my head.

There were in the end sixteen abstainers who, under the lead
of Captain Waterhouse, diffident rebel to the last, sat out the
vote on the benches of the House.

But I was not amongst them. Yet I was perhaps not the only
Conservative backbencher who entered the Government lobby
on 6th December, 1956, with the feeling that this was the end of
an era.

THE TWO FACES OF OPPOSITION

"BY Jese, those boys have certainly got it," remarked my friend, Mr. Stageberg from Minnesota, admiringly, after spending an evening watching our deliberations from the strangers' gallery. It had been a 'Suez' debate.

After my first bewilderment at this remark, I eventually appreciated that Mr. Stageberg was referring to Her Majesty's Opposition. Though perhaps it was not so surprising after all that it should be so.

"Since our last meeting, sir, the scene has totally changed. Instead of negotiation with colonies, we have a war to carry on against free and independent states: a wicked war, which has been occasioned solely by a spirit of violence, injustice and obstinacy in our ministers, unparalleled in history."

No, this is not Mr. James Griffiths speaking with hand on heart, once again. It is Mr. Wilkes speaking in the Debate on the Address in October 1776: and he was, of course, speaking of the newly independent United States of America and of the War of American Independence.

It is understandable that, since then, Americans must look in sympathetic fashion on all Oppositions in the Parliament at Westminster: that, in particular, such an Opposition as is ours must bring up nostalgic sentiments of anti-Colonialism from any one hundred per cent American subconscious.

There is no question of the effectiveness of the present Opposition at Westminster—as an Opposition.

These terrifying people! Who on the Government side can avoid the feeling of utter dismay and amazement at the waves of

131

political passion that sweep the benches opposite? At this
manifestation of the Freudian 'death wish' translated from the
psychiatric text books into real life. At this relentless machine of
destructive criticism—with no holds barred—geared to Party
advantage, and Party advantage only, come what may, regardless
of national advantage.

Has our historic Parliament of Westminster come to this?
Admittedly this question has been asked through the centuries
by sages and the commentators. Yet can destructive parliamen-
tarianism extend too far in range? Or be brought to *too* fine
an art?

It has often seemed to me that the most valid argument in
favour of the televising of parliamentary debates is that not only
a wide public should see the Labour Opposition in action, but
that perhaps the Labour Opposition might also see themselves
as others see them—for instance, from the point of view of an
observer on the opposite benches, as I was when, after a brief
hour or two of fitful sleep, unable to compose myself longer in
the dubious comfort of the armchairs in the House of Commons
Library, I walked into the Debating Chamber in the early hours
of the all-night session of the 17th November, 1955.

How far can an Opposition go without bringing parliamentary
democracy into disrepute? How far can it go without in-
validating the dictum of Jefferson that "opposition to a Government may be often exercised when wrong, but better so than not
be exercised at all".

This is the despairing question that has inevitably come to
mind on occasions.

Such an occasion was the all-night sitting to which I have
referred, which was occasioned by the debate on the Committee
Stage of the Finance Bill of the autumn of 1955—that ill-starred
endeavour of Mr. R. A. Butler, when Chancellor of the Exchequer, to arrest the decay of the national finances by the
introduction of his interim Budget, and to bring this home
to the average citizen and his wife by the increase of one-

fifth in the purchase tax of, amongst other things, pots and pans.

The synthetic rage of the Labour Opposition at the imposition of taxes which, in the words of Mr. Henry Brook, speaking as Financial Secretary to the Treasury, would cost the ordinary household an average of 4*d*. per week—the price of two cigarettes—knew no bounds.

In circumstances in which every Socialist M.P. visualized himself headlined in his local paper as a protester against this iniquitous impost, there was, even given the facilities of an all-night sitting, not time on the Committee Stage of the Bill for every Opposition speaker who wished to speak. The un-made speeches were accordingly sublimated into a concatena-tion of noises of indeterminate nature.

The tide of exhibitionism ebbed and flowed throughout the night as the Opposition, their frustrations from an unexpectedly lost General Election only just behind them, and oblivious of their real position as the not unprosperous representatives of a prosperous working class, gave their spirited and nostalgic rendering of a Committee of Public Safety, thrown up by a starving and revolutionary mob, with those self-appointed Robespierres, Messrs. Sidney Silverman and Leslie Hale, in the van.

As one sat through the small hours listening to this bogus show, this ersatz indignation, it was difficult to feel anything other than the most intense sympathy with the silent Chancellor who, a slightly contemptuous smile on his face, sat and listened to the streams of vituperation that unceasingly descended on his undeserving head.

Little wonder that at the end of this night's debate between 7.30 and 8 a.m., Sir Charles MacAndrew, the Chairman of the Committee, found himself in the strange predicament of being unable to bring the debate to an end without reversing what he regarded as a binding decision and having finally to accept a motion "that the Chairman do leave the Chair forthwith".

Little wonder that this impasse came about when we find such extracts in Hansard as:

The Chairman: I cannot reply unless I get a little bit of peace.

The Chairman: I can only ask for one hon. Member to speak at a time. I cannot answer any point unless there is quiet.

The Chairman: I am already trying to answer one point of order, but if the right hon. Member has another to raise, I do not mind.

The chaos and confusion were indeed such that it was virtually beyond the power of one person to control them. It is not a night of which the Labour Opposition has reason in retrospect to view with pride.

*   *   *

How far can an Opposition go in modern circumstances of intensive day-by-day debate without paralysing completely the operation of the armed forces of the Crown at a time of crisis? One asks this consequent on the interchange of Questions and Answers concerning the actions of Commanders in the Field in regard to the distribution of air-raid-warning leaflets to the Egyptian population, that took place in the course of the Suez Debate on 5th November, 1956.

I have already referred to the Opposition at the time of the American Revolution, but in those days, and indeed for long afterwards, parliamentary debates were at only infrequent intervals—strong as may have been the feeling on the War with the American Colonies, there lacks record of any debate on this between, for instance, Mr. Fox's Motion for an Enquiry into the Causes of the Ill Success of the British Arms in North America in February 1776, and the Debate on the Address in the same year, to which I have already referred.

This is a different state of affairs to the day-to-day questioning on military operations to which Sir Anthony Eden's Government was subjected at the time of the Suez operations.

The answer to my question on the part of Labour sympathizers will no doubt be that it was not the object of the exercise for the 'armed conflict' of the Suez campaign to proceed to success anyway. That it was a war being waged against 'the moral sense of half the nation'—though, in the light of the known views of large numbers of the rank and file of Labour supporters on the Suez issue, one has to question this.

None the less, we must look deeper than this. Why was it that the viewpoint of Mr. Gaitskell in the debates of mid-September and early October differed so much in comparison with the viewpoint of that same Mr. Gaitskell speaking on 2nd August, only a few weeks earlier? What are the true reasons for Mr. Richard Crossman, the resister against aggression of September 1938, becoming Mr. Richard Crossman, the appeaser, 18 years later?

There is a school of psychology, that of Dr. Watson and the Behaviourists, founded on the belief that the human mind is merely a highly complicated mass of reflexes—conditioned reflexes. I do not hold with Dr. Watson. None the less, his theory has received substantial support from the political scene.

Here are our intellectual Socialists. Here have been our Pavlov's dogs. And we have had two bells. One has been marked 'Nazi Germany' or perhaps just 'Fascism'. The other is marked 'Soviet Russia'. Ring the first bell and your Left Winger foamed at the mouth in unmistakable fashion. But ring the second and he puts on his rose-tinted spectacles and purrs like any titillated cat. Have we, in fact, got a parliamentary Opposition and alternative Government, imprisoned by the archetypes of its collective thinking, a living demonstration of the theory of Dr. Watson and the Behaviourists, so that 'the moral sense of half the nation' will always blind them to realities whenever the stimulus of a potential conflict with Soviet Russia is applied?

Do we enter a new era of Appeasement in which our Defence Forces, whether traditional or nuclear, will be paralysed as against our principal potential enemy during such time as present attitudes persist?

The developments of current foreign policy debates suggest that this may be so.

Can any foreign policy conducive to the national good be pursued at times of crisis, when, to use the words of Mr. Selwyn Lloyd, "The sayings of the Opposition come easily to the lips of Her Majesty's enemies."

Can even the remnants of a far-flung Empire be successfully governed when there is no subversive element throughout the hemispheres that does not lack its defenders and protagonists on the Socialist benches?

As a frequent attender at Question Time, I am inescapably reminded of my days in the general practice of medicine, of the dreary routine of my former regular surgery patients—the same appearance of the same querulous people with the regularity of clockwork at the same time on the same day each week.

On Tuesday it is Mr. Fenner Brockway, whose strained face shows all too plainly his sufferings on behalf of all black and brown humanity, to ask the Secretary of State for the Colonies what decision has been reached by the Government of Tanganyika regarding the lifting of the ban on open air meetings addressed by leaders of the Tanganyika African National Union.

Or maybe it is Mr. Zilliacus, rising from his seat in blowing fashion like the sea-dwelling animal he so closely resembles, to ask the Prime Minister whether, in view of the statement of Her Majesty's Ambassador in Bonn that the stationing of United States nuclear bases in this country would make it a target of nuclear attack, he will renounce the manufacture of hydrogen bombs, prohibit the use of British territory for launching nuclear missiles, and propose a summit conference to discuss proposals for the unifying of Germany within an all-European treaty.

Then, on Wednesday, it is Mrs. Barbara Castle to ask the Secretary of State for the Colonies whether Chege, alias Kinyungu, son of Gakungu, Ngethe, son of Mutumbu, Kumau, son of Negethe, Harrison, son of Kamau and Wamungu, son of Karaungu, who were arrested in Nairobi on 25th last and sent to Manyani detention camp, are still in detention; what charge has been brought against them; and what is the evidence on which it is based. Or alternatively to ask what has been the result of the enquiry by the Governor of Kenya into the conduct of the administrative officer concerned with the case of Kamau Kichina.

"The officer's appointment has been terminated," replies Mr. John Hare. "While warmly welcoming that reply, may I ask the Minister whether he agrees that I was perfectly justified in the charges that I brought against this man's professional conduct, for which the Colonial Secretary bitterly attacked me?" asks Mrs. Castle, jumping up in indignation.

(But whence this Maenad fury? "Lucky, lucky Mrs. Barbara Castle!" I cannot help but muse. Lucky, indeed, that Kamau Kichina was Kamau Kichina, a Kikuyu and a Mau Mau, rather than plain John Smith, a law-abiding British citizen, who had been removed into detention under the operation of the Lunacy Act 1890. No enquiry would be made then. Least of all, the dismissal of an administrative officer!)

And here on Wednesday is Mr. Zilliacus too, to ask the Prime Minister whether he will give the names of the independent scientific organizations on whose report Her Majesty's Government have relied for their view that there is no danger of genetic damage from continuing hydrogen-bomb tests.

Then on Thursday it is Mr. Fenner Brockway again to ask the Secretary of State for the Colonies on what evidence of intention to resort to violence the *Union des Populations du Cameroun* has been declared by the Governor-General of Nigeria to be an unlawful society; and on what charges 13 leaders have been arrested and ordered to leave the country.

This is democracy. But the danger to democracy is that its otherwise admissible processes can be used in the interests of faction and partisanship—words that can apply to two Parties as well as a multiplicity of Parties. Sufficient for me to ask briefly whether the idea of parliamentary Opposition conceived in a more leisurely age, does not require some exercise in self-restraint in the common interest of all in the more intensive circumstances of modern times. The answer must be left to others: and it is at least encouraging to know that, since this chapter was first written, the idea of self-restraint at Question Time in regard to military operations was mooted on the short interchange following the present Prime Minister's statement on Defence on 24th April, 1958.

This, however, is one face of Opposition.

*   *   *

What is the other face of the Opposition? It is one I record with greater pleasure.

Let us start at the beginning. In the beginning, as it were, I wrote a book entitled *The End of Socialism*. Published first in 1946, the purport of *The End of Socialism* was to show how I, a Liberal, had 'chosen Freedom' in my decision, subsequent to the 1945 Election, to join the Conservatives in Opposition rather than the Socialist Party in Government. It can be recorded that the ideological argument of *The End of Socialism* made an instant appeal to Conservatives in Opposition.

Its thesis was a simple one. It was that of the inevitable evolution of a socialist society into dictatorship and, with the establishment of a class of administrators and officials, of the decline in the liberal values of society and an inevitable loss of personal liberty. Later on, though I make no claim to be in any way responsible, this became the battle-cry of rampant, opposition Conservatism. One cannot do better than offer the quote from my right hon. Friend Dr. Charles Hill's famous broadcasts, a record of which—retained for its technical perfection—is still kept by the Conservative Central Office: "We all know our official people, we know them personally, decent, kindly folk the same as we are ourselves: yet when they get into their offices something happens to them, etc. etc."

The End of Socialism was published, of course, in the days of the sweet by and by, long, long before my active interest as a parliamentarian in the laws relating to mental health, long even before the incident that precipitated this interest.

However, since then, it has frequently come to my mind that there could be no better instance of welfare-statism run riot at the expense of the individual than in the evolution of mental health legislation during the first half of the twentieth century. This is no place to show in detail how the operation of administratively convenient practices gradually undermined the protections of individual liberty written into the original Lunacy Act, until such time as the National Health Act 1946 in its Ninth Schedule regularized the arrangement whereby all and sundry could be certified by one doctor after a minimum time of observation and compulsorily removed to mental hospitals, by the same casual process as that originally designed for the 'pauper lunatic' of 1890. These things have been set out by me elsewhere in *A Doctor Returns*.

These, at any rate, were the arguments I used when, for instance, searching for allies and helpers in those far-off days of lonely struggle, I called on that well-publicized and active body, The Society for Individual Freedom. The Ark of the Covenant of Individual Freedom in the tradition of the Liberal era of Queen Victoria's day reposes by their own claim with the Society for Individual Freedom, founded as a tabernacle by the late Sir Ernest Benn for just that purpose. Yet when I called on them, back in 1951, or 1952 was it, as an ordinary member of the public, they were as bewildered and as helpless on the question of the law relating to mental illness as was any unsanctified person.

(In *The End of Socialism*, I posed the question as to why, despite its efforts, the Society for Individual Freedom is so ineffective a body. Is it, I have since wondered, because, while they go frantic over any matter relating to property rights, they appear at so great a loss over any matter of freedom of the person as such?)

It perhaps should not have dismayed me as much as it did that when, on my arrival at Westminster, I started to raise these questions—pestering my own Minister on this exotic and little-known subject of mental health, casting aspersions on the efficiency of the National Health Service which (as I have pointed out) is these days every bit as much the pride and joy of the Conservative Party as it is of the Socialists—I was not immediately welcomed and understood, that I failed to rally overmuch support to my banner on my own side of the House.

Where, however, did those expressions of approval come from, when I made a more than usually telling point?

This was my surprise. They came from the Opposition benches. Nor were they the ironical cheers such as had greeted me when I had asked about the credit squeeze. They were ungrudging and heartfelt good wishes in a struggle for humanity and human rights, often expressed to me privately in the lobbies of the House in addition, on a matter in which, quite rightly, Party political differences can be put aside.

My well-wishers of the Opposition, admittedly, have in few cases been identical with those other hon. Members opposite who were the main protagonists in the events described in the early part of this chapter. None the less that this zeal for human welfare, mistaken though its forms may be on occasions, is a genuine one in the Labour Party has been evidenced by the Opposition Press which has in no way either grudged me support or stinted me some meed of praise when occasion arose, despite my being a member of the hated Tory Government benches.

Thus let me quote the *Daily Herald* leader of Thursday, 30th May, 1957, on the announcement of the enlightened recommendations of the Royal Commission on the Law relating to Mental Illness:

"Sweeping reform of our mental health laws is urged by a Royal Commission after two years studying them.

"Praise M.P.s Mr. Norman Dodds and Dr. Donald Johnson. Praise the National Council for Civil Liberties and the countless men and women up and down the country who awakened public opinion."

("No wonder the b—— *Daily Herald*'s going under," was heard to exclaim a prominent and outspoken woman Labour M.P., "when it spends its time building up Tory M.P.s.")

Thank you, however, *Daily Herald*, across the barriers of Party politics, for your generous attitude.

Thank you, also, of course, Norman Dodds. However, I anticipate.

AN UNEXPECTED ALLY

RUMOUR had reached me, before I arrived at Westminster, of that strange phenomenon whereby, so it was reputed, closer personal friendships are formed between M.P.s of opposite Parties than between those of the same Party. I had been inclined to greet this information with that same measure of incredulity as perhaps does the reader of this book, who may think it only proper that the unceasing factional strife between the two great political armies must extend into unrelenting personal animosity between every member of each.

Our personal affairs do not always work out that way. A moment's reflection will show that the big parliamentary battles concern by and large only the main protagonists of each Party and this allows friendship to flourish across Party division in an atmosphere unsullied by any direct clash of personality and characterized by the sense of detachment created by the already pledged lobby vote through Party allegiance, which, in all ordinary circumstances, no amount of persuasion is likely to alter.

Moreover, with the complexities of modern society and the right concern of Members of Parliament to give a lead in all aspects of our national life, an ever-widening scope has been found for fruitful co-operation between M.P.s of opposite Parties on a non-Party basis, which, for many, forms a welcome relief from the hag-ridden atmosphere of Party political debates. Many a backbencher on both sides, unable perhaps to find scope for his abilities in his own Party, has found an outlet in devotion to such non-Party causes, in which he has possibly been surprised himself at the common ground he has found between himself and members of an Opposition which he had previously considered damned beyond redemption—and possibly still does so consider, when viewed on a collective basis.

Thus it is that my association with Norman Dodds, on the question of mental health, though more informal, and possibly also rather more dynamic than most other cross-bench companionships, has been the most pleasant and the most fruitful to date, of my brief parliamentary career.

No extra publicity puff from me is needed to familiarize the name of Norman Dodds to my readers. A 'Geordie' by birth, a successful career in the 'Co-op' led Norman to adoption in 1945, as a last-minute choice, as the Co-op candidate for Dartford, for which place he has been M.P. (and after its division into two, for the constituency of Erith and Crayford) since 1945. During these years a trail of glory has followed Norman Dodds through the popular press consequent on his zeal at Question Time on such a variety of subjects as mock auctions, sales of Government surplus, gipsies and some hundred or more different subjects. No Question Time is complete without the intervention of Norman Dodds on some matter of human and practical interest—in contrast to the ideological basis which underlies the questions of so many of his colleagues on the Socialist benches.

Norman brought all the necessary attributes to our campaign to secure justice for those afflicted by the harsh and often capricious operation of the laws relating to mental illness, and I have much reason to be grateful to him. We share certain qualities of persistence that have been of use to us.

How did our association start?

I have already recorded my first parliamentary question in which I asked for the number of people certified annually and removed 'involuntarily' to mental hospitals under the provision of the Lunacy Act, 1890 (as amended). A year later, on 2nd

July, 1956, I asked a similar question, and I obtained an almost identical answer, consequent on which I applied for an Adjournment Debate. I moved this a week later, on 10th July, 1956, and this is what I said:

Dr. Donald Johnson (Carlisle): I rise to raise the question of the admission of involuntary patients to mental hospitals. The occasion of this debate arises from the Answer to my Question last Monday concerning the admission of certified patients to mental hospitals, which revealed what seemed an alarmingly high figure of some 20,000 people annually being put into mental hospitals against their will, only some 15 per cent of that number having been under outside observation in hospital beds.

In other words, some 17,000 people are swept up, in this way, mainly on summary reception orders, and detained in mental hospitals for an indefinite period up to a year. This is done on the opinion of two or three people who, though of official and professional status and empowered to sign certificates, are as liable to error as the remainder of mankind. This is an extraordinary large number of people in such a liberty-loving country as ours, to be detained on no other criterion.

In reply to my supplementary question last week, my right hon. Friend stated that a further 20 per cent of patients, representing about 4,000 people, were annually placed in observation wards of mental hospitals.

Before proceeding further, I wish to ask a further question on this point. If my hon. Friend cannot give me the answer tonight, or if she has not the figures with her, perhaps she could let me know at some future date what percentage of the number of those placed in observation wards of mental hospitals were already certified under summary reception orders before they went to hospital, or whether they were admitted merely under three-day emergency orders, and, if so, what percentage of them were discharged from observation wards at the termination of such urgency orders?

The reason why I ask this is because it is my impression, rightly or wrongly, that once a person is in a mental hospital his or her transference from one ward to another is, on occasion, something of formality and is by no means the same as if the patient were moved from a general to a mental hospital.

To return to my main point. The matter of these 20,000 people annually entering mental hospitals is a vast human problem. My first intention is to convince my right hon. Friend the Minister that, apart from anything else, the way in which people are placed in mental hospitals is really not particularly good business from their point of view.

How can we solve the problem of our overcrowded mental hospitals? According to the figures, at the end of 1954, 140,487 patients were occupying bed space authorized for only 121,555 patients, which represented an overcrowding of 15.6 per cent. There are, of course, two ways of solving the problem. One is by building more hospitals, but that in the present economic situation is only practicable to a limited degree, and the other and far more practicable and economical way is by exercising far more discrimination than at present over admissions.

This can be done by the establishment of observation wards in general hospitals in which patients can be viewed in surroundings as detached as possible from mental illness and where they can be seen by general physicians who are not quite so preoccupied with their own specialty as are psychiatrists. Such surroundings would provide a respite during which the patient could, perhaps, surmount an acute crisis and resume his or her place in the community without having acquired the stigma of having been an inmate of a mental hospital which, whatever may be said, is quite inseparable from such treatment.

K

What I have said is confirmed by the experience in the observation wards in the L.C.C. area. According to the figures supplied by the L.C.C. in their evidence to the Royal Commission, there were 4,746 patients admitted into the observation wards in the L.C.C. area during 1953. Out of these, 1,274, or almost exactly a quarter, were discharged at the end of the 17-day observation period, while a further quarter were moved as voluntary patients rather than involuntary patients.

Concerning the quarter who were discharged, it is clear to anyone who has even the most superficial acquaintance of the ways of mental hospitals and the time factor which operates within their walls, that these people were discharged very much quicker than they would have been once they were entangled in the mental hospital machine. It is equally clear that if a quarter of the admissions to mental hospitals in the country can be cut down, even if only with short-stay cases, it will go some way to solving this problem of overcrowding. Indeed, it seems to me that this policy offers a dazzling prospect to my right hon. Friend in that at a comparatively small cost he can solve the problem of overcrowding in mental hospitals.

I will, however, turn from this splendid vision to the more sombre human angle. It is probably one of the most distressing experiences that anyone can undergo to be forcibly put into a mental hospital, and we must dispense with euphemisms for a moment and call a spade a spade, because force is the ultimate sanction of putting these unfortunate people into mental hospitals, conducted by a local authority official and perhaps also a policeman if there has been any show of recalcitrance. Such an experience is hardly conducive to the improvement of mental health which, after all, is supposed to be the object of the exercise. It behoves a civilized community to soften the blow and to ensure that where detention is necessary not only is justice done but also that it is seen to be done, and this is far from the case at present.

The law of lunacy is antiquated, muddled and obscure. The Lunacy Act, 1890, has been amended and re-amended in such a way that practically nobody understands it at present. The hon. Lady the Parliamentary Secretary will, I hope, pardon me if I say that she is herself one of the most outstanding instances of this. We all admire her competence and grasp of her Department's work, yet when she comes to talk of the law of lunacy she seems to me to be at sea with the rest of us.

On 19th November, 1952, when she spoke in the debate on geriatrics, in reply to the accusation of over-zealous certification of elderly people, she said that patients can only be certified first on medical examination and then on the order being signed by two justices. I hope she will excuse me correcting her when I point out that according to the 1953 figures, there were some 20,000 people put into hospital by summary reception order and only 350 by petition. A summary reception order requires the signature of only one justice—any justice who is available.

The Section 16 procedure, under which most people are sent into mental hospitals, itself is a direct inheritance from the Victorian Poor Law arrangements which were incorporated into the Act of 1890, and it is characterized by the same lack of humanity. This can only be softened with alteration of the law—in such a way as I have suggested, namely by the establishment of observation wards such as those which are working very successfully in the L.C.C. area and which could be made to work in other places equally well, so that there would be proper medical observation, proper diagnosis, before this dire and rather terrible step is taken.

I need only reproduce the first part of the speech by Miss

Patricia Hornsby-Smith who, as Parliamentary Secretary to the Ministry, answered me.

"The hon. Member for Carlisle (Dr. D. Johnson) has, I know, a very great interest in this topic, but I think that he has done less than justice to the great work that has been done towards removing the stigma from our mental hospitals. In fact, the whole tenor of the debate has unfortunately been to put back the stigma which we have worked tremendously hard to get removed."

(Miss Hornsby-Smith spoke for her Department. It was a 'brush-off'.)

In the meantime, it was the day after my original Question that, while standing in the Members' Lobby, I encountered Norman Dodds coming out of the Debating Chamber with the Hansard Report in his hands.

"That's a hell of a lot of people put away each year," remarked Norman, indicating the figure of 20,256 that had been given in answer. "What a small proportion under observation too!"

He was the only one of my parliamentary contemporaries of either Party who commented on this.

Norman's interest in the subject had been stimulated by his constituency case of Mrs. Thornton. On Monday, 9th July, the following questions were put by him and by myself to the Minister of Health:

Mr. Dodds asked the Minister of Health what progress has been made in the independent medical examination of Mrs. Harriet Thornton who has been detained in a mental home for over three years.

Mr. Turton: It is for the relative who applied for an independent medical examination to arrange with the selected doctors for this examination.

Mr. Dodds: When the examination has taken place, will the Minister do his best to expedite a decision, which I am certain will set Mrs. Thornton free? Will he bear in mind that, when this has been achieved, I shall be asking for a thorough investigation as to how she got into a mental home in the first place, and what justification there is for depriving her of her liberty for over three years?

Mr. Turton: This is a matter for the Board of Control and not for me. When the report on the examination is received, it has to be sent to the Board of Control for consideration. It is within the power of the Board to order the patient to be discharged at the expiration of ten days.

Mr. Dodds asked the Minister of Health if he will make a statement giving the reasons why Mr. Alan W. Cripps, 25, Clive Avenue, Crayford, in writing to the Board of Control on 24th April, 1956, in respect of the case of his niece, Miss Harriet Thornton, did not receive a reply until 13th June, 1956, details of which have been given to him by the hon. Member for Erith and Crayford.

Mr. Turton: I have written to the hon. Member on 4th July, and again today, explaining the reasons for this re-grettable delay.

Mr. Dodds: While thanking the Minister for the splendid way in which he dealt with this case when it was brought to his attention, may I ask whether he is aware that this is not an isolated case of delay and that there is deep concern that the Board of Control is not doing the job for which it was set up, namely, to look after the interests of the individual, because more and more it seems to be moving as a machine? Not only does it lock people up, but it keeps them locked up. Will the Minister look at this matter to see whether the process cannot be humanized?

Mr. Turton: I will certainly have a look at it. This delay was most unfortunate. It was an instance where the machine broke down. Steps have been taken to guard against a recurrence of such a breakdown.

Dr. D. Johnson asked the Minister of Health if he is aware of the confusion in the public mind created by the fact that the Board of Control, previously located independently, has now an identical address with the Ministry of Health; and if he will arrange for adequate recognition of the separate existence of the Board as an independent body.

Mr. Turton: I think that the separate existence of the Board as an independent body is widely recognized. It is convenient for administration that the Ministry and the Board should be in the same building.

Dr. Johnson: May I, none the less, ask my right hon. Friend if he can make it quite clear that the functions of the Board of Control are to protect the liberty of the subject and—at the risk of repeating what the hon. Member for Erith and Crayford (Mr. Dodds) has already said this afternoon—whether he is aware that, admirably intentioned though the Board may be, it has in fact given the impression in recent times that it is both lethargic and inefficient in dealing with matters related to the individual and in reply to individual communications addressed to it?

Mr. Turton: I can assure my hon. Friend that proximity to me does not induce lethargy or inefficiency.

After this, our joint campaign was on!

It was a fortnight later that the news of my personal incident exploded, announced, as I have already said, as the opening shot of the campaign.

This was my announcement as it appears in the *Cumberland News*.

"During my time in Parliament I have, I hope, by questioning, laid bare the faults in the law, whereby this type of thing could happen to me and can, in perhaps somewhat different ways, happen to other people. Anyone who has come into contact with the laws as to mental health, will readily appreciate that I speak the truth.

"There is urgent need for a change in the law. The Royal Commission reports in the autumn and we must press for it then.

"There is only one thing more to say. I am a Conservative. But there are issues that arise from time to time in which there is no room for Party feelings. This is one such issue. The news 'broke' in *Reynolds News*, the Co-op paper. I am glad on this to co-operate with *Reynolds News*. Another collaborator is Mr. Norman Dodds, the Labour M.P. for Erith and Crayford. Mr. Dodds and I shout at each other across the floor of the House on a dozen different issues. I do not often find myself in agreement with Mr. Dodds. But on this occasion I am pleased to work with him. When we come to think of the 20,000 people who are detained yearly in some such manner as I was detained, there is no scope for Party differences."

This was not, perhaps, the best way to secure for myself the approbation of the Party hierarchy. None the less, Norman Dodds and I have seen life together during our association in mental health campaigning.

Fame is the spur which the clear spirit doth raise,
That last infirmity of a noble mind,
To spurn delights, and live laborious days.

Perhaps our enthusiasm for publicity, which we have shared, is decried and can rightly be decried, for I am the first to consider that reform should come about through reasonable argument and moderate statement of upright principles. But, in this imperfect world, I have known of no instance in which this has occurred. Few reforms occur, in fact, without agitation, of which publicity is an essential part. Moreover, it is impossible, at a time of reform, to embark on reform satisfactorily, unless there is some clear idea of what has to be reformed. This is not always visible to those acting in an official and administrative capacity, in as much as they are apt to suffer from that natural human failing of being unable to see their own actions in the same light as others, not least those who suffer from those actions, see them. Likewise the case for any given reform must clearly be demonstrated to the public in order to obtain public sympathy and support for it. It is in the light, therefore, of these important considerations, that we have had to guide ourselves.

A friendly rivalry ensued between Norman and myself following the episode of the publication of my book: and it has been something of ding-dong struggle between us all along, as to which should hit the headlines—each sharing appropriately in the pride and joy of the other's triumphs.

*   *   *

The opening of the new Parliament in November of this year of 1956 gave me the opportunity for the first time for eighteen months to bring the subject of Mental Health Reform on to the floor of the House of Commons in regular debate during the Debate on the Address. This was what I said on Friday, 9th November:

I thank you, Mr. Deputy-Speaker, for allowing me this opportunity to take part in the debate on the reply to the Gracious Speech.

While I agree with so much which is in the Gracious Speech, I deplore, however, one omission—the omission of any mention of the Health Service. This expression of regret applies particularly to the subject of mental health. Here I believe that the old-fashioned organization inherited by the National Health Service in 1947 has as yet failed to adjust itself either to modern developments in the problems of mental health or even to the changes in public opinion which are taking place at the present time. I am therefore anxious to say something of the Measures which I should like to see proposed in future speeches from the Throne during my present term as a Member.

The first essential is that we should have an early change in the law relating to mental health and mental illness. I hope that during the coming year we shall have the Report of the Royal Commission, which has already been in session for three years, and that we shall be able to discuss action consequent upon that Report.

I am the first to appreciate the many endeavours which are being made at present to remove the so-called stigma from the mentally ill. There have been the mental health exhibitions, speeches by my right hon. Friends, the opening up of mental hospitals to visitors, and the suggestion that mental illness should be looked upon in the same light as physical illness. These are all steps in the right direction, and have my whole-hearted support.

At the same time, this kind of propaganda is totally ineffective while we leave the legal arrangements in their present state. In comparing mental with physical illness I will try to do so in the simplest terms. If a man has appendicitis and refuses advice to go into hospital, he does not have the experience of being hauled off there by one or two policemen. That is what happens if he is considered to be mentally ill. Again, if he goes to hospital with a physical illness, he does not find himself in a locked ward, deprived of all civic rights, and wondering when, and under what circumstances, he will ever get out again. That, too, is what happens to large numbers of mentally ill people. If he refuses an operation in hospital he is not forced to undergo it, as is the certified mental patient.

I appreciate the development of the voluntary patient system, which has led to voluntary mental patients making up about 75 per cent of admissions to mental hospitals, but the fact remains that there are still some 20,000 certified patients being brought into hospital every year under various forms of compulsion. There has been no decrease in that figure over the past 25 years; it is practically identical with that quoted in 1929.

People are being certified, and removed to hospital under arrangements directly inherited from the less satisfactory aspects of the Lunacy Act, 1890, which still forms the background of the whole situation in our mental hospitals, even for voluntary patients. It is reported to me that in many hospitals even voluntary patients are put into locked wards. Why, I do not know. They go in voluntarily, but find themselves in locked wards and, in some cases, with the possibility of certification hanging over them.

If anybody doubts this kind of statement, I would refer to the autumn edition, 1955, of the magazine *Mental Health*. There is there quoted an extract from a letter written by a former patient, in which she says, quite baldly:

"Even in the apparent liberty and friendliness of an 'Open' ward I still found a background of threats that made me feel something between a prisoner and a pauper."

It will only be when it is fully recognized that these widespread detention arrangements belong to an out-of-date code of behaviour that the stigma will be removed. I do not believe that it can be done merely by a change in terminology, such as calling certification 'temporary detention'. To pretend that is merely self-delusion. It will mean using phrases which, although appearing all right at the time, will become equally as discredited, in the course of time, as is the word 'certification'.

While, as a doctor, I have to deplore the unsatisfactory arrangements as to methods of treatment to which I have referred, as a citizen and as a Member of this House I wish for a moment to look at the law from another angle. In other contexts I have emphasized the dangers to the individual arising from the present laxness of the law. The present state of the law is a standing invitation to the more unscrupulous members of the community to dispose of unwanted people, whether by false witness or by other sinister means. Certainly, no action can render a victim more defenceless than this.

The alarm which one feels at this is equalled only by the alarm one feels on coming across cases where the law of lunacy comes into contact with the criminal law. We find cases, and I have one which I hope shortly to bring to the notice of my right hon. and gallant Friend the Home Secretary, of people entering police courts and receiving short terms of imprisonment, but regaining their liberty only after many years, without having had the opportunity of an independent doctor's opinion in the meantime. I can only hope that the enactments which govern these matters, and which are older even than the 1890 Act, are being reviewed by the Royal Commission, together with the more ordinary and everyday mental health enactments.

I now come to another aspect of the problem. There is a general impression abroad that the ease with which a man can be put into a mental hospital is equalled only by the difficulty he experiences in getting out of it again. I believe that impression to be right. It is, in fact, borne out by statistics. According to the Ministry of Health returns which have just been published, the average mental patient going into hospital can expect to stay there for no less than twenty months before being released, either by discharge, or, as in so many unfortunate cases, by death. This is a period four times as long, for instance, as he would suffer while being cured of the longest curable physical disease known—tuberculosis. And, of course, this leads to the condition of overcrowding.

At the risk of repeating the obvious, I say that the first thing we need is a sifting process of admissions by means of observation wards. As I have made a speech on this question in an Adjournment debate, I will not go over it all again now.

The least we can do, however, is to prevent people who are physically ill, either from delirium or from some other cause, from drifting into mental hospitals as potentially long-stay patients. I have had a very large correspondence in recent weeks, and people have even written to say that because they were in pain of some kind, for which the doctors in the particular hospital to which they went could not discover the cause, they found themselves transferred to a mental hospital. That sort of thing is very wrong indeed and is a blot on the doctors and on our National Health Service.

I turn to the question of discharge. I cannot do better than quote from an authority higher than my own. To every hon. Member who is interested in the matter I recommend a small booklet. It was published recently by *The Lancet* under the title *In the Mental Hospital* and the price is only half a crown.

The first article is 'The Forgotten Patient', by Dr. J. A. R. Bickford, physician superintendent of the De la Pole Hospital, Willerby, in Yorkshire. He says that

"by far the more important reason"—for overcrowding in mental hospitals—

"is that psychiatrists have failed to cure and discharge their patients. . . . The business of a hospital is to cure patients, not to hoard them; and the sheltering of patients in hospital without continual efforts to make them fit to return to the world is a complete denial of the functions of medicine. If attention is mistakenly concentrated on building additional wards and villas, the almost invariable result will be that these too will become overcrowded, because the last incentive to discharge patients will have gone. It would be wiser in fact for the hospital to knock down a ward every five years or so."

I entirely concur with those remarks. I believe that by the proper rehabilitation of patients in systematic fashion and the establishment of the appropriate social service to this end, the population of our mental hospitals could be cut down by one-third, if not by a half, in a very short time.

We want rehabilitation, first by a system of sheltered workshops where patients can work in appropriately sheltered surroundings, while living at home or perhaps in hostels in cases where the home surroundings are not suitable. The establishment of such workshops and hostels could surely be explored as a less costly alternative to establishing more hospital beds.

Finally, to back all this up, we need—to use again a long-sounding title in regard to which, when I have used it before, hon. Members have always asked what I was talking about—the development of a domiciliary psychiatric social service. All that that means is that mental patients should have the essential service which can look after them in their own home surroundings under the aegis of the local authority.

I am not talking of anything nebulous. Such a service was established in the City of Amsterdam some twenty years ago at a juncture similar to our own, when the Dutch had over-crowded mental hospitals and only a limited amount of money with which to solve their problems. In August last year I took the opportunity of going to Amsterdam to observe it for a few days.

This system is run by the local authorities—the Amsterdam city authorities—with the aid of psychiatrists who are part of the local authority set-up. The duties of the psychiatrists include visiting people in their homes, and include—and this is the important thing—an emergency service. Thus, if anybody is taken mentally ill in Amsterdam he is not seen, as he would be in this country, by an untrained duly authorized officer, who is not specially trained in mental illness. In Amsterdam, anybody who is taken ill with mental illness is seen by a psychiatrist who is on emergency duty.

The psychiatrist's brief is an entirely different one from the brief which is given to our own officers in this country. It is not to get the patient into hospital, but to keep him out of hospital, to try to solve his problems in the first place in home surroundings, and to save hospital beds. It has the consequent effect of controlling admissions to mental hospitals—a control which is very necessary in this country. The service has a similar function on the discharge of patients, and that is to see they are properly and well settled in home surroundings, and to prevent a relapse, which again is one of the big problems in our mental illnesses in this country.

It is interesting that this experiment in Amsterdam was introduced at a time of financial stringency, to solve the problem of overcrowded hospitals. For general reasons and that particular reason, I recommend it to my right hon. Friend when he considers this matter. There can be little doubt that in establishing a service of this kind, accompanied by a geriatric service which will give proper care to our old people, we have a real opportunity during the next few years to develop our social services, and to solve one of the most urgent problems which the community has today.

Apart from a kindly mention in the editorial of the *Manchester Guardian*, this, however, made little impact. "Members ride their Hobby-Horses," commented the *Wolverhampton Express and Star*. It probably expressed the general attitude.

*   *   *

However, in the meantime, Norman Dodds, who does not enter into any struggle half-heartedly, had been taking up the case of Mrs. Harriet Thornton in a big way, with a view to obtaining her freedom. To every action, so one has learnt, there is an equal and opposite reaction. I have written in *A Doctor Returns*, my views on the evasiveness and secretiveness of our British bureaucracy and need not expand on my remarks here. The reaction to this is to produce Norman Dodds.

Thus we find in the Hansards of that November 1956:

Mr. Dodds asked the Minister of Health how many

doctors were concerned in the certification of Mrs. Harriet Thornton which resulted in her detention in a mental home for three and a half years: and on how many occasions, and for how long, did each doctor see her before a decision was taken to send Mrs. Thornton to a mental home.

Mr. Dodds asked the Minister of Health why a box of important documents taken by Mrs. Harriet Thornton to hospital was allowed to remain in a ward for three and a half years despite correspondence on the subject from the official solicitor appointed to look after Mrs. Thornton's affairs: and, in view of the fact that this is a breach of the lunacy law, what action does he propose to take.

Mr. Dodds asked the Minister of Health (1) under what authority the Cane Hill Hospital Management Committee asked for and received from the official solicitor acting on behalf of Mrs. Harriet Thornton payment of money from her estate whilst she was still certified and a National Health Service patient; (2) why an approach was not made by the Hospital Management Committee to the husband of Mrs. Thornton for payment towards her maintenance whilst in the care of Cane Hill Mental Hospital.

(Mr. Dodds—*a few minutes later*—"Owing to the very unsatisfactory nature of the answer, I beg to give notice that I will raise the matter on the Adjournment at the earliest possible moment.")

There were more civil servants listening to Norman's Adjournment Debate on Mrs. Harriet Thornton than I have seen listening to an Adjournment Debate at any other time, before or since.

In the meantime, Mrs. Harriet Thornton (who had attended my House of Commons party as one of my guests) was freed amidst columns of 'notice' in the national press.

"You must meet Pathé's man in the Central Lobby with me

at 3.30 tomorrow," invited Norman, generously anxious to
share his triumph with me.

We met Pathé's man and a few minutes later our unusual
cavalcade of Norman, myself, Pathé's man, and Mrs. Harriet
Thornton, this mildly eccentric lady whose abnormal mental
traits appear to have been that she believed the spirits talked to
her and that she wrote 'Belsen' across the garage door of her
rather unhappy married domicile, was wending its way along
Wardour Street to our rendezvous in front of Pathé's news
cameras, where, talking to Mrs. Thornton, I made my only
cinema feature in which I have so far played.

Despite a wait of an hour in the rain outside our local cinema,
Betty and I did not, alas, see this film, which was the foundation
stone of Norman's and my own joint fame throughout the
country. But I appear to have been amongst the few people who
did not do so.

It was a stimulating start. "I intend to re-double my efforts
in 1957," declared Norman. The zest that glinted in his eye was
that of the tiger who had tasted blood.

When the first parliamentary order paper for 1957 appeared
on the 24th January, on it, for Written Answer, were 82
Questions. Out of these 82, the first 22, with only one exception,
were in the name of Mr. Norman Dodds, and there were three
more in his name in addition—all on the subject of mental
illness. There were 10 in my own name on the same subject,
mainly concerning my constituent, Cathlene Murray, who had
been detained as a mental defective for 23 years and was still
in Moss Side Hospital, Liverpool There were 29 in the name of
Captain Harry Kerby on a variety of subjects. While the
remaining 21 were distributed amongst our several hundred
parliamentary colleagues.

Our campaigning year had started.

MENTAL HEALTHMANSHIP

I have intimated how my first question on mental illness may
well have been the first one on this subject on the parliamentary paper for a long time.

Threats to liberty can manifest themselves in many ways.
Liberty can be undermined by the capricious exercise of well-
meaning authority as well as destroyed outright by malevolent
tyranny, by local authority as well as by centralized despotism.
Obsessed as we are in our Parliament at Westminster with the
dangers of centralized authority partly as the outcome of our
own history, partly as a reaction to the main political threat of
modern times, we tend to overlook this fact. Loss of liberty, for
him who suffers it, is however no less a serious matter, whether
it results from the action of the uniformed minion of a centralized
police force, or from that of a plain-clothed duly authorized
officer of a local health authority.

Indeed we should remind ourselves that the threats to liberty
in the early days of Western civilization came not from central
authority, but from the exercise of capricious power by the
feudal baronage, which was only curbed by the establishment
of the King's Justice.

The baronial castle, where it still survived, had become a
historic relic over many hundred years, when during the course
of the nineteenth century a fresh collection of fortress-like
structures started to encumber the British countryside. These
were the gigantic lunatic asylums built by local authority for the
custodial care of the mentally afflicted. Nobody talked of what
happened in these places. Nobody even liked to know they

L   161

existed, just as, so one understands, nobody in Hitler's Germany liked to know that concentration camps existed. For instance, a desirable residential area south of London containing several 'asylums' was wont even to omit them from its local maps.

It appears one of the inalterable laws of human affairs, operative long before the famous dicta were propounded by Professor C. Northcote Parkinson, that any institution, once established, will acquire its own dynamic in expanding its establishment. Add this to the fact that the medical superintendents of these institutions found themselves over the years in just that same position of unchallenged authority as the feudal barons, and we have a system of sinister potentiality.

For who are the mentally ill? Are they not those afflicted with a different set of perceptions, a different way of thinking, a different code of behaviour to ourselves?

What is 'unsoundness of mind'? It is a phrase which, as the Board of Control has written to one of my correspondents, an ex-certificatee, 'lacks definition'. It can, in these circumstances, become merely a matter of opinion.

To what extent must a person differ from the human 'norm' to be considered as 'of unsound mind'? (What is the human 'norm' anyway?) Is it enough that, like Mrs. Thornton, she should hear the spirits talk to her and write 'Belsen' on the garage door? Is it enough that, like my correspondent Mrs. Jane Woodhouse, she should "suddenly burst into a temper with her husband—would become suddenly quiet and harp upon 'the official line' taken by us. Accused her husband of being against her". Or that, like my correspondent, Mr. Harry Jones, he should "have an obsession that his wife is in dire straits after an operation and that the hospital is to blame". Or, like my correspondent, Miss Edith Williams, that she should "say all doctors are stupid and behave aggressively to the present officers".

It would seem so, as these are all quotations from written certificates of unsoundness of mind warranting removal to mental hospitals, denoting 'signs indicating insanity'. In these circumstances almost any facet of human behaviour might qualify for inclusion on such a certificate. Be careful, for instance, how you joke about your own behaviour, for my schoolmaster correspondent, Mr. T., came home one day and jestingly remarked that, for keeping the peace in the atmosphere of acrimony amongst his colleagues that he had to put up with, he "deserved the Nobel Peace Prize"—at a later date, sure enough, he found this statement written down on his certificate as "evidence of signs of insanity communicated by others".

One can, in fact, find only one common denominator to the medley of reasons given on certificates of unsoundness of mind to the effect that the subjects of these should be detained in a mental hospital—namely that, in one and every case, they were unwanted people; unwanted by husbands, unwanted by wives, unwanted by relatives, unwanted—let us face it by local authority, either professional or lay. Hospitals for the care of sickness: or Bastilles for the detention of the unwanted? That has been the query heavily overlying the asylums in their evolution over the past hundred years. It is one which, let us hope, the present decade will solve.

In the meantime I have greatly to thank the *Spectator* for allowing me to set out these problems in a series of articles the first of which appeared on 18th January, 1957, under the title of 'Mental Healthmanship'.

"He ought to be locked up!" How many of us say this, half jokingly perhaps, but revealingly just the same—revealingly of the casually custodial attitude of the community towards even the mildly eccentric.

"He ought to be locked up!" The enticing thought comes readily to the unscrupulous mind as an obtrusive and embarrassing husband or a tiresome and ailing wife bars the way; or perhaps an elderly and penurious relative occupies a room that might be put to better use or better profit.

Laboriously, I have written no fewer than three books to show how easy it is to drug an unwanted person and get him into a mental hospital—for a long time, perhaps, if the right drug is used.

But greater knowledge—acquired through the correspondence which an M.P. attracts—brings disillusionment, though not perhaps in the same way that my critics would desire. For there is little need to resort to drugs.

Amongst the variegated activities of a big city, there is one activity that should be more generally known than it is. It is that of the Duly Authorized Officer of the Local Health Authority, who is sometimes known as the Mental Health Officer. His statutory duties are to take action in the case of anyone within the area of his authority whom he has 'reasonable ground for believing to be of unsound mind' and if he is satisfied that it is for 'the welfare of any person' that he should be detained in a mental hospital, he is authorized so to detain him. He can enforce his authority, if necessary, with the aid of the police.

The statute does not stipulate in any way how or in what manner the D.A.O. should come to his 'reasonable beliefs', what evidence there must be to support them, nor, in fact, whether there should be any enquiry as to motive behind such evidence. The D.A.O. acts 'on information'. (Nor, in the vast majority of cases, can the person informed upon discover subsequently who lodged the information.) But, acting upon information, he has his daily list of calls. He may take action alone, under which conditions he can make Urgency Orders authorizing three days' initial detention: or he may call for a doctor and a J.P. and, with the aid of a single doctor's certificate, make a summary reception order which lasts up to a year.

Let me say it loud and clear. One doctor's certificate is sufficient to 'certify' an alleged mental patient and deprive him of all civil rights, including his liberty, his control over his property, his access to the courts of law. The overwhelming majority of certified patients entering mental hospitals go in on summary reception orders supported by one doctor's certificate.

"The length of time taken in the medical examination of a person alleged to be of unsound mind is a matter for the discretion of the doctor concerned," said the Parliamentary Secretary to the Ministry of Health in the adjournment debate as recently as 21st December. "In many cases the patient is in a very sick condition and it does not take long for that reason. There is no legal requirement that he should have seen the patient previously."

Mr. Norman Dodds obtained a copy of the summary reception order relating to his constituent, Mrs. Harriet Thornton, as a consequence of which she began a stay of three and a half years in a mental hospital, and raised the matter in the Adjournment Debate from which I have already quoted.

"Is it not amazing that the J.P. and the doctor saw Mrs. Thornton only once and for no more than five minutes?" asked Mr. Dodds. "During those five minutes, the J.P. asked not a single question. They spent about half an hour with the husband, but since the husband was not a true advocate for his wife, that is not good enough.

"On the second part of the Reception Order the doctor gives his reasons for declaring Mrs. Thornton insane . . . there are seven reasons given, only one of which cannot be checked—that she was unco-operative and excited. Who would not be in that state on knowing that an effort was being made to put her into a mental home?

"There are, however, six reasons given, each one of which can be completely destroyed, had anyone taken the trouble to get evidence other than from the husband. For instance, it is said that Mrs. Thornton 'had delusions of persecution'. She said, 'My husband nearly killed me; he tried to push me over the banisters.'

"That is not a delusion," continued Mr. Dodds, "it is a fact. Luckily the son had to fight with his father for ten minutes to prevent Mrs. Thornton from being thrown over the banisters, but the son, who knows more about what happened in the house than anyone, and from whom I have evidence, has never been asked by anyone to give a statement."

Mrs. Thornton's is not an isolated case.

"It is with hope that I address you on the subject of my detention in this mental hospital," comes a letter to me dated 27th October, 1956, headed with the address of a large mental hospital near London. "I am aware that what I write will perforce be interpreted with the utmost caution. None the less I swear to the truth of every word of it.

"A month ago a monstrous and outrageously wrongful order was signed for my reception in hospital, as the result of the most trivial domestic incident. (A person damaged my belongings and I mildly retaliated by sprinkling some water in the kitchen.) An over-enthusiastic official, who I thought at the time was a welfare worker, but subsequently learnt was a Mental Health Officer, persuaded a magistrate and a young doctor (whom I had never seen before in my life) to sign this iniquitous order. It was done in a matter of minutes—five at the most. The magistrate spoke not a word, nor did he make known his decision. He just took a few notes.

"A disturbing aspect of this lamentable affair was, the said M.H.O. promised to bring the family doctor, who has been our family doctor for ten years, and who is thoroughly acquainted with both sides of the question. However, he failed to do so.

"I am of irreproachable character. I have never been in hospital before. From the first day of my detention I have persistently maintained I am perfectly fit both in mind and body. As a matter of absolute and disquieting fact I was apprehended in full vigour of health and strength, and in the full amplitude of my mental powers."

Fortunately for Mr. S., who wrote this letter, he has a brother who also wrote and confirmed his statements. On return from war service, Mr. S. had come back to live with his sister and stepmother in a house that he had partly bought. There began (as Mr. S., the brother, put it) "a campaign to ease him out of the house". The first step was a suggestion to the family doctor that he should be certified because he was eccentric—which was turned down flat. The next was a solicitor's letter instructing him to move—which was proved invalid. Then came attempts to torment him by damaging his clothes and other property. Finally, there was the by-passing of the family doctor and the culminating achievement of having him certified.

"Dear Dr. Johnson," the family doctor's letter lies here in front of me; "Mr. S. was a somewhat eccentric man with a grievance against his stepmother. He was certainly not of unsound mind. He struck me as an intelligent, thoughtful, kindly man. He shared a house with his stepmother, and as he had contributed towards the purchase price he naturally felt somewhat aggrieved, especially as they did not get on amicably. Increased domestic dissensions led to petty acts of damage to each other's property and with accusations of mutual damage. Two years ago I was asked to certify him, but I could find no facts indicating insanity and refused to proceed. Finally, on 26th September, he was visited by the M.H.O., accompanied by a doctor and magistrate and two policemen, and driven off to hospital. He was told by the M.H.O. that I was away on holiday, which was untrue. I was appalled at the manner in which this certification took place."

It was fortunate for Mr. S. that he has a brother who was able to obtain his discharge within a month by the appropriate relative's application. He had been diagnosed as suffering from delusions—delusions about damage to his property which (as his brother pointed out) was never subjected to inspection by those who made this diagnosis. But for his brother, Mr. S. would undoubtedly have been in hospital yet.

"THE MINISTRY OF HEALTH ACTS AS AN OGPU" declare the bold headlines of the small periodical *Gothic Ripples* as, in its issue of 27th April, 1955, it reports the case of both a husband

and a wife detained for ten days in the observation ward of a
London hospital, as a consequence of information coming from
they knew not where (nor did they ever find out), before they
were declared sane by a psychiatric specialist.

"We are merely tidying up a few odds and ends," said Mr.
Aneurin Bevan, a Celt and not a Goth, in breezily reassuring
fashion, as he introduced the committee stage of the 9th Schedule
of the National Health Service Act, under whose statutory
umbrella all the above actions have taken place.

"It was a race as to which of us reached a mental hospital
first," admitted a husband to one of my parliamentary colleagues, concerning his wife whose certification he had successfully arranged.

What he meant was that it was a race as to who got to the
Mental Health Officer first to lay the appropriate allegations.
He, of course, won; and since, once he had got his wife in, he
was the only person who could obtain her discharge, he
managed to dispose of her for a considerable time.

Clearly a new social science opens out. As from Gamesman-
ship we have had Lifemanship, now we come to Mental Healthmanship. Why, indeed, commit murder as in the old days as
release from a discordant or inharmonious marriage? Why the
expense and uncertainty of divorce? Why the complications
and risks of poisoning by drugs? Go to the Mental Officer.
But—and this is the first rule—*get there first*.

*   *   *

The only rider to my article is to the effect that my Mr. S.,
being both a persistent and an intelligent person, and one moreover imbued with the impression that he lived in a free country,
endeavoured to take legal action against the Mental Health
Officer of the local health authority. After taking Counsel's
advice, he was advised not to proceed further, as he had no case.
This would naturally be so, when any such definition as a doctor

or official wishes can be placed on the words 'of unsound mind'.

This is of interest, for it becomes important to see what happens when, as an alternative course of action, the case of a former certified patient is pressed by an M.P. in the House of Commons with a view to an enquiry. I reproduce the Adjournment Debate of Tuesday, 30th April, 1957, in which I put forward such a case and was answered by the Parliamentary Secretary, Mr. John Vaughan-Morgan:

* * *

Dr. Donald Johnson (Carlisle): I wish to raise this matter for a double purpose. The first concerns the grievance of a former certified mental patient, and the second is to discuss its background and to examine the problems which it illustrates. This case is only one example taken from a considerable correspondence which hangs, rather like the albatross, round the neck of any Member of Parliament who is interested in these matters, as a burden which he has to carry alone owing to the singularly unhelpful replies which he receives when he approaches authority.

This lady, according to her own submission, was arbitrarily and unnecessarily deprived of personal liberty for a period of four or five months. In defence of individual liberty, I feel that I cannot do better than quote the recent words of my right hon. Friend the Home Secretary (Mr. R. A. Butler) that:

"deprivation of liberty must always be a punishment."

He made that remark in relation to prisoners, but it surely applies to innocent people as well as guilty ones, and to sick persons as well as fit ones, though I must make it plain that the lady whom I am representing avers that she was a fit person during the entire time of her detention.

Under the working of the Lunacy Act, with its various

Amendments, the principles of liberty have fallen into disregard in recent years. It is, naturally, necessary that powers of restraint should exist in regard to those who are mentally afflicted and are a danger to themselves and to others, but it is equally necessary that the individual should have the fullest protection against either the misuse or the mistaken use of these powers, otherwise we may find that instead of sane people locking up mad people we shall have mad people locking up sane people. Under existing conditions there is nothing to prevent it happening. As this case shows, the protections have now become illusory.

This lady is a lady of some considerable academic distinction and also of considerable personality. She plays an important part in the public life of the district where she lives. She came back in middle-aged retirement some years ago to live with her two sisters in the family home. She was the member of the family who had broken away and achieved success in the outside world while her less brilliant sisters stayed at home. This appears to have been a basic cause of friction and ill-feeling in the family.

Shortly after she came home her mother fell ill, and was attended by a young assistant doctor who was fresh to the district. Miss X was dissatisfied and wanted a second opinion. This was refused by the doctor. The refusal led to a request by Miss X to the local executive council to supply a second opinion and the doctor got to know of this. I have here a letter which shows—that the council wrote to the doctor, so that he was well aware of this fact. This may or may not have a connection with what happened subsequently. I am putting the facts in chronological order and not with a view to connecting them as to cause and effect.

It so happened that four months later, quite unexpectedly, what one might term a 'posse of authority' descended on Miss X at her home. It included the doctor, local authority officers and a justice. I think there was also an ambulance. Naturally, Miss X took fright and attempted to evade capture, and she went to the house of a neighbour. The party entered the house and I imagine a somewhat angry scene ensued as Miss X resisted what she regarded as her capture. However, she was removed to the local mental hospital where she was detained for four to five months.

She found herself subsequently—as have many others in similar circumstances—deprived of the customary human rights in respect of this period of incarceration both at the time and also after her discharge. I give only one example. I submit that it is an elementary principle that those who lose their liberty, whether they are sick or well, at least should be notified of their rights under the law. As my hon. Friend knows, this lady is a voluminous correspondent. Yet, in spite of her appeals to all forms of authority, including the Minister of Health, the Lord Chancellor, the Board of Control and others, no one saw fit to inform her of her rights under Section 82 of the Act, by which she was entitled to obtain copies of the certificates which sent her to hospital.

The Parliamentary Secretary to the Ministry of Health (Mr. J. K. Vaughan-Morgan): I am sorry to interrupt my hon. Friend, but this is supposed to be an Adjournment Debate on a question of administration. Is my hon. Friend suggesting that the authorities transgressed any of the laws or regulations in not giving that information? Where is it laid down that this information has to be supplied?

Dr. Johnson: I am not suggesting that at all. I am making no suggestion of that kind. I am merely saying that this lady did not receive any help. I am stating that purely as a fact, that she did not receive any help, and I leave it there as a stated fact without further comment. I have not said that the laws were transgressed. I am merely talking about the position in which this lady found herself. She found herself in

that position until some three years later, when I was first
able to inform her of this right. Then, I fully admit, when she
wrote to the Board of Control and asked for these certificates,
she received them without delay. There is no dispute on that
point.

These certificates arrived. I have them here in my
possession, and had time allowed I would have liked to deal
with them in full; but I have only three more minutes. The
main thing that can be said about the certificates is that they
are confirmation of the story which I have already told,
namely, of considerable family animosity, on the one hand,
and what seems to be outraged professional feeling, on the
other.

The main point of substance is that I do not see any medical
evidence of insanity in any of the statements on the certificates.
An insane person could act as the certificate describes, but
that is not the point; so could a sane person. The day after
I received these certificates I was watching a football match.
Behind me were two supporters of the rival teams. I could
quite easily have given certificates just as good as the one in
this case for either of those gentlemen about the state in
which they appeared to be at that match.

There was a justice of the peace at this ceremony. A
statutory duty is laid on him to make such enquiry as he
thinks advisable. He appears to have conspicuously failed in
his duty. My correspondent alleges—and I put this forward
merely as her allegation—that the justice of the peace said
some eight words and they were, "Where are the papers?
I will sign them."

I appreciate that the lady was in hospital for five months.
The only comment I have in this connection, because of the
very brief time available, is that we are sane until we are
judged insane, unfortunately by only one doctor, while once
we are in a mental hospital we tend, particularly under a
certificate, to be judged insane until we can prove ourselves

sane. For many people, and perhaps for most of us, that is somewhat difficult.

I have put the complainant's side of the case. I do not deny at all that there may be another side, which my hon. Friend the Parliamentary Secretary will present to the House. At the end of it all the matter will be left somewhat indeterminate. That is why I regret that, since the good name of the service is involved and the rights of the individual, my right hon. Friend does not feel himself empowered to appoint an independent enquiry.

He has told me in answer to my Questions that the remedy is at law. I am sorry not to be able to develop my answer to this point, too. I can only state that since the Amendments introduced into the Mental Treatment Act, 1930, there has been no successful case of a doctor being sued—not that I want doctors to be sued—but there is no way in which a patient can restore his or her good name. While we must protect people who have difficult jobs to do, none the less we have to protect the individual also and give him or her, particularly in a case like this, an opportunity to re-establish his good name and bring evidence forward in some form or another.

The Parliamentary Secretary to the Ministry of Health (Mr. J. K. Vaughan-Morgan): May I, first, thank my hon. Friend the Member for Carlisle (Dr. D. Johnson) for his courtesy in giving me full and early notice of all the points he was going to raise in this debate. I realize, and the House realizes, the interest which he takes in the problems of the mentally sick. I share his anxiety that the greatest possible care should be taken at all times to ensure that the safeguards which Parliament has provided to protect those dealt with as insane are scrupulously observed. After listening to his speech, I must say with deep regret that he has used this occasion to make these general allegations of maltreatment, and of an abuse of the spirit of medicine. I will deal rather more fully with that later.

My hon. Friend talked about protection for those who are certified and has quite rightly reminded us that we need protection also for those carrying out very difficult duties, but I do not think he has thought of that side of the matter at all in his speech. However, since I am not going to say very much to commend my hon. Friend—I will be quite frank about that, I deplore some of the things he said—I do commend him for one thing; he has kept the name of the patient out of this debate. I think it is quite right that we should not use the privileges we have here to bandy names and reputations about. Incidentally, that applies not only to the patient but to all others concerned in this case.

I cannot agree with my hon. Friend in any way in the case he has raised either as to the facts he has given or the conclusions he has drawn from them. He has ranged over a very wide sphere, and I cannot answer everything he has said in the time left at my disposal, but I have one general criticism which I would apply to most of what he said, and I ask the House to apply it also. Of all the principal parties in this case—and there are many people involved—my hon. Friend has chosen to believe, and apparently to believe implicitly and unreservedly, the one least likely to be impartial or to judge impartially—that is, the patient herself. In a recent letter he wrote to me, which I hope my hon. Friend will not mind me quoting, he said that he has seen and cross-questioned the lady

"and believes what she says to be substantially true".

All right, I am not denying that what she says may be true, but there is absolutely no evidence that my hon. Friend performed the same service for the doctor—he has taken the word of the patient against the doctor—or for the justice of the peace—he has taken her word that the justice dismissed the whole thing in eight words——

Dr. Johnson *rose*——

Mr. Vaughan-Morgan: No, I am going to finish this—for the duly authorized officer, or for the patient's relations.

He has taken her view against the view of her sister, and there are two sides to that question. He did not mention that the police were witnesses of this 'disgraceful scene' which he represented, nor has he taken the trouble to question the neighbours who witnessed the certification. He has done this in other cases. He believes in some sort of conspiracy, whether consciously formulated or not, against Miss X, as he called her, in which her doctor and her sisters took the leading part. I do not doubt my hon. Friend's sincerity. I would accuse him, perhaps, of a certain streak of naïvety, but I think it is irresponsible to base so serious a case in Parliament as a court of law on a patient's unsupported story without having the views of others closely concerned.

I want to stress a point which my hon. Friend has mentioned and which I put to him in correspondence. It has always been open to this lady to seek legal redress if she thinks she has been wrongly certified. My hon. Friend pointed out that she was a lady of education and of some standing. I refuse to believe that in what he calls 'a friendless world' she did not know that the right person to go to was a solicitor, or at least a citizens' advice bureau.

Despite the voluminous correspondence which she has had with various Government Departments and other authorities, she has always evidently failed to take the legal advice which is her obvious remedy. Could this be because she lacks confidence in the strength of her case? That is the conclusion which I draw and which I think the House would draw and which my hon. Friend himself should have drawn.

My hon. Friend argues that there have been few successful actions against allegedly wrong certification, but I suggest to him that that might be because there have been few cases which have been sufficiently strong to persuade the courts which have tried them. He tries to prove that because there have been no successful actions it is, therefore, useless to use the machinery of the courts; but supposing there were many successful actions, my hon. Friend would be the first person to try to use that to prove how bad the present administration of the law was. He cannot have it both ways. It is not the function of the House to judge cases which should properly be decided in the courts.

Let me turn to a more detailed study of the case and tell the House some of the facts which my hon. Friend omitted. I will not go through all the legal ramifications. The lady was removed and admitted to hospital as a certified patient on the authority of a summary reception order dated 26th April, 1954, made by a justice of the peace under Section 16 of the Lunacy Act, 1890. That was done on a medical certificate in statutory form. Proceedings were initiated by a duly authorized officer, whose statutory duty it was, incidentally, to bring this case to the notice of the justice of the peace—that is under Section 14 of the Lunacy Act of 1890.

My hon. Friend made some criticism of the general practitioner in the case and suggested that he was inexperienced and had no special psychiatric experience. But Parliament has never laid down that the doctor called in by the justice of the peace should have special psychiatric experience. It is for the justice alone to select the doctor to examine the person and then to decide, after his own examination and enquiries, whether such an order can properly be made. There is no doubt that the doctor called in to examine Miss X was, in fact, of reasonable experience and qualifications. Some of what my hon. Friend has said, coming from a doctor, is very definitely to impugn the ethical standards and behaviour of a member of his own profession whom he has not examined.

My hon. Friend commented on another point. At the end of his speech he referred to what, in correspondence, he called the 'non-medical' nature of the certificate. However, the fact is that the Mental Treatment Act, as he should know, requires a doctor to state the facts which indicate insanity; in other words, the behaviour disorders which cause him to conclude that certification is necessary. It does not fall on the general practitioner to give a psychiatric diagnosis of the patient. The answer to my hon. Friend in his analogy of the football match is not unhappy. What would have happened if he had certified those patients and gone to the hospital? I cannot believe that he seriously suggests that any responsible medical superintendent would have accepted those men. To draw an analogy from a casual contact like that to what has been done by a doctor and justice of the peace in full accord with the law, is highly irresponsible.

My hon. Friend has painted a distressing picture of an unfortunate patient being seized by a posse of authorities from a neighbour's house. My information discloses a very different picture. It comes from the duly authorized officer concerned and it is agreed and approved by the police sergeant who was there. My hon. Friend has the evidence of the patient. I have the evidence of the duly authorized officer and the police sergeant and I cannot seriously think that any disorders within the family could have affected the impartial testimony of either of those two, and I think that my hon. Friend should agree.

I understand that the officer concerned went by taxi to the lady's house, having arranged to meet the doctor there and for the J.P. also to meet him there. When he arrived the doctor was already there and so were some of her relations, but not the lady. It then appeared that she had run over to another house and that the taxi-driver driving the duly authorized officer told him where she had gone.

The owner of the house then came up in a very agitated condition and said that he had seen Miss X run into his house, that she had locked herself in the house, and that he

M

was very worried because his wife was there and in a very poor state of health. The police were informed, and about a quarter of an hour later a police sergeant came to the house; that is, to the house of the man where the lady had taken refuge, as my hon. Friend has put it. The husband was there as well.

On the question of forced entry, the police sergeant called through the door several times to Miss X, and eventually the door of the house was opened from the inside. The lady of the house was inside at the same time, and they were both inside when the doctor and others went in. It is denied quite categorically that there was any forced entry into the house. One of the lady's sisters was present and went into the house as well. There was no question of ordering anybody out of the house, or of any unruly, disorderly or illegal behaviour; and I could expatiate on the report which I have received for a very long time.

My hon. Friend also raised the question that the lady had not received all the information she should have had. I would have liked, if there had been time, to draw the attention of the House to the very many safeguards which do exist against improper detention, and I think that, on behalf of those who have to administer this very difficult sphere of the Health Service, we ought to express some resentment at the suggestion that there can be these ghastly cases which my hon. Friend has suggested. I am not denying that there may not be occasions when something is wrong, but surely we want rather more evidence than has been given.

This lady's case was reviewed throughout her stay in hospital, and she was specially visited by a Medical Commissioner of the Board of Control and every step was taken to see that she was rightly and properly treated. On the question of an enquiry, neither my right hon. Friend nor the Board of Control has power to investigate the circumstances under which the justice made an order for this lady's reception into mental hospital care, since such an order can be quashed or set aside only by the courts.

Therefore, I end by repeating what I said at the beginning. Throughout this case, the right course was for this lady to take legal action if she felt that she was wrongly deprived of her liberty; and until she takes those steps, I think that we are fully entitled to say that the case which my hon. Friend has made is not proved.

My hon. Friend suggested that nobody had given the lady the documents which she wanted. I think that my hon. Friend is really asking a little too much. He admits that the documents were given as soon as they were asked for, but does he really suggest—for this is what it amounts to—that the Board of Control should give a copy of the certificate to every discharged patient? That certainly is not the law at present. I am sure that my hon. Friend has a very kind and good heart. As I have said, I think he has a rather naïve approach to these matters and I think we want to be rather more responsible in our approach to those who are doing a very difficult task under the law as it stands.

In any case, as the House knows, a Royal Commission has been appointed which will study all the evidence, and I think we can await its Report with great confidence. I am quite certain that if there is anything in the administration of the law which is wrong, it will bring it out into the light of day, and I am quite certain that it will produce rather more evidence of injustice, if it exists, than has been produced to the House tonight.

Thus Mr. John Vaughan-Morgan and I went our several ways: he to become Minister of State to the Board of Trade: I to write this book.

Almost the last of my long series of oral questions to the Minister on mental health legislation was on 17th February, 1958, when I asked if he was aware that Dr. Walter Maclay,

a Principal Medical Officer of his Ministry, had stated in the
course of a speech at Toronto that "doctors' reasons for
certifying patients as being of unsound mind, 'often make one
wonder whether it is the doctor or the patient who should be
certified' ". And with these final words, we can leave this aspect
of the subject.

*   *   *

Is liberty of value?

One sometimes feels that it is of little value at all, when it can
be abolished by the single sweep of an official and judicial pen on
the strength of a hurried and perhaps erratic certificate—a
decision which then has to be defended to the death by the whole
weight of the official machine—including a Minister's personal
prestige.

Yet let us look at the matter in another, perhaps more old-
fashioned context—the context of the rather extraordinary case
of Mr. Frank Higginson. Mr. Frank Higginson, then a duly
authorized officer of the Lancashire County Council, on
18th May, 1954, took out an order under the Lunacy Act
against a Mrs. Emma Sutcliffe of Monton Road, Eccles,
concerning which it was subsequently stated in court that
"his action was prompted entirely by the animosity which
existed between the plaintiff (Mrs. Sutcliffe) and Mr. Higginson's
wife". Notwithstanding this, the duly authorized officer had
managed to arrive at Mrs. Sutcliffe's home, with an Order, an
ambulance, a nurse and a police constable, with the intention of
removing Mrs. Sutcliffe to custody in a mental hospital. It was
only by the intercession of the husband that he was persuaded to
stay his hand and merely ordered Mrs. Sutcliffe to stay in her
own house until the following day. As a consequence of this
he was subsequently the defendant in an action at Manchester
Assizes in which his employers, the Lancashire County Council,
paid £250 damages to Mrs. Sutcliffe for the inconvenience to
which she had been subjected.

This case provokes interesting speculations to the political philosopher. What course, for instance, would it have taken had the duly authorized officer not lost his nerve: and had he succeeded in getting Mrs. Sutcliffe to hospital under an Urgency Order, which he was entitled in the nature of his duties to sign alone? Would he not then have had the whole official machine coming down in his defence—just as another and not altogether dissimilar action, which took place in another part of the country at the same time, was defended, in which, when a wife protested at the arbitrary removal of her husband by a duly authorized officer, she also was removed to a mental observation ward for ten days, together with her husband, before they were both released?

Was it, in fact, Mr. Higginson's only shortcoming that he failed to fill in the proper form at the proper time? And, by failing so to do obeisance to the shibboleths of a modern age, he thus laid himself open to more old-fashioned forms of justice? It would seem so.

What, therefore, is the price of liberty as sanctioned by the more old-fashioned procedures of our Law Courts? Is it £250 per night? So it would seem. If that is so, it would appear that the whole amount of the British National Debt might well be insufficient to compensate those who have wrongly— wrongly from a moral point of view, rather than wrongly from an official view—suffered its deprivation.

A QUESTION OF PERSPECTIVE

MY second article in the *Spectator* followed on 8th March: it dealt with the position of the Certified Patient once he was in hospital. This is it:

Anyone who is the loser in the contest in 'mental healthmanship' which I described in my first article finds himself in the position of being a certified patient. The term 'medieval pantomime', so properly ruled out of order on a recent occasion, is in this connotation perhaps more applicable. "The house was filled with policemen," declared a charming inoffensive lady visitor as, sitting in the lobbies at Westminster, she told me how a brutal husband, to distract attention from his own shortcomings, had reported that she had attempted suicide; as a consequence of which she spent some ten days imprisoned in a mental observation ward before being judged sane.

The majesty of the law is, indeed, at no time more evident than on such occasions. The harlequinade enters the hospital grounds with perhaps as many policemen as would accompany a condemned murderer. Then comes the slightly frigid reception; the walk down the stone-flagged passages to the observation ward; and the ritual of stripping—doubtless a necessary precaution, but not always performed with the utmost degree of tact.

Is it a necessary precaution to remove rings and trinkets—for which a receipt is not always given? A small matter; but the certified patient has no defence against petty pilfering. Nor, since he has lost access to the law courts, has he defence against anything else. A single doctor's certificate, signed perhaps in the middle of a busy round, has abolished the Habeas Corpus Act. A deceased Portuguese gunman, a Polish stowaway, may be the subjects of most exacting enquiry in our courts of law; yet anyone who, thus easily, enters the strange country of insanity becomes a *caput lupinum* and devoid of natural human rights. And the full appreciation of this fact, which comes to a certified patient within twenty-four hours of admission to hospital, is unlikely to produce a fillip towards recovery.

Has he, however, any complaints? Then, indeed, the notices on the walls (always provided that these are displayed as they should be) tell him that an imposing list of dignitaries wait only to hear from him. He may write unopened letters (provided that the ward nurse does not throw these on to the fire) to the Lord Chancellor, the Minister of Health, any Judge in Lunacy, the Chancery Visitors, the Members of the Hospital Management Committee, the Board of Control, or any Commissioners of the Board. But, in fact, these avenues of correspondence lead back to the same ultimate destination—the Medical Superintendent of the Hospital.

The Board of Control may concern itself with 'matters relating to the liberty of the subject' as its Memorandum to the Royal Commission explains; but to those who have encountered the Board of Control, it must sometimes have seemed that it has much the same relation to the liberty of the subject who is a certified patient in a mental hospital, as does a Russian trade union to the welfare of the worker in Soviet industry.

The philosophy underlying the working of the Board of Control is, in fact, that it does not matter how or in what circumstances a patient is admitted to a mental hospital, provided that he is admitted in the proper form. This objective the Board pursues with an earnestness that is worthy of a better cause. It is thus able to ensure that, when the Minister is questioned, he may conscientiously reply that "the documents of admission have been found to conform to statutory requirements". Should the Board receive documents which are not in order, it sends them back to the signing doctor for correction; it does not investigate the circumstances of admission.

The vast majority of certified patients, to the number of some 20,000 annually, admitted into mental hospitals today are admitted by summary reception orders made under Sections 14 to 16 of the Lunacy Act, 1890 (as amended). These are the sections of the Act which, in their original form, applied to 'the pauper lunatic' and 'the lunatic wandering at large'. Amendments to these sections have omitted the word 'pauper' and changed 'relieving officer' into 'duly authorized officer' (now becoming the 'mental health officer'); but the inheritance of these Poor Law procedures still informs both the procedure of admission and, in many instances too, the attitude to the patients, with all the personal humiliation thereby involved.

However efficient may be hospital treatment, this is a poor background to it; as is the fact that, in most hospitals, the patient (even if he is a voluntary and not a certified patient) will find himself behind locked doors. Why are there locked doors in mental hospitals still on such an extensive scale? Even the knowledge that one's 'husband or wife or, in default of husband or wife, nearest relative' may apply for discharge is of little consolation when it is just that person having the right of discharge who may be most anxious to keep one in. ("My husband gets me clothed and fed here for nothing," comes the plaintive cry; "why should he get me out when I know him to be living with another woman?")

The average length of stay of a patient entering a mental hospital is twenty months—a period no less than four times as long as that of a TB patient, the most protracted physical disease. Almost every mental hospital in the country has its considerable quota of chronic patients whose stay can be measured in years rather than weeks and these people tend to set the tempo of institutional life. Only by adjustment to this tempo can the beatitudinous state of being the 'co-operative' patient be attained.

What of the unco-operative? Here is one: "The whole aim of
the mental hospitals is to alter our personality, to change our
outlook on life, to reduce us into servile, dependent idiots—our
every action is dictated by the staff. Unthinkable brutality is
permitted—if they strike us, they are 'maintaining discipline',
or 'safeguarding themselves'—if we resist them, we are dubbed
'obstructive', 'unco-operative', etc., and subjected to insulin and
electric shocks, solitary confinement in padded rooms. If we
still remain rebellious we are subjected to the ghastly pre-frontal
leucotomy, which destroys the reasoning, thinking parts of the
brain for ever, reducing its victims to mere automatons, who
will scrub floors, peel potatoes meekly for their jailers."

Unco-operative definitely. Paranoiac and deluded, perhaps.
Not the type of patient suitable for production on the B.B.C.
programmes. But lest these statements are dismissed as lunatic
ravings, I quote from Dr. Richard A. Hunter's article, 'The Rise
and Fall of Mental Nursing', in *The Lancet*'s publication, *In the
Mental Hospital:*

In insanity the dividing line between treatment and restraint
is very fine. Since the 1930's psychiatry has seen a spectacular
rise and spread of 'physical methods of treatment'. Like the
drugs which they replaced, they were also not abandoned in
mental hospital practice when they failed as therapies. Like
drugs they remained as instruments of restraint in the guise of
treatment: hypoglycæmic (insulin), electrical, neurosurgical.
. . . When patients are controlled or suppressed by drugs or
electricity all respect for them as mentally sick is lost.

Those who seek to abolish the stigma of mental illness find
it as elusive as the Scarlet Pimpernel. It is hoped that the above
paragraphs will have provided pointers in the search. Re-
formism is in the air. The word 'certification' has by now
acquired such abominable associations that it is generally agreed
that it must go; it is futile, however, merely to replace it by
another brand of nomenclature while still retaining similar
attitudes and similar procedures. The solution of the problem

of the mentally ill is wider than a legal one and, indeed, there are many signs that new ideas are afoot both in medical and in administrative circles. It is important, however, that the impetus to reform should not peter out in isolated experiments at the periphery and pious aspirations at the centre. While our legislators can well bear in mind that the possession of a medical degree, or a nursing badge, does not thereby confer immunity from the dictum of Lord Acton.

*   *   *

I was not to gain universal acceptance for these observations. These articles in the *Spectator* mark, however, an important watershed in my own campaign. Prior to then, nothing I had written or said over a matter of years in criticism of our anti-quated mental health arrangements had been thought worthy of any form of answer. Haughty and aloof, the bureaucracy could safely afford to go its own authoritative way and ignore the likes of me. However, it was now evidently felt that I should not get away with this sort of thing unopposed. My opposition appeared in the form of the following letter in the *Spectator* of 22nd March under the name of Mr. Kenneth Robinson, M.P., Labour Member for St. Pancras North, and a member of the Council for the National Association for Mental Health, in which he spoke as a champion of all those authorities whom I was alleged to have traduced.

SIR—I know that Dr. Donald Johnson underwent a distressing experience in a mental hospital described, vividly if imprecisely, in his book *A Doctor Returns*. It is under-standable that he should champion the cause of the certified, but he should do so with some regard to fact. In his two recent articles 'Mental Healthmanship' and 'Certified', he attacks not only the law relating to certification but also the good faith and integrity of the Board of Control, the medical superintendents, the hospital authorities, the nursing staff and the mental health officers. He sees them all involved in a vast conspiracy against the liberty and welfare of the patient.

What conclusions would a credulous reader draw from these articles? That the mental nurse pilfers patients' belongings, burns their letters and beats them up as a matter of course. That the medical superintendent is sadistic, incompetent and corrupt, concerned only to ensnare more and more victims into his already overcrowded hospital. That the legal safeguards are illusory and that the Board of Control does not give a damn. If the picture he draws of a mental hospital were even half true the seventy thousand patients discharged last year would march in a body to Westminster clamouring for reform.

What are the facts of certification? Far from a single doctor being able to deprive anyone of his liberty the consent of a second doctor in some cases and a magistrate in all cases is required. A duly authorized officer on his own responsibility can only arrange admission to an observation ward for a maximum of three days. Once certified a patient may be discharged by the Board of Control, by the hospital management committee, or at the request of his next of kin or of any relative or friend who undertakes the patient's care. The medical superintendent can, it is true, issue a barring certificate, but this reserved power is subject to the closest scrutiny and infrequently used. One medical superintendent of my acquaintance has never once made use of this procedure in twelve years. Furthermore, if the patient disappears from the hospital he ceases automatically to be certified after fourteen days. Such are the safeguards under existing law. They will undoubtedly be further strengthened following the report of the Royal Commission which is expected soon. There will inevitably be, however, patients who are a danger to themselves or to others, and society will always need the power to detain such patients against their will. This need is

high-lighted by the recent case of the acutely disturbed
Nigerian who was with the utmost difficulty removed to
hospital. The removal was effected, at great personal risk, by
one of the duly authorized officers whom Dr. Johnson so
bitterly maligns.

Dr. Johnson appears to base his wholesale indictment upon
his own isolated experience, supported by the allegations of
other patients. To be mentally sick is perhaps the most
distressing of all experiences. The mental patient should
command all our sympathy, but by the nature of his illness he
cannot expect our unquestioning acceptance of all his
assertions. For example, Dr. Johnson quotes approvingly a
patient's letter which includes a statement that leucotomy
"destroys the reasoning, thinking parts of the brain for ever,
reducing its victims to mere automatons". For any journalist
to give currency to so blatant a fantasy would be irresponsible.
For a doctor of medicine and a barrister to do so is, I suggest,
unforgivable. Indeed, the whole tenor of the articles is of a
sensationalism more appropriate to the less reputable mass-
circulation newspapers than to a serious journal like the
Spectator. To secure progress and reform in this field we need
first of all an interested and informed public opinion. I
cannot think that Dr. Johnson's articles have helped in that
direction. Should not the public at least be told that, out of
every four patients admitted to mental hospitals, three enter
of their own free will, and that most of them are discharged to
their homes within a few weeks or a few months? Is it not
relevant to mention that, thanks to modern treatments, the
number of those who become chronic patients is falling
steadily? Or that inroads are being made at last into that
tragic hard-core of degenerated, long-stay patients, the
forgotten men and women of yesterday?

These facts, encouraging as they are, offer no excuse for
complacency. Much needs to be done. But where does
Dr. Johnson make one single constructive suggestion for the

benefit of the patient? He seems content to allege mal-
practice in the most general terms, and to leave it at that.
Like him I want to see great improvements in the Mental
Health Service, but I gladly recognize the admirable work
being done, often in wretched surroundings, by our doctors
and nurses in treating the mentally sick. Dr. Johnson's
smears and innuendoes will hardly encourage the recruitment
of staff so urgently needed. Though we need more psychiatrists, more nurses, more modern buildings, more out-patient
facilities and day hospitals, more money and, above all, more
research into mental illness, we possess even today a service
which compares favourably with that of any other country.
To denigrate this service and those who work in it, to
exaggerate and distort its difficulties while ignoring the
dramatic advances of recent years, far from assisting reform,
can only tend to thrust the whole subject of mental illness
back into the limbo from which it is beginning belatedly to
emerge.   Yours faithfully,
                                      KENNETH ROBINSON
House of Commons, S.W.1.

Notwithstanding any remarks of Mr. Kenneth Robinson's,
my heart warmed at the thought that at last I had brought the
adversary to battle. This was my reply which went in the
following week:

SIR—Mr. Kenneth Robinson and I agree on the necessity
for the reform and improvement of our mental health services.
There is, doubtless, a school of thought which believes that
you can get reform without criticism. I do not belong to that
school. Nor, on many other issues, does Mr. Robinson.
Your readers will, however, wish me to answer a number of
the charges he raises against me as your contributor.

Mr. Robinson states: "Far from a single doctor being able
to deprive anyone of his liberty the consent of a second

doctor is in some cases required." This statement is perhaps correct—though, if I may say so, imprecise. The comparative figures are given in the Memorandum of the Board of Control and the Ministry of Health to the Royal Commission now sitting. "In 1953," states the memorandum, "it is estimated that just over 20,000 non-paying (i.e. National Health Service) patients were admitted under summary reception order (the 'one doctor' method) and about ten by order on petition (the 'two doctor' method)." In other words, for every National Health Service patient certified by two doctors, there are 2,000 certified by one doctor. It is reasonable therefore to regard the 'one doctor' method of committal to hospital by summary reception order, which was the target for my criticism in my 'Mental Healthmanship' article, as the usual one. The figures are unlikely to have varied since 1953.

Mr. Robinson blisters me for mentioning the pilfering of patients' belongings. It would seem that, though he is a prominent member of a regional hospital board, he must be unaware of Ministry of Health Circular H.M. (56) 85 of 4th October, 1956, which 'advises Boards and Committees on arrangements for internal financial control and precautions to minimize the risk of loss due to fraud and theft'. The Appendix to this circular gives 'notes of various types of irregularities reported to the Minister'; and Section 8 of this, dealing with 'Theft of patients' money', states: "The majority of cases have concerned mental and mentally deficient patients and the offenders have taken advantage of the fact that these patients are incapable of looking after their own affairs." No one suggests that mental hospitals are staffed entirely with thieves and rogues: but that such thefts occur on a plural scale is beyond controversy with evidence such as this. One can only hope that, in the light of Mr. Robinson's unawareness, his regional board are taking some of the precautions suggested by the Ministry to prevent these undesirable occurrences to which I drew attention in my last two articles.

Here is corroboration on two points. If there are any others on which he wishes me, in particular, to supply it, I will gladly do so to the best of my ability. In regard to my book, for instance, which he describes as 'imprecise'. Though I suspect that he cannot have read my book. "Where," asks Mr. Robinson, "does Dr. Johnson make one constructive suggestion for the benefit of the patient?" Where else, indeed, than in my book, where I describe at some length the Amsterdam Experiment in the domiciliary treatment of mental patients and how, in my opinion, it can enlighten us in our backward ways here. Also, incidentally, in my parliamentary intervention on the Debate on the Address on 9th November last; and again on the more recent Social Services Debate. If Mr. Robinson was not there to hear me on either occasion, he might at least have paid me the compliment of looking me up in Hansard's excellent index before making a comment of this nature.

There *is* a conspiracy in this matter of mental illness. It is, as all can agree, a 'conspiracy of silence'. It is this conspiracy which I am endeavouring to break. I publish patients' letters—of which I get a large number, not just a few—in my articles and elsewhere because there are no other circumstances at the present time in which their grievances can be ventilated. I shall continue to do so until I see genuine and basic reform of the arrangements for the mentally ill along the practical lines that I have put forward and that are identical with those propounded by the most forward-looking thinkers on the subject; and until there are sufficient safeguards for individual liberty written into our statute book. In the meantime, these people are men and women and they have a point of view. I hope to be instrumental in propounding that point of view further when, in two months' time, my firm expect to publish under the title of *The Plea for the Silent* a symposium of ex-patients' stories. I will send Mr. Robinson a copy.

There must, of course, be powers available to restrain the violent mental case, such as the 'acutely disturbed Nigerian' Mr. Robinson mentions. There are not, however, 20,000 acutely disturbed Nigerians in the country each year. But this is the approximate figure of certified patients who are taken against their own will to mental hospitals—a figure that has remained virtually constant for some twenty-five years. It is, I submit, one that can, under more modern and sympathetic arrangements, be drastically reduced. It is only proper that, when individual liberty is affected on such a large scale as this, the question should be one for public debate, both in your columns and elsewhere. It is others who would wish, so it seems, for the subject of mental health to be 'thrust back into limbo'. I can claim, if nothing else, that I am making it the matter for discussion that it should be.   Yours faithfully,

DONALD MCI. JOHNSON

House of Commons, S.W.1.

*   *   *

"To be mentally sick is perhaps the most distressing of all experiences," writes Mr. Robinson. "The mental patient should command all our sympathy, but by the nature of his illness he cannot expect our unquestioning acceptance of all his assertions."

"There *is* a conspiracy in this matter of mental illness," I reply. "It is, as all can agree, a 'conspiracy of silence'. It is this conspiracy which I am endeavouring to break. I publish patients' letters because there are no other circumstances at the present time in which their grievances can be ventilated."

The House of Commons is a fair-minded and humane place. It will listen with patience and attention while Miss Jennie Lee reads out a complaining letter from a detained Cypriot terrorist a column of Hansard long, as it did in the Debate on Cyprus on

15th July, 1957. It will rise as one man to ensure that fair treatment is given to a Hungarian stowaway, or a Spanish deserter. It will be moved by waves of sympathy for transported cattle or hunted stags. Yet the following is an extract from the Debate on the Government's Social Policy on 19th March, 1957, when I presumed to read a brief extract from a letter of a former certified mental patient.

Dr. Johnson: I will read to the House a letter from a former mental patient, describing what happens when a patient is considered to be mental and is taken to hospital. It shows what happens in contrast to what should happen—the patient being seen by a tactful and trained psychiatric social worker and a skilled psychiatrist.

This man, in a letter to me, describes, first, how he was certified as a result of a sudden and unexpected visit by a doctor, a duly authorized officer and a justice of the peace. He continues:

"After the aforesaid meeting in my house, and the departure of the four visitors, there was an interval. Towards 12 noon there was an amazing scene. Two uniformed policemen (an inspector and a constable) arrived at the door, demanded admission, and an ambulance drew up outside. My removal was effected in the best traditions of the old Nazi Gestapo. Without explanation, without a moment's notice, I was bundled into the ambulance. An attendant inside hugged and held on to me as though a murder had just been committed. I had to tell him to desist, and even the policeman sitting opposite smiled."

That is the sort of thing that happens today. It is only one instance and I quote it because it has been better described than a number of others which have been brought to my notice.

It shows how the mental services in the country are getting into a quite unnecessary disrepute, because this man was not

N

in the least violent. It was completely unnecessary to bring
a policeman in this case, just as it is unnecessary in any case
of mental illness that can be tactfully and skilfully handled.
I submit, therefore, that the service which I have described to
the House all too briefly is urgently needed.

Mr. Shurmer: I cannot let the hon. Member's statement
pass. I have been a member of a mental hospital committee
for thirty years and I have never known a policeman attend
such cases, unless the person has been brought from a prison
where he had been confined and certified. This man must have
had hallucinations. Two policemen could not have been sent
to fetch him, and even the uniforms of our male nurses would
not suggest that they were policemen. I have never heard of
such a case.

Dr. Johnson: I assure the hon. Member that this is one of
several cases where policemen are employed. I will give him
particulars later if he wishes.

Mr. Christopher Mayhew (Woolwich, East): I have
warmly sympathized so far with the speech of the hon.
Member for Carlisle (Dr. Johnson), but may I ask whether, in
fairness to the mental staff and the nurses concerned, he
checked the facts with an independent source?

Dr. Johnson: Yes, I checked them with a relative. The best
check that we can have is the fact that one has more than
half a dozen such stories from different sources, where there
can be no possible collusion. This is only one case out of a
number.

Mr. Mayhew: I, too, have received a number of letters of
this kind, but one has to realize that they are not all of equal
validity—that is, the letters one receives from former patients
at mental hospitals. We must be fair to the people who have
this hard job which the hon. Member has described. I wish
that he had been able to assure us that he was not merely
quoting a letter, but had made independent enquiries himself.

Dr. Johnson: I can quote another incident. I was talking

earlier about Amsterdam. This is the effect that our mental services have on people abroad. I went round her visits in Amsterdam with a psychiatric worker. She came over to London to see our mental health services here and she went out with a duly authorized officer.

Sir Leslie Plummer (Deptford): A police officer?

Dr. Johnson: No, a duly authorized officer. These officers are known as mental health officers. The identical thing that I have just described happened when this visitor was over here. A patient would not go into a hospital and a policeman was sent for. The psychiatric worker I have mentioned expressed her complete horror to me at that incident. That is just another example.

Mr. Shurmer: But the police have no right to interfere.

Dr. Johnson: Oh, yes they have. Apparently the hon. Gentleman does not know the Act of 1890, where that procedure is laid down. He should know his law in this respect. May I ask him to look at Section 16 of that Act, under which people are moved to mental hospitals? It provides for a constable to be sent for. That is the legal procedure at present, and that is why I am intervening in this debate, because I want a social service which avoids that kind of thing.

Mr. Surmer: They may have done those things in years gone by, but today things are very different.

Dr. Johnson: If the hon. Gentleman will meet me afterwards, I can give him perhaps half a dozen cases of the police being called for, and he can see the people himself. They are not figments of my imagination. I have met and talked to these people and I should be glad to introduce the hon. Gentleman to them. Perhaps we can arrange that.

This attitude of scepticism is perhaps permissible in dealing with the genuine lunatic whose perceptions are playing him false. However, if we are to rate the certified mental patient

less worthy of our credence than the Cypriot terrorist, the
Spanish deserter, we ought at least to be careful whom we put
into that category. It is, therefore, perhaps, of interest to state
that my certified patient whom I had quoted was none other than
my friend, Mr. S.—whose mild eccentricities had caused him
to be removed into detention by a strange doctor after a few
minutes consultation, consequent on maliciously given information.

My aim, throughout all these endeavours was not, of course,
to make dogmatic judgments on the basis of the witness of
mental patients—to suggest that I have done so has merely been
a convenient form of misrepresentation. It has been, on the
other hand, to secure a basis for an independent enquiry on the
strength of the evidence that was available, so that there was
facility for aggrieved patients, who could produce sufficient
evidence, to state their case and be listened to impartially.

I can find no better plea for such kind of an enquiry throughout the Hansard record than I do in the following extract from
the Debate on Cyprus to which I have already referred:

"My hon. Friend the Member for Cardiff, South-East,
referred to the allegations of ill-treatment and brutality by
certain members of the security forces in Cyprus, and my hon.
Friend the Member for Cannock (Miss Lee) and the hon.
Member for Windsor devoted their speeches to a specific
aspect of the matter. It is no good the Government merely
writing off the allegations of ill-treatment as E.O.K.A.
propaganda. If they have not heard the gravest concern
expressed by responsible British observers in Cyprus, I can
only surmise that they have been closing their ears. I have
certainly heard from many responsible people that they are
not at all happy about the situation in respect of the security
forces. I do not think that even the Colonial Secretary would
regard Mr. John Clerides, Q.C., as a spokesman for E.O.K.A.,
and yet he has been unremitting in his attempts to obtain a
general impartial enquiry into the charges. It may be that

charges are entirely fabricated—that is within the realms of possibility—and hon. Members on both sides of the Committee will hope profoundly that that is the case, but it is just no good the Government of Cyprus merely producing a White Paper and saying that in its view the charges cannot be substantiated.

"There are some rather extraordinary things in the White Paper. Paragraph 16 states the reasons why the Government are unwilling to have an independent enquiry. It says:

'. . . a public enquiry would play into the hands of the detractors of Government and do more harm than good; not because Government has anything to hide, but because it would tend to focus attention on these malicious allegations, which is exactly what E.O.K.A. and its supporters want.'

That is roughly what the Under-Secretary said this afternoon.

"However, I cannot believe that an enquiry in Cyprus could not be conducted in such a way that witnesses would be prepared to come forward and speak the truth. Indeed, if the fear of intimidation of witnesses is the main reason against having an impartial enquiry, how do we stand about the investigations which have already been made by the Government? *A fortiori*, the witnesses would be more frightened of talking to the Government than to an independent judicial enquiry. Are we to assume that all the investigations—as a result of which the Governor is satisfied that there is no foundation for the allegations—have been made without any consideration of the facts that could be brought forward by Cypriots? Have the investigations been anything more than a questioning of the men who have been accused or of the men who have been in contact with the prisoners alleged to have been ill-treated? It is difficult to see how they could have been more than that."

These three paragraphs are extracts from the speech of none other than Mr. Kenneth Robinson, M.P.

CRUSADE ON A SHOE STRING

CRUSADE! There are few of political bent in whom this magic word does not bring about some reaction. To me it is irresistible. I am an inveterate crusader. We are likewise a country of crusades which, from Lord Beaverbrook's Empire Crusade on the right to the anti-H-bomb march to Aldermaston on the left, have usually a common denominator of ineffectualness.

There have been few more unusual crusades, however, than that embarked upon by Norman Dodds and myself in the month of May 1957. There were just we two and no more, but at least we sallied forth in person and did not sit by the fire, leaving the brunt of the day to more gullible supporters. From platform to platform, from the Caxton Hall, London on Friday, to Edinburgh on Monday, Manchester on Tuesday, Leeds on Wednesday, Birmingham on Thursday, Bristol on Friday, we made the news on behalf of the cause we had at heart.

Of the various accounts that appeared about us, probably the following from the *Birmingham Mail* is the most descriptive.

CRUSADE

A Tory (quiet persuasion) and a Socialist (forceful challenge) tell why they have teamed up to fight a battle.

Two M.P.s from opposite sides are absent from Westminster this week—by leave of their Whips.

They are visiting some of the main cities, Birmingham included, to further their campaign to amend the laws governing mental health.

To Dr. Donald McIntosh Johnson, the Conservative representing Carlisle, and his Socialist partner, Mr. Norman Dodds (Erith and Crayford), this tour is in the nature of a crusade timed in advance of the publication of the report of the Royal Commission on the subject and concurrently with the launching of their book *The Plea for the Silent*.

Published by the firm of which Dr. Johnson is the managing director, this book originates from the human stories he and Mr. Dodds have culled from their Westminster postbags.

In an interview room in the House of Commons on the eve of their crusade these earnest men told me how they came to team up.

According to Mr. Dodds, their constant barrage of questions to Mr. Robin Turton, the first Minister of Health in the present Government, and to Mr. Dennis Vosper, his successor in the office, convinced them that they had a common interest sufficiently strong to surmount the obstacle of political differences.

Dr. Johnson, the less voluble member of this two-man team, emphasized the non-political nature of the meetings being held this week at Leeds, Edinburgh, Bristol, Manchester and Birmingham.

"To ensure complete impartiality, we shall have a chairman from the Liberal Party at each meeting."

The main complaints to be voiced from the Dodds Johnson platform are that far too many of the nation's mental patients— 63,000 classed as defectives and 110,000 as lunatics—are wrongly detained in our public institutions, and that our mental laws are far too slapdash.

Dr. Johnson claims that the report of the Royal Commission is likely to prove that reform is in the air. "But we feel you cannot reform unless you know what is wrong. No one can tell you what is wrong better than the aggrieved people—the 'grievance committee' whose cases are in the book."

That is why some of the former mental patients will be at this week's meetings. They will tell their stories, if called upon, but their identity will not be disclosed. They will be the silent witnesses, known only by a number.

Dr. Johnson, a former general practitioner and house physician was once certified as insane after a mental disturbance, and was not released for six weeks.

His sympathy with others who have suffered is very real.

"It is time we created an informed public opinion regarding mental illness," he told me.

"The public have been kept in the dark for too long. Sick people can so easily be put away in our mental hospitals."

Even if his partner is likely to stick to a persuasive bedside manner, Mr. Dodds is determined to make his voice heard throughout the land. "I am ready to stick my neck out," he declared.

"At our meetings, we may be told that we are being unfair to those who administer the laws as they exist. Should expression be given to such objections, I am prepared to return to any of the cities we visit to debate the matter in public.

"What appals me most in the cases revealed is that the safety of the individual has been undermined. The Board of Control, primarily set up to safeguard the individual, has ceased to control once there is certification.

"The person suffering from mental illness stands no chance."

And so the crusade is on its way. This week the Minister of Health may be free from the constant prodding of Dr. Johnson and Mr. Dodds.

They will soon be back at Westminster, however, continuing their barrage of questions on such cases as that of Miss Mary Betteridge and others.

Mr. Dodds will discuss the case of the girl in St. Margaret's Mental Hospital, Great Barr, on the spot with the medical superintendent tomorrow, a few hours before he joins Dr. Johnson on their joint platform at the Imperial Hotel.

*   *   *

The Plea for the Silent, a symposium of personal stories, was the outcome of the feelings of desperation at official refusal to consider the grievances of former mental patients. To deplore publicity is all very well, but there are certain circumstances in which publicity is the only course to draw public attention to grievances. Thus, with deaf ministerial ears, the only alternative was to fall back once again on the facilities of my publishing firm for the publication of a book. It was late December 1956 that we decided on this. The decision taken, it was necessary to gather the material together for our spring publication list. We suggested, therefore, to seven or eight of our most expressive correspondents that they might expatiate on the accounts of their mental hospital experiences, which they had written to us, for the purpose that we had in mind. In this suggestion we received the fullest co-operation. Indeed I am glad to place on record that our allegedly paranoiac authors (for a reader of the reviews of *The Plea for the Silent* which subsequently appeared, will have appreciated that anyone who disagrees with a psychiatrist or criticizes the mental health services is automatically a paranoiac) were models of behaviour and indeed set an example of author–publisher relationship to many whose sanity has never been officially disputed.

Having got our book the next thing was a title. My mind instinctively flew to *I Speak for the Silent*, the book published these many years ago by Professor Tchernavin, one of the first to escape from and tell the truth (at that time not believed) about the Russian concentration camps. I got the nearest to this that I could in *The Plea for the Silent*. The analogies in the title were not altogether inept. Professor Tchernavin had struggled through the barriers of ice and snow and the tundras of Arctic

Russia to tell his story to a then incredulous world: these people, our authors, were penetrating an equally difficult barrier—the thought barrier of official indifference and of human aversion to mental illness—to tell an equally disturbing story.

Given a book and a title, the next thing to think of was its promotion on publication. Few people will accuse me, I imagine, of exploiting the situation financially in my publication of a book such as *The Plea for the Silent*. To settle any remaining doubts on the subject, I would say that a book of this nature is by no means 'a natural' as far as the book market is concerned. Apart from any consideration to do with its distasteful subject matter, the only classification which it could fall into for the book market was that of symposium, or a book of short stories—both of which are a format, popular perhaps in Victorian times, but anathema to the market of today.

The only antidote to this state of affairs was once again that of publicity, of combining the publication with our crusade, in which Norman Dodds generously accepted the proposition that he would join me for a week. But even a crusade presents its problems. No large hidden funds were available to support our crusade—it was, as I have said, a crusade on a shoe string, one that had to be supported out of two alternative sources, one was the profits from the book, the other was my own pocket—it would be my own pocket in the first place. Needless to say, it had to be done at a minimum of expense, in which endeavour Norman Dodds helped considerably by refusing any form of remuneration other than his bare expenses.

Our crusade, actually, cost just about £80. This included our railway fares (in which we broke all tradition by two M.P.s travelling second class!), hotel and meal expenses and hire of meeting rooms and local advertising.

All this booked and arranged, Norman and I went forth into the unknown just as crusaders have done before us and crusaders will do again—neither knowing who would come to listen to us, nor what adventures the morrow would bring.

We have to thank many people for such modest success as our efforts achieved. We have to thank, first of all, Dr. Nathaniel Micklem and other distinguished members of the Liberal Party for completing our non-Party platform by appearing as chairmen at each of our meetings. We have to thank the enthusiastic audience of 120 or more who turned up to our initial meeting at Caxton Hall in response to a few personal letters and a couple of small advertisements in the *Spectator* and the *New Statesman*—possibly nothing shook official complacency more than the numbers at this meeting. We have to thank the generous lady at Edinburgh who contributed a cheque of £15 to our funds; we have to thank the manager of the Grand Hotel, Manchester, for letting us have a meeting room without charge; we have, in particular, to thank the members of that excellent organization, The Friends of Menston Hospital, who, at Leeds, provided us not only with the hospitality of a hall but also strong reinforcements for our meeting—thus giving the direct lie to the curious accusation that, by our efforts, we were upsetting the relatives of hospital patients.

Various other recollections remain from our two-man touring company. Most prominent of all is that of the harmony that prevailed between us, differ as we might on many contentious matters, throughout a full week in each other's company— the question of the Suez Canal, for instance, did not come under discussion between Norman and myself during the entire week! There remains in my mind, also, our arrival at Birmingham, when, surrounded by the aura of excitement round the Mary Bettcridge case, we were met by the local Press at the station, swept round the city in a large car amidst batteries of flash bulbs and their accompanying photographers: and the consequent delusions this reception evidently gave rise to in the mind of the manager of the restaurant where we lunched, who laid on special (and incidentally almost totally inedible) steaks for us, with mushrooms to boot, which we had willy-nilly to eat at a cost of some fifteen shillings a head. This poor man must have thought, at least, that we were film stars working on expense accounts supported in turn maybe by Government subsidy. Need it be said that, for our evening meal, we patronized the popular café round the corner.

I have also in mind our meeting at the Grand Hotel, Bristol. "Lively, vigorous, and sometimes noisy question and answer were still going on after the meeting had been in session for nearly three hours," reported the Bristol Press. What seemed to be the entire Mental Health Sub-Committee of the Bristol City Council, which has a large Labour majority, turned out to defend the good name of their local services. I have in other contexts, in one of my previous books, described Bristol as being a somewhat quiet and subdued city. It was not so on this occasion. Seldom have I heard so much noise in one comparatively small room, as the personnel of the Mental Health Sub-Committee on the one hand and Norman Dodds on the other joined in altercation.

"Just like a Trade Union meeting," remarked Norman subsequently, a note of satisfaction in his voice.

We have, of course, to thank too the local Press in all the places we visited for putting us on the map in no uncertain fashion.

What was the final result of all this? I have to report that, despite our ballyhoo, despite the full-page feature laid on in *The People*, despite our supporting display of the book by booksellers throughout the country, *The Plea for the Silent* has sold to date exactly 1,172 copies out of the edition of 2,000 that we printed. (Compare this to the first printing of 135,000 done for Thor Heyerdahl's latest book *Aku-Aku*, or to the fact that 4,000 copies of a 4-guinea book on Tropical Fish sold in *Birmingham alone*, if you wish to make publishing comparisons and draw your own conclusion). As regards finances, the book, despite the fact that our authors forewent their rights to royalties for any sales under 1,500 copies, has made a small surplus of £13 1s. 4d. after paying for our tour, but *without reckoning anything for our firm's overheads*.

"To think," as I sometimes say to Norman, "that during our tour we were often mistaken for business men." This remains the standing joke between us.

*   *   *

Was, however, our crusade successful in its main object? I think so—indeed we can claim, I think, that in the history of British crusades we were outstandingly so. Though this is perhaps more to the credit of coincidence than any virtue of our own.

For, in the sphere of mental health reform, we have been but the guerrilla troops, the advance skirmishers—or, alternatively, as we have been designated in some quarters, the nuisances and the irresponsible critics. Behind us, there was limbering up the main artillery—the Royal Commission under the chairmanship of the late Lord Percy, which had by this time been occupying the times and energies of some dozen distinguished, experienced and erudite people over a space of three years at a cost of £26,925.

I have no wish to arrogate to myself any responsibility for the Royal Commission's Report. I had no connection with the Royal Commission. I had no part or share in its appointment—this was, of course, prior to my election to Parliament. Nor, for that matter, did the Royal Commission have any connection with me—it declined to accept my offer to give oral evidence to it—this too being before I was an M.P. While even when, in my capacity as a Member of Parliament, I communicated with the Chairman of the Royal Commission about the grievances of my correspondents, I was told that it was by then too late to accept further evidence.

Nobody therefore could be more dissociated from the work of the Royal Commission than I am.

However, two things happened. The first was that the Report of the Royal Commission with its 306 pages and 883 paragraphs was by coincidence published the very week following our tour. The second was that the conclusions which it had formed, working from its own official point of view, and its consequent liberal and enlightened recommendations, were closely in accord with such ideas as we had formulated ourselves and were such as we could support with only few reservations.

When, therefore, by a species of poetic justice, I was invited on to the B.B.C. 'Tonight' Television Programme the day the Royal Commission's Report was announced, having hurriedly digested the Ministry of Health's précis of its recommendations, I had no hesitation in recommending it to the nation at large. And confirming that recommendation two nights later, when I appeared on the B.B.C. Television Press Conference with Christopher Mayhew and others, questioning Professor Hargreaves of Leeds University.

Norman Dodds and I, therefore, had no part whatsoever in the Royal Commission's report.

However we did perhaps do something of equal importance. The shelves of Whitehall lie littered, as we know, with the Reports of Royal Commissions which Government after Government has not seen fit for various reasons to act upon. We did ensure that the Royal Commission Report was noticed by the public and given its due meed of attention by the Press when it was published.

The Report of the Royal Commission was debated on Monday, 8th July, in the House of Commons and my own speech was as follows:

Dr. Donald Johnson (Carlisle): I rise to welcome this Report as much as any hon. Member who has so far spoken in the debate. My admiration for it is equalled only by my admiration for the Parliamentary Secretary, who told me the other day that he had read it through twice. It has been my constant companion, but I regret to say that I have got only as far as paragraph 458 in my own thorough reading and have to content myself with just a smattering of knowledge picked up here and there of subsequent recommendations.

When one tries to look at the Report from a detached point of view, what inevitably strikes anyone is the revolutionary nature of its recommendations as compared with the general mildness of its criticisms of the existing system. Indeed, I think any newcomer to this House listening to the opening speeches of this debate, would really wonder whether there was any necessity to make changes at all. It was to some extent, therefore, in anticipation of this situation that the hon. Member for Erith and Crayford (Mr. Dodds) and I, over the past year, have worked together, sinking our Party differences, to fill what we felt might be a gap. We, perhaps, have formed one of the pockets of disaffection to which my hon. Friend the Parliamentary Secretary referred in his opening remarks.

Mr. Vaughan-Morgan: May I correct my hon. Friend? I did not refer to 'disaffection'; I just said 'irresponsibility'.

Dr. Johnson: I stand corrected, but I think that hon. Members who, apparently, will not find sufficient reasons in the Report as such for this or that recommendation, may well find them in the speeches and Questions which have been asked in this House and possibly in publications outside.

Rightly or wrongly, it is the custom for any criticism of our health and welfare services at present to be expressed in somewhat muted tones. Therefore, it is natural and proper that, when we come to the recommendations of the Commission for the abolition of the Board of Control, the Commission should distribute bouquets such as we find in paragraphs 788 and 791 of the Report and such as have been repeated in this House. I, on the other hand, will be sending no orchids to the obsequies of the Board of Control. It has outlived its usefulness in the manner which has already been stated by my right hon. Friend the Member for Thirsk and Malton (Mr. Turton).

It is proper, also, that we should pay every tribute to those who work in these services and to the undoubted advances that have been made in treatment and the general improvement of conditions but, if we are going to reform, it is essential to know not only what we are going to reform, but why we are going to reform.

What one finds in taking a view of the mental health services of the country is an extreme variability between one district and another and one hospital and another. It is insufficient that here and there we should have the best. We must also think of the worst. To get a satisfactory service we must bring up the worst to the level of the best.

At the risk of continuing in heresy, I maintain that no one can give us better criticisms of what is wrong than the patient, even when the patient, as occasionally he does, complains. After all, there is nothing like being at the receiving end and, where compulsory powers exist, it is very easy for those who exercise them to live in a world of self-delusion.

We are united in our anxiety to take the stigma out of mental illness. In this process we can start now, because if there is one thing more than anything else on which the mental patient and the ex-mental patient feel they are stigmatized it is that they are discredited people, that no one will believe them, no one will listen to them and give them facilities for putting their case. We have already heard it jestingly stated that anyone who differs from the psychiatrist is dubbed a psychopath. That is, perhaps, an exaggeration, but there is an underlying truth in it.

In particular, I welcome the fact that the Royal Commission examined a number of witnesses who were former mental patients, and published their evidence as a supplementary Report. At the beginning of what I hope will be a series of debates on this subject, I ask hon. Members to believe, not that everything mental patients say should be implicitly believed, but that no evidence should be disregarded, just because it comes from mental patients, without carefully weighing it.

The effect of the Commission's Report on any further legislation would be to reform and bring up to date the Act of 1890, so it is appropriate that, as a basic consideration, we look at that Act.

It is a reasonable Act in its way and in the context of the times in which it was enacted. Let us see what was the context of those times. If a man was mentally ill in those days, he did not go to any early consultation to see what was the matter with him. He hung on and on, until he was mad in the proper sense of the word; his personality became disintegrated; he became impossible for others to deal with, and was then put away out of society, perhaps indefinitely, by the operation of this Act. That was the atmosphere that overhung the whole situation—an atmosphere of indefiniteness, of incurability, of general hopelessness.

In those days the asylums were places far more isolated even than is the case today, in the age of the motor car. Consequently, they became populated with these people and infected with this atmosphere of hopelessness. The people in them were those who, it was thought, would never recover; although there were occassionally included those who were not so ill, but who had, nevertheless, slipped into the net. To prevent a man slipping into the net too easily, various defences of individual liberty were written into the Act.

Fortunately, times have changed. But they have not changed as much as all that, nor have they changed everywhere alike. For instance, the continuity of tradition, associated with the continuity of the law has remained very strong inside many of these institutions. I hope that it will not be thought that I am just cracking at medical superintendents when I say this, because the more enlightened medical superintendents will themselves say that it is this tradition

o

which is their most formidable obstacle to effecting improvements in their own institutions.

This tradition which is the patients' main burden of complaint is, first, the attitude with which they are regarded by those they meet in the institution when they enter it. Coming from the outside world as they do, and being not always dull people, but frequently specially sensitive people, they feel that very strongly. This attitude varies, naturally. In many hospitals the patients do not sense it at all. In others, where the tradition has remained stronger, the patients are very conscious of it indeed.

Their complaint, secondly, is their isolation—the fact that they are frequently cut off from friends and relatives and, above all, occasionally from legal advisers. Then, thirdly, the fact that, if they are removed to an institution compulsorily under certificate, they are deprived of their civic rights and— and this is immensely stressed by them—they are unable to deal with their financial affairs, which are taken right out of their hands immediately by the operation of law.

The primary cause of all this is the legal formalities which still surround the fact of admission to mental hospitals, particularly in the case of certified patients. A certified patient today immediately becomes a second-class or third-class citizen. That is why one welcomes the de-designation of the hospitals which is recommended by the Royal Commission. I particularly welcome paragraph 849 of the Report, in which the Commission recommends that even compulsory admission to hospital should not necessarily involve the patient being deprived of the control of his financial affairs. I welcome the remarks in that paragraph about the Commission's realization of the distress that people feel over this, and I hope that that realization will be noted when it comes to effecting new legislation.

We can look forward to vast changes in the whole atmosphere of our mental services through the de-designation of mental hospitals. It is fair to predict that the area in which compulsion has to be exercised will be greatly reduced, and will become very much more manageable than it is at present. Compulsory powers are, of course, occasionally necessary, just as it is necessary to have protection against their wrongful use.

I welcome the recommendation that, where compulsory powers are exercised, two doctors should be called in, so that there is at least some chance of establishing a proper diagnosis. I welcome, too, the independent tribunals which are so desperately a missing feature of the present system. I should like to echo what the hon. Member for Gosport and Fareham (Dr. Bennett) has said about the dislike doctors have of being completely responsible for the exercise of these compulsory powers. In any case, where there is compulsory detention, there should not be too long a period before legal procedure is taken, and the suggested period of six months is, I think, rather lengthy.

Whatever protections we put into future legislation I suggest that they should be tied up completely. We must not allow them to degenerate into the mere paper protections, of which there is no better object lesson than the 1890 Act. That Act is full of protection for individual liberties, which one after the other have gone by the board and have in many cases become valueless because of the loophole in the Act and because of the easy process of certification which in recent years has been found convenient to use.

I should like, in conclusion, to express my pleasure at two recommendations in this Report which cover the mental deficiency, or psychopath, field as we shall probably be calling it. The first of these recommendations is that relatives shall have the right of discharge of all patients who come under the psychopath and mental deficiency laws, as well as the mental illness laws, except where there is court procedure; and, secondly, that psychopaths will not be detained over the age of 25.

I think it is agreed that we can do very little by way of treatment for psychopaths over the age of 25. If they get on the wrong side of the law and it is necessary to detain them for that reason, that is quite another matter, but treatment as such is of very little use.

Mental illness is a large and unwieldy problem, but problems are apt to create themselves, and if they are tackled competently, thoroughly and on right principles they reduce in size. The Royal Commission's Report shows such a way to meet this problem of mental illness. We should appreciate that it cannot perhaps be implemented all at once. In fact, it may well be advisable to contemplate its introduction in two stages. The first stage, and the immediately urgent one, is the de-designation of hospitals and the revision of the admission procedures. The second stage, which is admitted to be the more difficult, is to get the local authorities services functioning, to deal with the question of expense, to get them to work new duties and so on.

I am confident that, given good will, the Commission's Report, looked at from a practical point of view and carried forward with enthusiasm, will introduce a new era in the general treatment and administration of mental illness in the country.

*   *   *

My own speech, however, was not the most important part of this debate.

The most important part was that towards the end of the debate when Mr. R. A. Butler intervened as Leader of the House, speaking on behalf of the Government. I need only quote two extracts from his speech:

"The debate we have had, like the debate we had the other day on penal reform, finds the soul and the conscience of the House, and they really make very much more repercussion in the country than some of our more reiterative debates followed by the perpetual perambulation through the Lobbies afterwards. I hope that we shall have a debate like this again.

"I unreservedly accept the recommendation of the Commission for a revision of the law, and that it should be broadly on the lines indicated in the Report."

RAMPTON

THE name of the Rampton State Institution probably conveys to the average person an idea of mystery, imbues him perhaps with contrasting feelings of a slight chill of terror on the one hand, and (providing he does not live in its immediate vicinity on the northern edge of Nottinghamshire) a strong modicum of comfort on the other that here is a nice, safe, remote place where dangerous and criminal lunatics can be locked away.

The first consideration to shatter these conceptions is that half the population of Rampton have had no convictions to their names in the Courts at all.

However, we will come to that later. The best theme on which to start this chapter is that propounded by someone speaking from a detached point of view, Mr. D. H. Howell, Labour Member for All Saints, in one of our Rampton debates:

"I have never been to Rampton and, therefore, I will not say a word against anyone at Rampton.

"But it makes one extremely suspicious, in the case to which I have referred, when I find it impossible to get any information. It is impossible to find out why this girl is still being kept there, what treatment she has been having and what progress she is making.

"I must say that, unless I can obtain some more reasonable information than I have so far, I shall feel like going to Rampton and I do not think it does Rampton or any other institution very much good if hundreds of Members of Parliament descend on the place. I do ask the Minister kindly to see to it that when we as Members of Parliament enquire of medical superintendents and the Board of Control about cases in which we are interested we are given, even if in confidence, the fullest possible information so that much of the suspicion which surrounds these institutions can be removed.

"Members of Parliament do not take up these cases until they have thoroughly investigated what they have been told by the complaining parents and others. We are entitled, I think, to the fullest possible information, and when we suspect that we are not getting it we really begin to think that there is something radically wrong—perhaps more wrong than is apt to be the case. I hope that the Minister will try to bring more light to bear on these cases and ensure that better information is provided for Members and other complaining bodies."

Six months before Mr. Howell's speech, a Parliamentary Party, with Norman Dodds and myself amongst its members, had already 'descended' on Rampton in July 1957 for an officially organized visit.

It was consequent on this that I wrote the following in the *Spectator* on 27th September, under the title of 'Heartbreak amongst the Roses':

Eleven of us had taken the 8.5 from King's Cross. "I have been trying to get to Rampton for twelve years," remarked one member of our parliamentary party; and here we were, at last, at the front entrance of the Rampton State Institution. With cine-camera laid on, we chatted affably with the medical superintendent and other doctors and were introduced to the senior members of the staff.

Under the heading of 'Helping to Make a Citizen of the Psychopath: Rampton's success belies a bad name', the *Manchester Guardian*'s special correspondent had already described a similar visit in flowery terms. ("An excellent article," commented Dr. Edith Summerskill in the House of Commons.) "Today there was opened at Rampton Hospital," the article said, "a new staff dining hall. In design it is neo-South Bank; the high arched interior is drenched with light from clear windows which take up most of the side walls; the colour is both cool and gay. Far from being an exotic in a grim setting, the new building is a natural and logical addition to the pleasant red brick villas, each with its own garden, and the existing nurses' wings, all set amongst rose beds and smooth lawns." And so on, and so on.

This is the impression of Rampton which remains with the occasional visitor; it is one that remains from our day spent amongst the rose beds and the pleasant red brick villas—with bars built into the windows so that you scarcely noticed them. The reaction to the more old-fashioned 'blocks' where half—the more difficult half—of the patients live was less enthusiastic.

But I carry another impression of Rampton. A crowded meeting in the Conway Hall with some 200 people present, many of them parents of Rampton patients; others ex-patients—two of them, embittered, on the platform; both, though previously labelled 'feeble-minded', as able platform contenders as I have seen at many an election meeting. Emotional scenes as methods of punishment were described: cheers as one speaker declares, "Thank God something is happening at last!" I spoke at the meeting: I have not known its like in a political lifetime.

I have another impression, too. Headlines in the *Star*—'GIRL'S HEARTBREAK LETTER'—a facsimile reproduction of a letter from Marie Mayo, since released on account of an alleged 'serious error' by a classifying school, where she had been sent by a Juvenile Court decision—Marie's school reports had shown 'good intelligence, average ability'. I have some two dozen 'heartbreak letters' on my own files from Rampton and its kindred institution, Moss Side—all saying the same thing. "I haven't had fair play." "I never had a chance." Heartbreak among the roses. . . .

What is Rampton? It started its career as an extension of Broadmoor in 1910—as a 'criminal lunatic asylum'. In 1921 it was closed as a Broadmoor extension and it reopened for another purpose—as a State Institution for Mental Defectives of Dangerous and Violent Propensities. It is now an integral part of the mental deficiency set-up. Its male nurses are, however, still members of the Prison Officers' Association and wear uniforms with peak caps.

"There is little difficulty," states the evidence of the Ministry of Health and Board of Control to the Royal Commission which has recently reported, "in diagnosing mental defect in the two lower grades of defectives, i.e. idiots and imbeciles. But when it comes to the higher grades many difficulties arise." They do, indeed! According to the National Council of Civil Liberties, in its memorandum to the Royal Commission, the term 'mental deficiency' is being applied 'to large numbers of young persons who appeared to everyone else as normal and whose "mental deficiency" could only be discerned by those functioning within the mental deficiency service.' A writer in *The Lancet* has said that some inmates have had intelligence quotients of 100; how can they be regarded as mentally deficient?

There is also difficulty in defining a psychopath. "Psychopaths have been described as having either predominantly inadequate or predominantly aggressive personalities," says the Royal Commission. These seem elastic terms. Anyone of whom a psychiatrist disapproves can have an 'inadequate personality', while, if he resents or protests at the treatment of his inadequacies, he can also easily be included in the aggressive category. In this the psychiatrist is no different from the rest of us; he merely has the more heavily charged magic of phraseology at his disposal.

The inmates of Rampton are psychopaths and mental defectives. Some have been convicted in juvenile courts of serious crimes—one broke out and terrorized the surrounding countryside with an axe, another set fire to his grandmother. But only a small minority of Ramptonians are in this category. Out of 1,092 inmates in March less than half had been dealt with by the courts; and of these some were in court only for trivial offences, and were sent to another mental deficiency institution in the first place. Here, they developed 'propensities'—for which, like the Erewhonians, they must submit to 'treatment'. This was what happened in the case of Marie Mayo: and of others.

Peter Whitehead was brought up in an orphanage and at the end of his stay was transferred to a Home: while there, he became involved, in self-defence, in a fight with another boy in which a knife was used, though without serious injuries; nothing happened at the time, but two years later, when the institution of which he was an inmate was closed down, he was sent to Rampton; he was there eleven years before obtaining his release.

Cathlene Murray, my own constituent in Carlisle, at the age of thirteen ran away from school continually to stay with her uncle: with her parents' consent she was sent for 'special education' to a mental deficiency home; the special education did not materialize but her detention was continued: her parents' consent could not be revoked and Cathlene smashed a window in protest; she was sent to Rampton and was there for twelve years during which time her parents, owing to travelling distance, only saw her twice.

James Mills was, like Peter Whitehead, an orphanage boy sent to a mental deficiency home; while at this home, he made friends with a girl from the female side and absconded with her to her own home, where they were soon recaptured; he denies fervently that any violence occurred; that was twelve years ago and he is still at Rampton.

These are typical Rampton stories told by the patients: and there are many more similar ones. The 'propensities' for which Rampton treats would seem to have arisen, as often as not, in other mental deficiency homes where patients have been under restraint, as in the outside world. Would not restraints on liberty in entirely normal young people result in the type of violence

which, when associated with an inmate in a mental defective
colony, becomes a 'propensity'?

As you go round Rampton, admittedly, it is impressed on you
a dozen times that these people are 'patients' and they are there
for 'treatment'. But it was disturbing to me that, in this motley
community, mental defectives who have committed no offence
against the community at all are mixed together with those who
have been through the courts, including of course the
dangerously violent cases. I was assured that this makes no
difference—that a court case, for instance, is merely 'an incident
in a medical history of cyclical aggressiveness', etc. etc. What,
in fact, this implies is that the psychiatrists have a higher status
in regard to depriving people of their liberty than any court of
law!

Anyway, here the patients are and they are being treated for
their 'inadequacies' or their 'aggressiveness'—for their 'propensities', in fact.

It clearly takes a long time to treat anyone for 'propensities'.
One quarter of the patients have been inmates for over ten years,
some have been there for more than twenty years, one or two
for more than thirty; only eighty-nine patients were discharged
last year—nearly all to other institutions. Considering the
amount of juvenile delinquency about, it is a highly selective
and expensive process; Rampton costs £7 10s. 0d. per patient
per week to run; almost £500,000 per year. This works out at
about £4,500 per 'cure'!

Obviously there is some confusion as between restraint and
treatment that needs elucidating; but it is difficult to get an
angle on what is the treatment given at Rampton. There are
seven medical officers employed there who 'classify' and deal
with disturbed and difficult cases (the patients themselves
allege that they only see a doctor when they get into trouble).
The workshops are represented as a feature of Rampton, part
of the curative and rehabilitation process. But observers are
dubious—they say the machinery is old-fashioned and only

produces what the place itself needs. Peter Whitehead, after ten years at Rampton, had to go to a Ministry of Labour Training Centre to learn a practical trade following his release.

In the meantime, while this expensive experiment is going on for a small number of people, the main problem of juvenile delinquency remains unsolved. Two-thirds of the crimes of violence in the Metropolitan Police area—which were double the number they were in 1938—were committed by offenders under the age of thirty.

If Rampton is to serve a proper purpose, its present population clearly needs sorting out. It should be a short-stay place for the redeeming of juvenile psychopaths—a medical Borstal, if you like. The Royal Commission in its recommendations obviously visualizes something of this character. It recommends (*a*) no 'psychopath' should be detained over the age of twenty-five except when there has been a special court order; (*b*) if a psychopath is detained without having a court order against him, he can be discharged by patient's order in the same way as a mental patient. If these two recommendations became law, a considerable proportion of Rampton's patients would be entitled to immediate release.

*   *   *

Mystery deepens! We are already involved in the strange mysteries of the mental deficiency law.

The first and major mystery—the fundamental mystery which is rightly the one of permanent concern to the national Press— is as to how the Parliament of a free country could have passed laws which authorized that people of normal intelligence, people who have not been convicted of any offence, be detained indefinitely on medical opinion alone: and without any appeal except the rather illusory one at intervals of years to visiting justices.

When we look into the history of this we find that Parliament,

cognisant, as it thought, of these dangers, did attempt to define
mental deficiency. In the Mental Deficiency Act 1913, it is
described as 'existence of mental defectiveness from birth or
from an early age'. Clear enough you might think? In that,
however, you reckon without the psychiatrists! "Psychiatrists,"
you will remember my friend, Colonel Drummond, saying,
"are modern equivalents of Greek sophists. Their aim is not so
much to enlighten as to bewilder." Thus, during the various
parliamentary debates that took place on the subject these many
years ago, it occurred to nobody to define the meaning of the
word 'mind'. It was left to the psychiatrists to declare that
"defect of mind" is "not necessarily defect of intelligence".
Once this idea is accepted, then almost anything is possible. It
is not difficult to proceed to the further assumption that anyone
you don't like the look of, anyone who is a persistent nuisance
to authority for whatever reason, is suffering from defect of mind.

To any young person who might be the subject of such a
train of action and reasoning, and who shows resentment at it,
Rampton could be his ultimate destination—Rampton for an
indefinite term of years in treatment for his propensities. Whatever the treatment may be at Rampton, and it is difficult to
discover what it is, it is invariably of a protracted nature.

Amongst such attributes as may be imbued by a term at
Rampton—and I use the word 'term' in ambivalent fashion,
for one has heard of Rampton boosted in authoritative circles as
if it were an invigorating, if slightly tough, public school—one
of them is unfortunately not that of hope.

For this we have the high authority of the Bishop of Southwell,
in whose diocese Rampton lies, who, when he spoke in the House
of Lords debate on mental illness on 16th February, 1958,
remarked of it in the following terms:

"I think there is a lot wrong with Rampton . . . I am not here
to whitewash it. . . . Out of 670 male patients, only 189 are
there because they have been sentenced by a court or transferred from prison. . . . Mental patients under treatment are,

inevitably, living together with murderers, rapers, or goodness knows what. . . . Over the whole place, like the shadow of a hawk, is the power of certification, with all its social stigma, with all its terror. As the law stands, these particular mental patients could not get mentally treated any other way, but by the same token they are all subject to an indeterminate sentence. It seems to me that that induces an awful sense of hopelessness and despair, a sense of having passed out of the world of human rights into a different kind of non-earthly order, administered at the mercy of some remote control in London, the Board of Control, with whom one can communicate only on an official form. I believe all that militates against the hope of recovery . . . There are people who have been for fifteen or twenty years immured . . . and at the end of that time they are completely unfitted for any kind of normal life anywhere. . . . A heavy sense of grievance and fogs of despair would be rolled away by the setting up of the Mental Health Tribunals which the Commission recommends."

Let us look, however, at a particular instance. A sizeable proportion of my total correspondence is from the inmates of Rampton and Moss Side; or their distressed and worried relatives from all parts of the country. Here is one to hand only a few days previous to these words being written. Despite its spelling mistakes, the penning of it is clearly motivated with a mother's love:

DEAR SIR—I am writing to ask you if you can help me get my son Ernest R. Smith home from Rampton Hospital as he was sentenced to one year in prison. He did three months then moved him to Rampton. He has been away from home seven year altogether.

He was sentenced but he was innocent as we have wittneses to prove where he was on the night he was spossed to have commited this crime these witnesses were with him all the time at a dance (in Cleethorpes) they also walked home together.

I would be very gratfull if you would look into his case for me as It would be very nice for him to be home as he is a bit backwards in his reading and writting they may be holding this against him but he is quite good at reckoning money.

Well I must close now as their is nothing els that I can tell you but we can get refrences to his character if you need them if you cant help me will you please put me on to some one els who will even if we have to pay for his case to be reopend

Yours truly,

Mrs. I. Smith

I advised Mrs. Smith that she should seek the advice of her own M.P. What reply however is she, or her M.P. likely to get to an enquiry? It is that her son is no longer merely a prisoner, he is now a 'patient' being treated for his 'propensities'—to whom, of course, since he is a mental patient, the ordinary rules of justice do not apply.

Let us say that the enquiry is pursued, as Norman Dodds pursued the case of James Mills, whom I have mentioned as being a patient in Rampton for 11 years, to a parliamentary Question, asking "what action is contemplated to end his detention, as his condition can only deteriorate if he is not given some hope of ending his long stay?"

The odds are that, since the following answer was given in identical form, both in the case of James Mills and another case, it will also be given to any enquirer in this. This is the answer:

"As with all other patients, the progress of this patient is being continually reviewed by the Medical Superintendent and the Board of Control. He will be transferred when he is well enough to go."

When is a patient at Rampton well enough to go?

Of a population of a little over 1,000 (1,092 in March 1957) out of whom only half have been through the Courts, 282 (in April 1957) have been there longer than ten years, 178 longer

than 15 years, 110 longer than 20 years, 53 longer than 25 years
and 20 longer than 30 years.

Even the circumstances of the most formally conducted of
parliamentary delegations could not prevent members of this long
stay population accosting us with pathetic eagerness as, on our
July visit, we circulated round the Rampton workshops and
attempting to tell us for a few moments their sombre stories.

Those haunting faces stay with me. I am reminded of them
by the story of the European detainee in a British mental
hospital told by Miss Aloysia Wingfield in her poignant book
The Inside of the Cup. This man, who had been inside for
seventeen years and "seemed very normal and convincing",
"made one surprising point". "It is better in a concentration
camp," he said, "especially under the Russians. It is hard, very
hard, but it is the same for all. You do get justice and you also
are told the terms on which you can be set at liberty. If you do
not accept those terms then you are captivitied partly at your
own will and that makes the heart lighter." There is little
evidence of light hearts in the Rampton workshops.

A total of over 40 parliamentary questions concerning
Rampton were asked during 1957 and 1958, 23 of which were
asked by Norman Dodds and 13 by myself. But we are not the
only Members of Parliament worried about Rampton. But here
are some of our answers.

How many patients detained in Rampton have had their
certificates revoked by visiting justices of the peace during the
past ten years at reviews taking place after their attaining the
age of twenty-one years? (The magistrates visit Rampton once
a quarter for the purpose of seeing patients and see seventy
patients in a visit of two days duration.) 'Two' was the answer.

What pathetic hopes indeed there are to place in Member of
Parliaments' interventions, when justices visiting for the purpose
of inspection and examination have been as ineffectual as this!

There is a children's villa at Rampton. The six youngest
patients admitted to this since 1950 are, one at 5 years of age,

one at 6, two at 8, and two at 9. There are (or were at date of asking) thirteen boy and three girl inmates of the children's section.

At the other end of the scale, the oldest patient at Rampton is 86 years old and has been a patient for 21 years: while the longest stay patient has been there 38 years and is 71 years old.

Both doctors and nurses at Rampton are compelled to sign a declaration under the Official Secrets Act, even though half their charges have not at any time been convicted by the Courts.

Most of the patients in Rampton come, however, into the age group 15 to 35. Even on an official visit it is clear that they are of many varieties and grades of intelligence. They vary from the higher-grade 'psychopathic' cases to which reference has been made, to the class of definitely low-grade mentally defective young girls just learning community singing. How the régime of a single establishment can be made to fit all these types, it is difficult to say. A crazy mixed-up place full of crazy mixed-up kids!

*   *   *

Curiosity not only moved Norman Dodds and myself to ask questions, but our anxiety to see for ourselves beyond the restricted confines of an officially conducted party, impelled us to make a further visit to Rampton.

Once again, therefore, a morning in January 1958, saw us starting a pilgrimage from King's Cross—this time, however, with second class tickets, and paying our own fare. The background to our visit on this occasion was Norman's adjournment debate on Rampton on 19th December, 1957.

In this Norman had been in his most minatory form:

"I believe that there are hundreds at Rampton whom Parliament never intended should go there. . . . I am satisfied that, with the poisoned atmosphere of Rampton, we are not getting

P

proper value for our money, etc. etc." He then went on to discuss such delicate questions as those of patients' hours spent in
scrubbing.

It need hardly be said that neither Norman's remarks that I
have recorded, nor his pressing of the allegations of ill treatment,
went down well at Rampton. Indignant protests from the
Prison Officers' Association had led to an invitation to meet
their local branch, consisting of the male Rampton staff, in the
canteen at Rampton. So, after a day of discussion with the
medical staff on rather more peaceable lines, at 8 p.m. prompt
Norman and I, in the company of Mr. Frank Bellenger, M.P.
for the Bassetlaw Division in which Rampton is situated, faced
a dour-looking audience of members of the Prison Officers'
Association.

As I sat in my wicker chair at the top table, I felt some sense
of relief that my part in these particular proceedings was a
secondary one.

"It's lucky you're a chap who likes trouble," I remember
whispering to Norman, after I had surveyed our audience.

Norman had asked for trouble. Indeed he had paid his own
railway fare across half the length of England to seek trouble
out; and, need it be said that, once our meeting started, he found
it. The question of rough treatment of the inmates of Rampton
has been a rather unsatisfactory one of bitter complaint from a
diversity of sources on the one hand, and equally bitter denial
and counter-accusation of irresponsibility on the other. ("The
staff at Rampton carry out their duties with sympathy and
devotion and precious little thanks from the public.")

Far be it from me to attempt to resolve this dispute. I can,
however, definitely state that, at times, during the meeting that
January night at Rampton, I felt some relief that I was an
honoured guest and not a patient.

"I enjoyed myself thoroughly!" exclaimed Norman when,
after the bad blood of angry tempers was let out and more acute
differences resolved in the after-meeting hospitality of the

canteen, we were back in the safety of the Olde Bell Hotel, Barnby Moor.

I really believe that he did.

*   *   *

So we must leave Rampton as far as this book is concerned with these few sketchy impressions. To those who wish to know more detail, I would recommend that competent book *Sentenced Without Cause* by David Roxan, being the story of Peter Whitehead who, as we have seen, was detained in Rampton for 11 years. This book has been condemned as 'deliberately suppressing facts that would help to present a balanced picture': the answer to that is that the author has, in his ably-told story, set down all the facts made available to him.

After all, even Authority cannot have it both ways!

BACKBENCH REFORMER

I<small>N</small> the preceding chapters, we might appear to have strayed some way from the main objective of this book. This is not so, however. For, just as the symptoms of the mentally ill are frequently exaggerations of normal human traits, so, in respect of mental health legislation, it might similarly be said that it demonstrates the defects of current legislative trends in their most grotesque and pathological form. The lessons learnt from a study of it may consequently be of immense value in relation to more normal life and activity. None the less, our return to this is overdue.

The General Election of 1955 was notable for two things. The first was the achievement of the Conservative Government in being returned to office after four years of power with an increased majority. The second was a shifting of the balance as from Party to personality in the electors' favour: the personal attributes of candidates counted to a greater extent than at any time during the previous twenty-five years. Seats were won that were not expected to be won, while other seats were held that, so it had seemed, should not have been held—to the no little consternation of the psephologists.

"This will be a Parliament of individuals, a Parliament of 'chaps', " prophesied the late Walter Elliot in a forecast of the nature of the forthcoming Parliament.

Unfortunately the late Mr. Elliot proved no more right in this than had the psephologists in their calculations of electoral swings. Indeed, no Government Party of modern times has seen a higher mortality of its independent spirits. "Parliament has lost yet another of its independent spirits," I wrote in my obituary of my friend, the late Bob Crouch, in *The Times* and this was in July 1957, before yet a further landslide of resignations took place. Mostly they have gone quietly, giving discreet, sometimes incorrect, reasons for retirement. But Mr. Angus Maude is made of sterner stuff.

"Let us face this fact," wrote Angus Maude in the *Sunday Express*, before leaving for Australia, "the influence of the backbench M.P. is now almost nil. His influence on Government policy is negligible. . . . The Party machines are responsible for degrading the backbench Member to the contemptible status of the lobby-walking robot. . . . At present M.P.s spend a great many hours at Westminster that are wasted in utter futility—mostly sitting around waiting for divisions, the result of which is a foregone conclusion."

To what extent is this slightly bitter epitaph to a parliamentary career correct? The answer is that Angus Maude was nobody's fool and that his case has a certain substance. Indeed, I would appear to have supplied him with corroborative evidence.

None the less, I like to think that my personal story to some extent belies it: and that given time, persistence, and a modicum of energy, combined with concentration on a popular cause, a backbencher can on occasions move mountains. The mountains that have to be moved are not only the artificial earthworks and fortifications thrown up by the Party Whips, but also the more natural ones that lie in the way of his persuading his 600 or more fellow Members that what he has to advocate is the right thing.

Maybe, of course, I flatter myself in thinking that I have been in any way responsible for the happy denouncement of the mental health story that I have told, with its promise of revisionary legislation. Indeed, there are those who aver that I have been but a nuisance, a clog on the natural action of progressive and beneficient authority; and that I delude myself in imagining it to be anything other than a coincidence that my campaigning is to be followed by a reform of the law. (The same might also, of course, be said about my colleague, Gerald Nabarro. It might well be that the Chancellor would have reformed and simplified the purchase tax, even if Gerald Nabarro had not asked his 100 Questions pointing out its absurdities.) These are things which the reader must judge.

But to deny that Norman Dodds and I have any responsibility for mental health reform, or that Gerald Nabarro has any credit for purchase tax reform is to give Angus Maude his case.

The truth is maybe somewhere in between the two points of view. But even that is fair enough for me. I have described in *Bars and Barricades* how, in the days of so long ago, when I fought the Bury election in 1935 as a Liberal, coming as was inevitable in those days at the bottom of the poll, I went up to congratulate the late Alan Chorlton—my victorious opponent. "The trouble is," replied the late Mr. Chorlton, with a gesture of resignation, "that one can do so little when one is there."

Even such sombre words as these failed to daunt me in my endeavours and when, twenty years later, I have entered Parliament, I have been surprised, not that I can do so little, but that I have been able to do so much.

Let it not be thought, however, that this idyllic picture is entirely devoid of snags.

"Soon after he was elected, Dr. Johnson set out on a lonely campaign to draw attention to the defects in the lunacy laws. *His methods have not pleased everyone*, but although travelling on a different route, he has advocated many of the same reforms and come to the same conclusions as the Commission."

I quote my candid friends, the *Cumberland News* in an editorial at the time of the publication of the Royal Commission's Report. I owe them nothing but thanks for their candour: what they say is all too true.

What have been my methods concerning which 'not everyone' is pleased?

As I examine them in this book for the benefit of my readers, and compare them to those of a previous generation of revolutionaries I have to confess that I find myself a disappointing performer. I have not, like J. V. Stalin, robbed banks. Nor have I, like Mrs. Pankhurst, chained myself to the railings in Parliament Square. I have not even, like Jack Beckett, run off with the mace. Nor yet have I, like some of our modern would-be reformers, either been called to order by Mr. Speaker (except for the modest misdemeanour of 'reading') or been guilty of abuse of parliamentary privilege—for there is nothing that I have said in Parliament that could not equally well have been said outside. Indeed, I have said considerably more outside in my books than I have ever said in Parliament.

Unable to reveal anything further, I am left to formulate speculations from the material in my previous pages.

Of which of my actions then has 'not everyone' approved?

Have I asked a total number of between 90 and 100 Questions to a series of Ministers on the subject of mental health? Have I pressed these persistently when I have found no means of getting satisfaction over cases of serious personal injustice? Have I been critical at times? Perhaps so; and I think rightly so. But hostile—scarcely, except in the very widest interpretation of that word. Though, indeed, perhaps it was rather wicked of me to ask Mr. Dennis Vosper if he would "give the House an assurance that it is not the policy of his Department to remove people to mental hospitals merely to cure them of aggression?" as I did relative to one of the more absurd certificates that had come my way.

Have I stridden across Party barriers in this humanitarian cause and campaigned the country with Norman Dodds, the very mention of whose name must cause a shudder to run throughout our bureaucracy?

Have I indulged myself in the limelight? Have I embraced publicity with almost childish abandon? Certainly I have done so in regard to the abuses of current mental health legislation, and injustices in connection with these, as a justifiable method of attaining my end.

Have I published books and made stunts of them? Perhaps so. But in surely harmless enough fashion.

Have I failed to restrain my uninhibited and, on occasions, garrulous correspondents from writing about their own special mental health problems to prominent people from the Prime Minister, the Archbishop of Canterbury, the Lord Chancellor, the Home Secretary and the Minister of Health downwards (thus doubtless adding considerably to the burden of secretarial work for the secretaries of the secretaries of Secretaries), including their own M.P.s? (Nor have I been able to avoid it when these same garrulous people have written back to me in their uninhibited way, telling me details of their encounters with prominent folk: so that I tend to keep a private score-board of my colleagues, rating them 'high' or 'low' as to how they treat their mentally-afflicted constituents. My score-board, I should say, yields some surprising results. One or two of our old Etonians score very high marks indeed: the lowest perhaps are those shared by a non-U Tory and a Labour old Etonian.)

Have I finally—most abominable sacrilege of all and equivalent almost to the robbery of a dozen banks—MENTIONED A NAME of an aggrieved patient on B.B.C. Television? To this I must confess. Though the name of James Mills was already on the Parliamentary Order Paper in a Question by Norman Dodds weeks before I referred to him in my interview on the 'Tonight' programme following our Rampton visit.

But apart from this last, these sins which I have listed are surely venial enough, when considered separately and individually?

Perhaps therefore it is not my methods to which exception is taken so much as their cumulative effect. I am reminded of my experience during the recent War when I was appointed by Army Command to the Regional Ministry of Health with the proud and sonorous title of Medical Military Liaison Officer—

an appointment, the duties of which, in my three years of occupation of it, I never accurately discovered. My appointment was coincident with the invasion threat of 1940 and the Command which appointed me was responsible for the medical arrangement for troops defending the coastline. But, alas, all the Army ambulances had been lost at Dunkirk! This problem was conveniently solved, however, by putting the responsibility for the evacuation of coast casualties on to the civilian authorities.

Elaborate and satisfying plans reposed at Command based upon the resources that the civil authorities were presumed to possess. Unfortunately, the first letter which I received on assuming my office at the Regional Ministry was from the Medical Officer of Health of Barsetshire. It is a letter which I still remember. The gist of it was that he (the Medical Officer of Health of Barsetshire) had been vouchsafed the sight of the elaborate plans, but that he had to report that, as far as they in Barsetshire were concerned, they had not the means to fulfil them. They had no ambulances any more than had the Army. They had nothing, in fact, but some adapted farm carts. Conceiving it my duty so to do, I conscientiously relayed this vital information to Command. When next day a special summons to Command Headquarters arrived I reported there eagerly, prospects of promotion looming enticingly in front of me. But, far from the commendation which I anticipated, to my dismay I received the worst reprimand that I have ever in my life experienced. I did not, at the time, appreciate what had hit me! But, of course, from the point of view of Command, if not a traitor, then I was next door to a traitor; for what had I done other than to destroy the great and comforting illusion that someone else was looking after all the vexing problems of coast-casualty evacuation? This was, as I have said, in 1940, when I was a captain. I stayed in the same rank for the remainder of the five years of War.

Now, eighteen years later, it seems that both 'authority' and I are running to the same form. Except that you will no longer

see in my eye the bright glint of expectation of promotion, as
you might have done that day so long ago when I travelled, a
young, eager and conscientious medical administrative officer,
between Regional Ministry and Command Headquarters.

"We often see your name in the papers," beam my hopeful
friends from time to time. "You'll soon be getting a job now."
I do not dash their hopes, but if only they knew that scarcely a
mention of me in *The People*, the *Empire News* or the *Daily
Sketch* has occurred without there passing through my mind
those significant words of the poet, John Donne, "I am mine
own executioner."

Which brings us back to Mr. Angus Maude and my friends
of the *Cumberland News*.

"It will take some months for the Government to examine the
Commission's findings and to announce if they will act on them,"
continued the *Cumberland News* in the editorial to which I have
referred. "If they do, Dr. Johnson's wide experience, both
personal and gained during his campaign, will be of great
service to the Government when the Bill comes up for
examination."

The Government, as we have seen in the last chapter, has
announced through Mr. R. A. Butler, its intention to act on the
Royal Commission's findings: it is expected that the legislation
will be promoted during the 1958–9 Session: and who will be
right in regard to any part that I may play in it? Will it be the
Cumberland News: or will it, on the other hand, be Mr. Angus
Maude?

The odds, I regret to say, at this moment of writing are
heavily on Mr. Angus Maude. Certain recognition has come
my way consequent on my efforts in the sphere of mental
health reform both in the publicity and in the professional
sphere—in some cases from those who, in the light of what I
have said from time to time, might well be expected to have none
of me! I have made three appearances on T.V. programmes, I
have had the privilege of a centre page feature article in the

Observer, I have had articles in popular newspapers throughout the country, I have written for such a professional paper as *The Mental Welfare Officer*, I am asked to speak to the Annual General Meeting of the Mental Health Tutors Association, and again at the Mental Health Course of the Residential College attached to Liverpool University.

There is, however, one quarter from which no invitation has come to me to speak on Mental Health; and that is from Smith Square, the Headquarters of the Conservative Party—other than on the single occasion on which my services were specially bespoken from the constituency I visited.

Thus, by the time the Minister descends from his Sinai of Saville Row with his clauses of a new Mental Health Bill engraved, as it were, on tablets of stone, it is unlikely, judging from all previous experience, that I shall be able to alter them. Indeed, I may well be sitting as the member of a Standing Committee set to consider a White Fish Industry Bill.

Thus my work in the mental health sphere, such as it has been, is perhaps already done. It may have been only to a small extent effective. For this little effect it may be that I have sacrificed the opportunities of a political career in the higher echelons of command. I will only say that, even if it has helped by a little to alleviate the treatment of these unfortunate people whose cause I have had at heart, it has been worth while.

THOSE WHO ARE DIFFERENT

As, some years ago, one drove northwards on Route A5 one would suddenly in the midst of the peaceful country-side come upon a series of roadside signs announcing THE INN THAT IS DIFFERENT. I believe some of the signs are still there, but I seldom drive that way now.

This chapter starts with THE MAN WHO IS DIFFERENT.

The House of Commons draws to itself a wide variety of human nature and human experience. It is said that it is unsafe to talk loosely in the House of any subject, of any walk of life, or of any part of the world, as there will always be someone who will interrupt and lay just claim to expert knowledge on it. But however variegated our experiences outside and away from the House, once inside, not only in our voting, but also in the patterns of our behaviour, we are all conformists. It was that admirable king, Henry IV of France, who said that "Paris is worth a Mass"; and I am a conformist too.

We are all of us conformists, save only one. HERE (as the inn sign finally remarks) IS THE MAN WHO IS DIFFERENT. It is Captain Henry Kerby, the Conservative Member for Arundel and Shoreham. The ubiquitous presence of my friend, Harry Kerby, is a feature of our parliamentary lobbies. The unabashed and companionable loquacity with which he pursues his course, the fluence and pointedness of his questions, are only matched by his self-denying ordinance in regard to speaking in the debating chamber. Curious at this, I have made a special search of the index of Hansard to discover if Henry Kerby had, in fact, made any intervention in debate during this present parliament. I found only one single reference. This must be some pearl of wisdom, so I thought. Hurriedly, excitedly, I looked it up. It was one word. The word was "Rot!"

Henry Kerby, however, finds expression through the medium of his pen. Readers of the *Spectator*, *Time and Tide*, the *Recorder*, and of the correspondence columns of the *Daily Telegraph* will be familiar with his critical articles and letters. Great truths and flashes of brilliance appear in these slightly discursive writings.

One such letter appeared at the head of the *Daily Telegraph* correspondence column on the 18th April, 1958, under the heading of 'THE SOCIAL DISEASE': MUTUAL MIS-TRUST OF RULERS AND RULED. (The theme of the letter was hung on the reference of the Home Secretary to the spread of crime as "a social disease, so perplexing as to demand our imagination and science".)

"It is imperative to mark another and more insidious change in the life of our people," says Henry Kerby, after covering the economic position in an introductory paragraph, "that change is the gigantic growth of the Bureaucracy and the rapid deterioration in the relationship of the public with the machinery of the State and its ubiquitous operators. . . . The origin of the 'social disease' need cause no perplexity. The State itself is the fundamental cause. . . . The social disease is a cancer generated at the centre, under the very noses of the Cabinet, and spread through the land by the Bureaucracy."

To write a critical letter to the Press, to make a challenging statement in Parliament is not unlike prospecting for oil. Should one tap a well of public sentiment, the pent-up emotion comes gushing upwards in the form of letters. I have mentioned the several hundred which I have received in the course of my mental health campaign. In this instance, Harry Kerby received over eighty letters as a consequence of this single incursion into the columns of the *Daily Telegraph*—all of them saying 'more power to your elbow' and that sort of thing. I have seen these letters, and as a contrast to the ones received by me, sometimes disordered epistles written on pieces of mental hospital lavatory paper, they were all well written, many on expensive and embossed notepaper, several from those who are, or should be, the natural leaders of the community—a collection of letters such as might give food for thought in the very highest quarters in the land.

To turn again for one moment to the field of publishing: I have in front of me *Parkinson's Law*, the collection in book form of the numerous, though slightly cynical, aphorisms of Professor Northcote Parkinson. '2nd large printing before publication' reads the blurb on the front flap. In a trade in which it sometimes seems that books have virtually ceased to be bought, unless they are either technical books or half-crown paper backs; customers in large numbers are paying 12/6 for Professor Northcote Parkinson's book. Should we therefore examine the author's numerous statements rather more seriously? If so, this is what he says:

"Solemn conclaves of the wise and good," says Professor Parkinson, relative to the science of political economy, "are the mere figments of the teacher's mind."

What therefore has happened to authority in this country to disturb the relationship between 'rulers and ruled' in such a manner as Henry Kerby put in his letter, and which produced so large a response? For it is not Henry Kerby's letters by themselves that are so disconcerting as is the correspondence which they elicit from his readers. What has happened to authority that it can be guyed so successfully—and evidently also so profitably—by Professor Northcote Parkinson?

Let us examine what has happened in the construction of those vast edifices of authority that have been the inevitable concomitant of the Welfare State. If, in so doing, I seem to state the obvious, then it is because the obvious does not appear to have been readily recognizable. Still less has it been commented upon.

In the beginning, the Minister has taken, and is taking, powers from Parliament by legislation of an enabling kind. As I write these words in the quiet of the downstairs interview rooms at Westminster here they still come, grinding through on our ticker tape boards that announce ensuing business in an endless procession—bills that are going through unopposed, bills that are voted through by the Party machine, bills that have been hatching in Departments for years, bills that may even be the brain child of some private member, bills that no one except perhaps a handful of specially interested people has time to read and understand—or even the least clue to what they are all about.

We know, however, that with the mass of detail that they involve, the Minister cannot possibly be exercising all these powers personally, but that in so many instances the words 'the Minister', as they appear in an Act of Parliament, are merely the archaic synonym for his Department. This much was explained to us these many years ago by the late Lord Hewart in his book *The New Despotism*.

We must, however, go one stage further in the appreciation of the position and realize that the central Departments, be they those such as the Home Office and Ministry of Housing and Local Government still situated in Whitehall, or the Ministry of Health in Saville Row, or the Ministry of Education in Curzon Street, are unable by themselves to exercise the vast powers of the prerogative of the Welfare State—any more than an Army Command can evacuate casualties without ambulances. They, therefore, bring in the local authorities as their administrative agents: and vast and arbitrary powers over the individual, taken from Parliament, are passed over from central authority to local authority for the purpose of the latter exercising these, so often without check or hindrance, in the implementation of policy. It is, in the course of this, that liberty can be lost.

Lord Beveridge in his Report worked on a number of 'assumptions': and assumptions can be dangerous. But, in the process I have described, lies the most dangerous assumption of all. It is that local authority is wise, honest and far-seeing: whereas the fact that, in its dealings with the individual, local authority is almost always dictatorial, is sometimes capricious and is occasionally even corrupt, does not come into the reckoning. On one side, therefore, is the assumption on which the façade is based: on the other is the less prepossessing reality. In being at the receiving end of the reality, the individual has little or no defence against the capricious exercise of power by local authority—apart from, in certain matters, an appeal to a tribunal, or a ministerial inspector. If the power is power over personal liberty, sanctioned by the 'rubber stamp' of a justice's certificate, there is not always even that. "I have no power to conduct an enquiry," states the Minister concerning the case of Miss X, that I raised in the Adjournment Debate which I have reported. But where has the power gone that was originally given by Parliament? That is the mystery which we should investigate.

Let it be regarded with appropriate suspicion when the plaintive cry goes up from local authorities that "they have no powers", that they are "dictated to from Whitehall". This may be so in matters of general policy. It is not so in regard to powers over the individual.

"The poorest man in his cottage," said Lord Chatham almost two hundred years ago, "may bid defiance of all the forces of the Crown. It may be frail—its roof may shake or the winds may blow through it—the storm may enter—but the King of England cannot enter. All his force dare not cross the threshold of the ruined tenant."

In the days of medical officers of health, of duly authorized officers of local health authorities, even of planning officers and borough surveyors, this proud dictum of individual liberty no longer applies.

It did not apply, for instance, in the case of Mr. A. G. Corbin.

"Here is my case," writes Mr. A. G. Corbin, aged seventy,

now of the Salvation Army Hostel, London, E.1: "I was a
Master Mariner 'retired' and living on my own freehold smallholding since 1923. I managed to cultivate my orchard and
occupy my time by chicken farming, etc. I interfered with
nobody. I was just carrying on quietly in my own free way
when suddenly at 10.30 a.m. on 3rd March, 1951, two policemen
in uniform accompanied by their police surgeon and two other
officials appeared. I ordered them off my premises as they had
produced no official warrant for my arrest. I was then seized by
the four of these bullies, dragged outside and thrown into their
ambulance (Black Maria) and rushed by them into a madhouse."

(*"The Medical Officer of Health of this district," confirms the
official version of this incident sent me by the Clerk to the Council
in reply to my enquiry, "applied to the justices on 2nd February,
1951, for an Order under Section 47 of the National Assistance
Act, 1948, to deal with Mr. A. G. Corbin as being a person in
need of care and attention. This was granted and as a result he
was removed to hospital."*)

"I was taken from there after twenty-three days," continues
Mr. Corbin, "again under strong guard of these bullies. Flung
again into an ambulance and thrown into a bed in a horrible
madhouse amongst raving lunatics. I was there only four days.
I was again manhandled and rushed again to another madhouse
where I found I was 'certified'. I found by spying on my
'confidential report' that I was to be *permanently detained* as
being in need of care and protection, forsooth."

(*"He is sullen and resentful," reads Section 3a of the certificate
giving the complete 'facts indicating insanity' in regard to
Mr. Corbin. "He has no insight into his condition. He has no
realization of his affairs. He has persecutory delusions. These
are not substantiated. He has exalted ideas of power and wealth.
He has written to the House of Commons about his delusions.
He lacks judgment."*)

But Mr. Corbin, having sailed the seven seas, and fought the
Turk and the German in the First World War—presumably

Q

in the name of liberty—has an element of indestructibility about him. After five years' detainment in hospital, he escaped and came to London where, a fugitive from the Welfare State, he is at present lodging.

He has visited his smallholding to find his cottage demolished and his belongings dispersed. He has nothing left to him other than his entirely able-bodied frame, his lively nature and his fiery spirit, which moves him to write me letters which— *eheu fugaces!*—read just like the more ebullient type of Conservative Party propaganda of those far-off days of the late nineteen-forties.

Here lies the stuff of tragedy, not only for Mr. A. G. Corbin— but also for the Conservative Party. It is not only that the Party, having come to power on anti-bureaucratic slogans, has found itself in the hands of those same bureaucrats whom it then attacked. (Would the Minister have power to investigate the case of Mr. Corbin? I do not think so.) But also that it is frequently those fiery individualists, who were amongst its most fervent supporters when it came to power, and who are now the most aggrieved parties against bureaucratic powers, either directly or indirectly. For what has been the position of anyone seeking still to pursue with enthusiasm the tenets of Conservative faith as expressed in days of Opposition, and to right the wrongs caused by capricious and irresponsible action by officials? It surely has been that of myself of twenty years ago, the young medical officer presuming to tell the General at Command that, where the latter expected and fondly imagined there to be ambulances, there were no ambulances at all. His is the worst crime of all—that of the destruction of the illusion of perfectionism with which authority sustains itself in its delegation of powers.

Meanwhile the Minister too is limited in any given situation, not only by his laws which he must administer, but also by the customs of his administration, so that on the one hand in such enquiries as he makes, he is restricted to hearing one side of the case only, that of officials speaking in their own defence: and on the other there must be application of the whitewash brush in the noble manner performed by Parliamentary Secretaries day by day in their replies to adjournment debates, so that not even the smallest crack must appear in the veneer. For there are few examples in recent years of concessions being given to criticism, however outrageous the apparent circumstances. Indeed recent history records only one independent enquiry being appointed— that concerning Crichel Down. Immense hopes were raised by Crichel Down. We now know, however, that the Crichel Down enquiry was more of a political freak event than a landmark of our constitutional history—even if only by reason that Sir Thomas Dugdale signed his own ministerial death warrant by appointing it. It is not thus that precedents are created!

Even though the enquiries instituted by a Minister in response to a parliamentary intervention may lead to good being done by stealth in the background, even though a long series of monstrous injustices to individuals will lead eventually to a change in the law—and this is likely to happen only slowly, since both Ministers and officials need much dissuasion to discount the perfection of their own arrangements—this is still little consolation to the aggrieved individual, who from then on carries his own ethos of disaffection with him, spreading it throughout society.

*   *   *

It is the basic attitude of bureaucratic officialdom that the individual complainant can be brushed off without danger. He is, after all, just one person. He can 'create' for a time, he may gain sympathy for a time—but not for long. The Press will perhaps feature him for a day; and then forget him. His sympathizers may last a little longer; but they too will grow weary. Finally, if he persists alone, he will be classified as a paranoiac, the victim of an obsession, or otherwise mentally peculiar. He will cease to bother authority and disappear from ken.

The advantages of this attitude are conspicuous: it makes for a protected and peaceful life for all in official places and for a smoothly running routine. Above all, it makes it easier to delegate powers, if you can do so on the implied condition that you protect your delegate from the consequences of the abuse of those powers. They are, however, advantages of a selective nature in that, while they are 'total' to the permanent bureaucracy, they are partial only to those whose tenure of office depends in the last analysis on popular favour—as, for instance, that of the Ministers of a political Party in power. For such, they are short-term advantages only. For, if you are dependent on popular favour in the long term, your ability to brush off individuals successfully and without harm to yourself will essentially depend on there being only a strictly limited number of individuals so affected.

These lost powers! How many people are there aggrieved by them? How far does the disaffection and moral devastation caused by them extend?

Meet my constituent Mr. John Smith, concerning whom I have had yet another Adjournment Debate, which space alone prevents me reproducing. His grievance—that, though practising as a chiropodist in Carlisle for 22 years, he is ineligible for inclusion in the Old People's Welfare Service owing to being rejected from the Minister's list—yet the Minister is unable to intervene.

Mr. Smith is one person: but soon the circle widens.

What of the people we have noticed in this book? What of the doctor on the dole, who, in the former days of medical freedom could have fitted into medical practice, but who is now unable to find a vacancy under the National Health Service? "It is a complete misunderstanding to suggest that the Minister is responsible for ensuring that every doctor is employed," said the Parliamentary Secretary in the debate on this question. But do we carry conviction in telling a doctor on the dole that he is lucky to be living under Conservative Government, and warning him of the dangers of Socialism?

There are, of course, only thirty to forty doctors on the dole— a negligible number—but their existence at all bedevils the conditions of the humbler ranges of the medical profession, the assistants and the unestablished practitioners, now, in many cases, reconciled to the possibility of a salaried service.

What of my several hundred bitterly aggrieved mental health correspondents? Not many, until one appreciates that 18,000 to 20,000 people yearly come under compulsory mental health legislation. Do they retain a belief in the fundamentals of liberty and democracy? Certainly not in all cases. "My documents are worse than the Star Chamber records I have examined," writes my adjournment-case friend, Miss X, who happens to be a scholar of medieval history.

What of the private doctors of the Fellowship for Freedom in Medicine, promised in the days of Conservative Opposition that their privately-treated patients should have the right of receiving drugs under the National Health Service, and who still at the end of seven years are denied this owing to 'administrative difficulties'? What of general practitioners as a whole, brought into the National Health Service in 1948 by specious promises, and who, 20,000 of them throughout the country, remain unhappy in their work and restive when it has been found impossible to fulfil these promises?

There is a small body of men belonging to the Aeronautical Engineers Association on whose behalf both Henry Kerby and I have asked parliamentary questions from time to time in the early days of this Parliament. These are fitters, many of whom are employed by the Air Force at R.A.F. stations, who were brought into the aeronautical industry before the War as 'dilutees' through Government training centres on various promises of 'good jobs'. Though in many cases now employed

for twenty years or more in their jobs, they are still in a dilutee
capacity owing to agreements subsequently signed between the
Air Ministry and the powerful Amalgamated Engineering
Union: this means that they will never acquire skilled status,
that they will be dismissed prior to non-dilutees in event of
shortage of employment, and so on. Their agitation is that they
should be accepted to a proper status in their industry. "I think
it best to work through the existing machinery," replies the
Minister to any approach concerning negotiations on this.
These people, at the time of the Rochdale by-election, took a
five-inch double-column advertisement in the *Rochdale Observer*
to call attention to the professions of the Conservative Party
in Opposition, and what they considered the pusillanimous
behaviour of the Conservative Party in Government in the face
of pressure from a large Trade Union. Did anybody read this
advertisement? Did it lose votes? I don't know.

There is another body of people, the Federation of Hospital
Officers. They are formed in the main from the senior administrators of the former voluntary hospitals. In that capacity they
might be said to have a specific point of view in regard to their
pay and terms of service. Indeed it was the origin of their
Federation that, once the Health Service had started, they felt
they could only be represented in negotiations concerning these
by a separate union. Their grievance, which again I have
represented for them? It is that they were not recognized for
membership of the National Health Service Whitley Council at
the inception of the service owing, so they allege, to the bias of a
Socialist Minister of Health and 'politically-minded trade
unions'. "None," states the President of the Federation in an
article in their journal, *The Hospital Officer* of January 1955,
"felt more strongly about this than our friends on the Conservative Benches of the House of Commons. To them it
seemed a classic instance of an attempt to blackmail hospital
officers into trade unions they did not wish to join. In 1949 a
Conservative Member raised the matter in the House. A lengthy

debate ensued. The Conservatives, many prominent members amongst them, were emphatic in criticising the Minister for not remedying a situation which was so patently inequitable and unjust. But political considerations remained paramount. . . . In due course," so the account goes on, "the Conservative Government was returned to office and a new Minister of Health appointed. At once the Federation made its formal application for recognition as a national negotiating body which, if granted, would enable its members to enjoy the rights of which they had been deprived so long. . . ."

But need I go on? The Federation of Hospital Officers also has 20,000 members scattered in influential positions throughout the community.

Here, then, are the men who are different, those who cannot be fitted into the pattern of a society which, even under Conservative Government, has ceased to be flexible. Well may these people ask, "Is this the Opportunity State?" And, even if we only tot up these few instances that have come within my personal scope, we can start to formulate an idea of the range of the crisis in confidence created by allowing unchecked rein to bureaucracy and by surrendering to trade union pressure.

QUIS CUSTODIET IPSOS CUSTODES

I HAVE so far discussed powers lost to Parliament. We now come to powers that Parliament would not appear at any time to have exercised.

By the Act technically known as 2 and 3, Vict., Chapter 93, it was provided that County and District Constables be established by the authority of justices of the peace. It is this Act, now almost 120 years old, which still governs our present police organization throughout the provinces. This creates the curious situation that, whereas the Home Secretary is in direct control of the Metropolitan Police, his control stops at the boundary of the Metropolitan Police District, beyond which the Constables of Counties and County Boroughs are responsible only to the Watch Committees or Joint Watch Committees who have appointed them—and this responsibility again appears on occasions to be of a tenuous character.

It is the popular idea that Scotland Yard is a nation-wide organization, ready to swoop on the malefactor in any part of the country at a moment's notice. But this is not so. Scotland Yard is merely the headquarters of the Metropolitan Police Force. It is unable to intervene in investigating crime outside its own London Area without being called in by the Chief Constable of the County or County Borough concerned, unless the case has started in the London area.

This arrangement has, by and large, received sanction in this country owing to the general sentiment of aversion towards any form of centralized police force. Indeed, it does not seem to have been seriously questioned over the past hundred years or more, right down to the present day. It has run on the basis of the traditional standards of integrity and the high sense of responsibility of the English gentleman with which, whether country squire, successful industrialist or professional man, he had imbued any public activity he undertook, or any service for which he was responsible.

Few people will dispute that these standards of integrity and this high sense of responsibility so congenially exercised in the circumstances of a subdued provincial life in a static age, have been amongst the casualties of the social and mechanical revolutions of our time. While an even more serious consideration than the actual decay of standards, has been the abandonment of social responsibilities by the class of people who previously formed the core of the local judiciary system.

In the meantime the situation contains a curious anomaly which has been the concern of certain of my colleagues, primarily Godfrey Lagden, Conservative Member for the Hornchurch Division of Essex. This is that, whereas a Member of Parliament for one of the constituencies from either London, or its immediate vicinity within the Metropolitan Police District, can represent a constituent's grievance against the Police in the House of Commons, a Member whose constituency is outside that charmed area is unable to do so owing to the Home Secretary having no direct responsibility for the provincial police—even if, as in the case of Godfrey Lagden, his constituency is only just outside. Indeed, there are one or two Members for constituencies in the Greater London area who, owing to the arbitrary boundaries of the Metropolitan Police District, are in the extremely curious position that they can represent their constituents in the House in respect of Police grievances for a part of their constituencies, but are unable to do so in regard to the other part.

This is the situation which my ever-cheerful friend Godfrey Lagden has set himself to combat, in a running battle with Mr. Speaker, successive Home Secretaries, and other dignitaries of the House of Commons. Of somewhat Herculean physique, Godfrey Lagden has set himself a Herculean task. For nothing—repeat NOTHING—is more difficult than to get any discussion concerning the duties of Chief Constables on to the floor of the House of Commons.

Let me give an example:

"It seems reasonable that every hon. Member should have the same facilities for protecting his constituents," said Godfrey Lagden during the Adjournment Debate, in which he had raised his dissatisfaction with the position, "whether he represents a Metropolitan constituency or one in a county."

I reproduce the remainder of Godfrey's Adjournment Debate exactly as it is recorded in *Hansard*, including my own brief intervention at the end.

Mr. Speaker: If the hon. Member is complaining about the present state of the law he must realize that that can only be altered by legislation, and that debate entailing that is out of order on the Motion for the Adjournment.

Mr. Lagden: Thank you, Mr. Speaker. I am not complaining; I am merely pointing out what in point of fact exists. Every hon. Member should have the same facilities and, more important still, all the persons whom he represents should be able to expect the same protection from him as that which any other Member of this House gives to his constituents.

Let me give an example. If, say, a police-sergeant in the Metropolitan area were seen in the act of seduction by one or more witnesses and the witnesses lodged a complaint with the hon. Member who represents them here, that hon. Member should, of course, look very deeply into the matter. As their Member of Parliament he should, and probably would, report the matter to the Commissioner of the Metropolitan Police. If he were of the opinion that the Commissioner—I think this is unlikely—was attempting to whitewash the conduct of the officer he could and should bring the matter to the House, where it could be discussed. If precisely the same thing happened in a county, say in Essex, the hon. Member could not refer the matter to this House.

Mr. Speaker: Surely the hon. Member is, by inference, complaining of the existing state of the law with regard to responsibility for the Essex Constabulary, and that cannot be altered without legislation. The hon. Member has gone into this matter very thoroughly. I admit that he is doing his best, but the matter is out of order.

Mr. Lagden: I will not continue on those lines, but will conclude that part of my argument by saying that the people of Essex would in that respect be indeed badly served.

If such a state of affairs exists as that to which I have previously referred, great public disquiet must be raised. The public will feel, and do feel in some cases, I have no doubt, that by reason of existing law their Member—I do not want to transgress your Ruling, Mr. Speaker, and I am trying very hard not to—is unable to protect them. They may also feel that the shadow of suspicion is being cast upon officers where it should not be cast——

Mr. Speaker: Surely, these are all reasons why the existing law should be altered by means of legislation. I can see no drift to the hon. Member's argument other than one which is contrary to our practice with regard to debates on the Motion for the Adjournment of the House.

Mr. Lagden: I thank you very much, Mr. Speaker.

In that case I should like to refer, if I may, to what was said by an eminent Home Secretary, none other than Sir William Joynson-Hicks. I understand that these are the actual words he used in this House on 20th July, 1928, and I take it that if he used them I am in order in quoting them. He said:

"I am the servant of the House of Commons, and every action I take, every decision I come to in regard to the police, can be brought up and discussed here."—(OFFICIAL REPORT, 20th July, 1928; Vol. 220, c. 840.)

What wise words the then Home Secretary used and this evening I am trying only to suggest that in 1928, he was saying, within the rules of order, what I am trying to say tonight——

Mr. Speaker: I do not know whether Sir William Joynson-Hicks was making that speech on the Adjournment, or what comment the Speaker of the day made upon it, but the hon. Member is in this difficulty. Either he is complaining about the Essex police force, for which the Home Secretary has no responsibility—and on that assumption, of course, the debate on the matter is out of order on the Adjournment because of lack of Ministerial responsibility; or, on the other hand, he is suggesting that the Home Secretary should have responsibility for it, in which case the hon. Member is out of order, because he is suggesting legislation. These are the rules of the House.

Mr. Lagden: In that case I will conclude and, with the deepest possible respect, will ask my hon. and learned Friend to convey to the Home Secretary what he thinks I have been trying to say this evening. I thank you for your assistance in this matter, Mr. Speaker, and I am perfectly certain that our united efforts will lead my hon. and learned Friend to see that the Home Secretary knows your opinion and mine.

Dr. Donald Johnson (Carlisle): I thank my hon. Friend the Member for Hornchurch (Mr. Lagden) for allowing me two minutes of the time allotted to this debate. It was my intention, Mr. Speaker, to endorse his plea, but if I do so at any length I shall be equally out of order. I think, however, that it will be in order for me to express fears similar to those of my hon. Friend, and at the same time to bestow a word of praise in a positive manner on the Chief Constable of Carlisle for the rapidity with which he called in an outside force in our recent murder case in Carlisle, which led to a quick and satisfactory solution——

Mr. Speaker: I am afraid that praise, equally with blame, is out of order in a matter connected with a police force for which the Home Secretary is not responsible.

Dr. Johnson: I have used up my available time, Mr. Speaker.

However, a persistent person is Godfrey Lagden: and almost a year later on 27th March, 1958, it seemed that his persistence on this question of Chief Constables would be rewarded through one of the most curious coincidences that have entertained the House of Commons for many a day.

It was Thursday afternoon, the afternoon for the Home Secretary to answer Questions: and the following question, the terms of which will already be familiar, is on record.

Mr. Lagden asked the Secretary of State for the Home Department if he will consider introducing legislation to extend to the Secretary of State for the Home Department such power over Chief Constables as would seem necessary in order to enable Members of Parliament to raise Questions in the House of Commons concerning the conduct of police officers in provincial forces.

Mr. R. A. Butler: No, sir. An essential feature of our police service is that it is organized and controlled on a local basis.

Mr. Lagden: Does not the Secretary of State agree that to debar some Members of this House from the right of Questions which is enjoyed by other Members is a serious thing? Would he not look at this matter further, having regard to the matters concerning Chief Constables which have recently been before our notice?

Mr. Butler: It is an anomaly that in the case of the Metropolitan Police hon. Members have a greater power of questioning than in the case of a provincial police force, but there are many curious developments in our Constitution upon which our liberties largely depend, and I do not think it would be a good thing to have absolute uniformity in this matter.

Mr. Lagden: In view of the unsatisfactory nature of the reply, I beg to give notice that I shall raise the matter on the Adjournment at the earliest opportunity.

It seemed that Godfrey faced another abortive Adjournment Debate after the same style as the one which I have reproduced.

On that same Thursday, however, it also happened that at the end of Question Time it was the private Members' ballot for Notices on Going into Committee of Supply on the Civil Estimates—an annual event in which, by custom, for a whole day Private Members' Motions are debated. Some two hundred Members put their name down for this ballot and are given numbers which are subsequently drawn from the box by the Clerk at the Table immediately after Question Time. It is a dramatic scene (which recurs fortnightly also for the privilege of moving Resolutions on alternate Fridays) as Mr. Speaker calls out the number and the name of the Member who has drawn it. The Member then rises to announce the terms of his Motion.

But whose number was drawn first on this occasion? It was none other than that of Mr. Godfrey Lagden, who rose without delay and, to the vast amusement of the House, announced his Motion in the following terms:

Mr. Lagden: I beg to give notice that on going into Committee of Supply on the Civil Estimates I shall call attention to the powers of Chief Constables, and move a Resolution.

This was so far, so good. It was fine. But then, during the succeeding days, doubts and uncertainties started to cast their shadow. Was Godfrey's motion in order, or was it not in order? Could he possibly construct an alternative motion that would be in order at all within the terms allowed for a debate on the

Civil Estimates? An expert contortionist of words, particularly of words in regard to Chief Constables, Godfrey constructed his motion and circulated it to all those interested. But, alas, as he sat at dinner on the Thursday night, prior to the Monday set aside for the debate, a note was placed in Godfrey's hand. The note was from Mr. Speaker. His motion was finally disallowed.

Nothing daunted, Godfrey Lagden was rising to point of Order sharp when the business of the House opened the following morning: and this is what transpired.

11.7 a.m.
Mr. Godfrey Lagden (Hornchurch): On a point of order. I must ask for your guidance, Mr. Speaker, in connection with a communication which I have received from yourself about a Motion relating to the powers of Chief Constables which stands in my name on the Order Paper and which is due to come before the House on Monday. You said that the Motion goes beyond the terms of my notice. If I rephrase the Motion so that it does not go beyond the original terms of notice, may I then expect that the Motion will not be ruled out of order? If your answer to that question is in the negative, Mr. Speaker, may I receive your advice as to what machinery I can use to bring before the House of Commons any questions affecting provincial police?

(*That an enquiry is desirable into the personal powers, capacities and previous training which influence the selection and appointment of Chief Constables, having regard to their far-reaching authority and their relations with Her Majesty's inspectors of constabulary and the public in general.*)

Mr. Speaker: The hon. Member was successful in the Ballot and gave notice that he would draw attention to the powers of Chief Constables. At that time, I had doubts whether that would be an appropriate subject to discuss on Supply because of the possibility of legislation, but I had to wait until the hon. Member expanded his Motion. This he has done with great ingenuity, I must say, but, nevertheless, he has expanded it to deal with matters about the appointment and selection as well as the powers of Chief Constables. The Motion also deals with their personal qualifications. These matters go beyond the terms of his notice.

In a Motion of this sort that the hon. Member seeks to move as an Amendment in Supply there are three hurdles which he must surmount. The first is that the terms of the Amendment which he proposes to the House must be within the terms of the notice which he has given. If it exceeds those terms, it is out of order. The second hurdle is that, this being Supply, the subject raised must be one for which a Minister is responsible. The third hurdle is that the grievance must not involve legislation for its remedy.

The hon. Member fell down on the first of these hurdles. He now asks me how he can deal with the matter which he wishes to raise and, at the same time, keep in order. I know the subject matter, because the hon. Member made a most gallant but unsuccessful effort to raise it on the Adjournment on 29th May last. I remember the circumstances perfectly well.

The crux of the hon. Member's difficulty is that the control of local police forces and Chief Constables is in the hands of the local authority. It is a question of considerable controversy whether that should be changed so as to make a Minister in this House responsible for them. That would mean legislation. At present, the Home Secretary's powers do not include responsibility for local police forces.

Therefore, the only advice that I can give to the hon. Member—and I am anxious to help him to raise the matter that he wishes to raise—is that he can, of course, proceed by way of a Bill. He can ask leave to introduce a Bill under the Ten Minutes Rule, telling the House exactly what alteration in the law he desires it to make. He can put down a Motion stating again exactly what he wants the House to resolve. That would not be shackled by the prohibition against topics involving legislation or for which there is no Ministerial responsibility.

A Motion put on the Order Paper and framed in proper terms can be debated, if it succeeds in getting a place. There are still some days left for private Members' Motions, such as we have today, on a Friday. The hon. Member, if he ballots hopefully, may yet be successful.

If he were again successful, he would not be trammelled by the rule about ministerial responsibility or legislation, but he could discuss his Motion and tell the House exactly what he wanted it to resolve. Under our rules, this is not a matter which he could raise either on Supply or on the Adjournment. I have given him the best advice that I can in the matter.

Mr. Lagden: I should like to thank you very much, Mr. Speaker, for the advice that you have just given and to say that you are probably more optimistic about my luck in the Ballot than I am. Nevertheless, I shall endeavour, under one of the headings on which you have guided me this morning, to raise this matter, which is of great importance to 37 million people.

Mr. James Griffiths (Llanelly): We sympathize with the hon. Member. May I ask you, Mr. Speaker, about the powers of the Home Secretary in connection with local police forces? Did I understand you to say that the Home Secretary was the Minister responsible to the House for police forces generally, but that he had no responsibility for the powers of Chief Constables?

Mr. Speaker: The Home Secretary has certain powers. For example, he has to approve the appointments of a Chief Constable, but the selection is made by a county council or other local authority. He has certain appellate jurisdiction in disciplinary cases, that is to say, if a Chief Constable is dismissed by a county council or other local authority, the appeal lies to the Home Secretary. He has control of Her

R

Majesty's Inspectors of Police, who report to him, under
Statute, to make sure that local police forces are efficiently
conducted so as to enable the Home Secretary to authorize
the grant from central funds, which, I think, is 50 per cent,
to the police funds all over the country. However, beyond
that he has no power. He has no power in day-to-day
administration of a county police force or other local authority
police force. That lies in the hands of the local councillors,
who are elected persons, and, ultimately, in the hands of
local government electors.

*   *   *

In discussions on parliamentary procedure, important as these
are, it is inevitable that a remote and academic quality should
enter. Constitutional anomalies are by their very nature
pleasing curiosities for the researchers and professors of political
economy to discuss.

What is it like, however, to be at the receiving end of this
particularly constitutional anomaly? What of the unfortunate
individual, anxious to uphold proper moral standards in his own
affairs, who may find himself helpless and enclosed in a corrupt
provincial police set-up? This is not an outrageous or improper
question, for conspicuous examples of personal corruption in
provincial police forces have come to light in recent cases at
Brighton and at Worcester—hence the public interest taken in
Godfrey Lagden's exchanges with the Speaker which won him
the honours of a full column on the centre page of *The Times*,
and yet another on the centre page of the *Daily Telegraph*.

It is well that, before answering this question, we should
examine a Chief Constable's position. In particular, what are
those powers to which Godfrey Lagden has wished "to call
attention and move a resolution"? What makes a Chief
Constable tick?

The immediate answer is that in regard to the organization

of the Police Force, and in regard to the investigation and prosecution of crime, a Chief Constable's powers are absolute in the area of the county or the county borough in which he operates. The Home Secretary's powers are limited in the manner set out by Mr. Speaker. Nominally, as Mr. Speaker has said, a Chief Constable is responsible to a local Watch Committee, and so to local government electors, but in assessing this responsibility I suggest to my reader that, as a local government elector, he asks one of his representatives on the local Watch Committee (particularly if it happens to be a joint Watch Committee) about this and see what answer he gets. Moreover, in the days in which we live, it may well be that this responsibility to a committee of local people is one of the complications of a Chief Constable's position.

By and large, it can be taken that, in his own particular area, a Chief Constable is a law unto himself—it is he and he alone who decides what is a crime and what is not a crime. To give a simple instance; *A* who is an ordinary citizen may park his car at the kerbside and *B* who is a councillor and much respected local figure may park it a little farther along, if a Chief Constable decides that *A* has committed a traffic offence and *B* has not, his word goes. *C* may be the only prosecution witness in a case of sexual indecency involving leading citizens and, if *C*'s body is found in the canal the week-end before the hearing in the Magistrate's Court, it is up to the Chief Constable as to what extent investigations into the circumstances and causes of *C*'s death are pursued. *D* may be a corrupt police officer whose defalcations are exposed and reported to his Chief; it is for the Chief Constable alone to decide what action he should take with, on the one side, evidence he is able to discount and on the other the prestige of his Force at stake by any public exposure. *F* may be an independent bus driver savaged by strikers during a Provincial bus strike in a Labour-controlled County; the Chief Constable responsible to a Labour Watch Committee full of Trade Unionists has to decide if he will prosecute or not for a breach of the peace: or, conversely, it may be a decision on an investigation which, in a fashionable county area, may affect a prominent family.

If a criminal act occurs and a Chief Constable does not wish to see it, then it is not a crime at all: if an accident takes place in circumstances that are suspicious, the circumstances are no longer suspicious at all if the Chief Constable does not say so. Even if Chief Constables and their officers were all men of 100 per cent integrity and high moral tone, then the maxim indicated by the Latin phrase *quis custodiet ipsos custodes* (who will guard the guardians themselves?) would still apply: but, as we too well know, this is not invariably the case.

In the meantime, as Godfrey Lagden has pointed out, there are some 37 million people in this country who have no appeal to Parliament with a personal grievance against this state of affairs.

In addition, there is a still stranger anomaly than that which has already come to light. On the 13th March, 1957, the following appeared on the Order Paper.

Administration of Justice
Mrs. L. Jeger to ask the Secretary of State for the Colonies to set up an independent judicial enquiry to investigate the irregularities in the administration of justice in Cyprus to which his attention has been drawn.

One may have such opinion as one wishes of this Question. Mrs. Jeger did not get her enquiry—but no matter. The only point I wish to make is that, whereas it was possible to get this Question on the Order Paper about Cyprus, as the Secretary of State for the Colonies accepts responsibility for grievances against the Police Forces there, it would not be possible to put down a similar one about Oxfordshire, Gloucestershire, Worcestershire or any other English county—whose unfortunate 37 million inhabitants have, in this respect, rights that are inferior to those in Her Majesty's non-self-governing Colonies.

However, I am glad to report—as Stop Press News—that Godfrey Lagden's efforts in this excellent cause have not gone entirely unrewarded. It will have been gathered that I have had something of minority interest in this Question. Indeed, I had originally had a Question down to the Home Secretary on the same day as Godfrey had on 27th March, which for various extraneous reasons I postponed until Thursday, 13th May. Here it is: and, when it has been read, it may be agreed that here, too, we make little progress:

Dr. D. Johnson asked the Secretary of State for the Home Department whether he is satisfied with his present powers of investigation relative to provincial police forces; and if he will make a statement.

Mr. R. A. Butler: The responsibility for maintaining an efficient police force is placed by law on the police authority for the force. The Secretary of State's duty is to satisfy himself that this responsibility is being properly discharged. He does so on the basis of reports by Her Majesty's Inspectors of Constabulary. I do not think that any additional powers are required for this purpose.

Dr. Johnson: Is my right hon. Friend not aware of the public concern at the recent revelation in regard to the provincial police forces? In addition to his present powers, will he not also take powers to investigate complaints made by members of the public when put through their Members of Parliament? Am I not correct in saying that, for instance, in the recent Brighton case the abuses that came to light had been going on for many years before they came to a head at the trial?

Mr. Butler: I cannot comment on the two cases which are at present *sub judice*, namely, Brighton and Worcester. The case of Brighton is *sub judice* because the appeal of the Chief Constable still lies to me, as Home Secretary, and I would rather not comment pending the determination of that appeal. But I understand the anxiety on this matter, and I have made

it the subject of enquiry, with the aid of my Inspectors of
Constabulary. If a Member of Parliament wishes to put
any point to me, he has immediate access to me, and I shall
be glad to hear anything he says.

Mr. Gordon Walker: Does not the right hon. Gentleman
agree that there is here a rather difficult problem which
should be looked into, namely, that it is anomalous that this
House has ultimate responsibility for the Metropolitan Police
but no responsibility at all, as far as I can see, for other
police forces in the country? He will be aware that very
grave problems are raised in this matter. Nobody wants to
turn the whole police into a politically controlled force, but
does not he agree that there is a problem which needs enquiry?

Mr. Butler: I do not think that the problem needs enquiry,
but it exists, because the Secretary of State is primarily
responsible for the Metropolitan Police Force and area—
and it is a very large force—but has direct powers only in
certain matters relating to Chief Constables, and a certain
responsibility, through the Government, for grants. Otherwise, he is not responsible for provincial police forces.

A MATTER FOR INVESTIGATION

MY last book, *A Doctor Returns*, was concentrated on my own personal mental hospital experience. In this book I have referred to this only obliquely. I may, perhaps, therefore be forgiven if now, towards the end, I arrogate a chapter for a further stage of my own story.

Few experiences have a more transforming effect than three years in Parliament. There is nothing like a term in Parliament, with the personal prestige that it brings, for inflating the ego—and no ego has been in greater need of inflation than mine. Thus, there is one difference in me as I am now and as I remember myself at the beginning of this book, a diffident new entry to Parliament, namely that I am purged of any lingering sense of grievance. It is only unfortunate that, out of the nature of things, all those people who have had experiences so similar to mine, are unable to undergo so esoteric a cure.

I have, as I write this, few reasons to be dissatisfied with my lot. I am thankful to be able to count life's blessings. While for the rest, I have learnt, like my old friend S.P.B. Mais, to thrive on trouble. I am able therefore to look on that other person that was me, the person who sought to enter Parliament and three years ago by the greatest good luck succeeded in doing so, the person even who published *A Doctor Returns* two years ago, with a sense of detachment—as if at a specimen in a glass case.

Here I am, or rather there I was—the specimen, the perfect specimen of the aggrieved and rejected person. At the University it has ever been the summit of achievement to be a Triple Blue;

champagne does not reach the highest quality unless it be *triple sec*, so this is I—or, at least, this was I—trebly aggrieved and trebly rejected, and, in this capacity, my own star case for the purpose of emphasizing the general thesis of this book.

Was it not I—that other I—who on that epoch-making day in the country town of X——, in October 1950, quite suddenly fell within a three-ringed circus of authority? So that when I look back—and indeed I can still look back in anger, as well as looking back in gratitude to Providence for the manner in which everything that I hold dear was rescued from the brink of ruin—I often feel an unworthy affinity with Daniel, who came through the lion's den unscathed, with Shadrach, Meshach and Abednego, who emerged unharmed from the burning, fiery furnace.

What were the three rings that encompassed me?

The first one was that of our antiquated and hopelessly slipshod mental laws according to which, without enquiry either precedent or subsequent, I was picked up from the pavement outside my own premises, pitchforked into a waiting car and driven off to the nearest mental hospital, there to be deposited under certificate in the refractory ward.

The second one was formed by the iron curtain of professional silence which descends when there is any possibility of a medical mistake having been made, particularly a mistake under the lunacy law. "Should a doctor tell?" No question of a doctor telling arises when there is doubt as to the diagnosis on a certificate of unsoundness of mind.

In *A Doctor Returns*, I wrote of my difficulties in obtaining any elucidation of my case. As, some two years later, I read my remarks over again, I am slightly horrified to find how closely they resemble in tone the letters of those who now write to me in my capacity as M.P.—remarks which professional colleagues tend so unhesitatingly and so glibly, to class as 'paranoiac'! It is, however, no longer revolutionary doctrine to state that our present legal and administrative system creates mental disease rather than cures it! Nor is it any longer a heretical statement to suggest that errors may occur when one single doctor is allowed the power of certification under the lunacy laws. When this matter last came up in the House of Commons at Question Time, far from being any longer a lone voice, I was unable to get in myself with a supplementary question owing to other Members wanting to make themselves heard. These deplorable laws are, as we have seen, now due for revision: I am glad to think I may have played some part in this.

I have shown, too, in *A Doctor Returns* how the whole great British National Health Service, the proudest boast of our country, could apparently not produce anyone who was either willing or able to diagnose my condition.

Fortunately, in regard to this too, there is a happier story to tell. In *A Doctor Returns*, in describing the effects of the drugs known as hallucinogenic drugs and the similarity of these to my illness, I refer to certain interesting experiments at the Weyburn Hospital, Saskatchewan. In due course my book, through the medium of my Canadian agents, reached Saskatchewan: whither it had been preceded by my small publication *The Hallucinogenic Drugs*, which, though derided in the medical Press at home, had, I am pleased to report, impressed these transatlantic researchers. Here it came into the hands of Dr. Humphry Osmond, Medical Superintendent of the Weyburn Hospital, who is one of those younger doctors to whom I have referred in a previous chapter as emigrating from Great Britain to Canada to find that opportunity denied under the National Health Service in their own native country. At the Weyburn Hospital, Saskatchewan, he has been engaged these several years in research into the psychomimetic (insanity-simulating) drugs. At the end of six years my story had travelled half-way round the world and here, at last, was someone both able and willing to give an independent opinion on my case, free from the inhibitions of working under the National Health. Service—the employer of almost all the doctors in this country

Humphry Osmond's feature on *A Doctor Returns* was published
in the December number of *Twentieth Century* under the title of
A Doctor Goes Mad. Here are the relevant extracts.

What happened to Dr. and Mrs. Johnson that week-end
almost seven years ago? While interpretations vary with
the viewpoint of the observer, the facts seem to be well
established. It appears that on a week-end in October 1950
while staying in a hotel, both Dr. and Mrs. Johnson suddenly
and simultaneously went mad. They had extensive distur-
bances in perception, thinking and mood, and became
convinced that they had been poisoned by some ill-wisher
who had managed to plant microphones in their room.
After various vicissitudes, Dr. Johnson found himself
certified as insane, while Mrs. Johnson, whose symptons
seem to have been very similar, though their duration proved
to be less, was allowed rather mysteriously to remain with her
relatives. She became well in about a week or ten days. He
took between six and eight weeks to recover. The general
practitioner who certified Dr. Johnson, the hospital where
he was treated and the Ministry of Health's psychiatric
advisers are apparently satisfied that he suffered from a brief
psychotic episode, presumably of a schizophrenic type.
He himself believes that he and his wife were poisoned
maliciously by a substance whose qualities resemble those of
hashish and datura mixed—a favourite prescription of the
devotees of thugee. After leaving hospital he sought advice
from learned counsel as to whether there were any steps that
he might take to clear his name and was advised that without
the Ministry of Health's co-operation there was nothing that
could be done. The Ministry proved reluctant to admit that
he could have been poisoned. He wrote a book on hashish
and suggested that something of the sort could happen. The
reviewers, particularly in the British Medical Press, were
openly scornful and emphasized that doctors would never

confuse an intoxication of this sort with a mental illness. One is glad to know they have such confidence in their colleagues. Their faith is touching.

His main complaint is that he could have been easily admitted to a general hospital psychiatric unit, where he would not have required certification, that he did not have access to his solicitor soon enough, that his wife was not told that she could have taken him home sooner had she been able to do so and, above all, that no one listened to his complaint that he and she had been poisoned. There seems no doubt that they each suffered a brief and severe madness. How did this come about? So far as I can judge there are three possibilities. They both may have developed acute, simultaneous, psychotic episodes of short duration. As neither of them had been afflicted in this manner before or since, this is very odd. Another possibility is that Mrs. Johnson suffered what is called a *folie à deux*—though not herself mentally ill, she became influenced to act as she did because she was disturbed by her husband's behaviour. It is unusual for such *folies* to develop as rapidly as this one is said to have done, though I have once seen one occur extremely quickly in identical twins, but what to my mind goes strongly against this is that Mrs. Johnson seems to have remained seriously ill several days after her husband had been taken to hospital. I feel that the *folie à deux* theory is difficult to support. Thirdly, of course, they could have been poisoned. Now there are poisonings and poisonings. Dr. Johnson's choice is for a deliberate, malicious and highly sophisticated attempt on his sanity and well-being.

Could the medical men who cared for him have made what must sound such an appalling diagnostic howler? It seems quite possible to me. Indeed, seven years ago I would have made just the same howler (if they did make it) and would have stood by my error just as tenaciously as they have done. I don't believe they are either ignorant or blameworthy, but as so often happens, nature may have played an unpleasant trick on the Johnsons which mislead their medical advisers. Doctors are never too keen to make public admissions even of the possibility of error, particularly when their patient is a fellow doctor. This reluctance is not lessened by his being both a publisher and a Member of Parliament.

The Johnsons could have been poisoned in three ways. They could have taken drugs themselves—either by design or accident, there is no evidence of this. Certain drugs could have been administered to them secretly by an enemy, which is what Dr. Johnson believes, though again he produces no supporting evidence. Lastly, they could have been poisoned accidentally.

Do we know any substance which could produce a prolonged psychotic disturbance of this sort? We do not. But we do know the sort of substance which could do exactly this. Naturally we can't prove that they took any such thing, but again we can't prove that they didn't. In 1950, even had someone looked for such a poison, it would not have been found.

In the last five years my colleagues of the Saskatchewan Schizophrenia Research Group with scientists in other centres all over the world have been pursuing substances which reproduce to a greater or lesser extent those symptoms from which the Johnsons suffered.

* * *

"Certain drugs," says Dr. Osmond, "could have been administered to them secretly by an enemy, which is what Dr. Johnson believes, though again he produces no supporting evidence."

My additional evidence—a full and exact description of the circumstances of our illness, omitted from *A Doctor Returns* for reasons of discretion, had been written into my previous book, *Bars and Barricades*, published in 1952. Copies of *Bars and Barricades* are still available for those who wish to obtain them. There was terrible talk of libel when *Bars and Barricades* was produced, but *Bars and Barricades* has stood the test of time and has now been in print unchallenged all but seven years.

I need only generalize in my present remarks. In a recent trial, in which the defendant, a person of some high authority in the community, had been acquitted of the charges against him, the judge remarked of him, none the less, that he had "failed to give moral leadership". It might be said that, in the year of our Lord nineteen hundred and fifty, our country town lacked moral leadership. In the declining years of the Socialist Government, the black market in food—which rotted the moral fibre of the community in the same manner as Prohibition did in America—was rife throughout all our agricultural districts. I do not of necessity regard it a matter for severe moral censure that alcoholic drinks should be served and drunk after 10 p.m. in a licensed establishment: it may well be, however, that this apparently venial offence is a symptom of a deeper moral decay, as it was in the establishment known as 'The Bucket of Blood' at Brighton. Did I, in 1950, in my country town hotel—of which I have, of course, written in *Bars and Barricades*—have a 'Bucket of Blood' on my hands? I do not know. I only know what subsequently happened when, disturbed at certain irregularities, I decided to keep a closer watch on these premises than the monthly visit I had been paying it hitherto.

Earlier in this chapter I referred to three rings of authority and described two of them. What, therefore, is my third ring of authority that still encloses me?

It is surely none other than Godfrey Lagden's old-fashioned system of Chief Constables.

For, naturally, it is my view that an investigation of the circumstances might well have yielded fruitful results.

"Your complaint has been carefully reviewed," states the

Deputy Chief Constable of the county in a letter of recent date, "and the Chief Constable is still of the opinion that there is insufficient evidence to justify further action by the Police."

There is no appeal against this decision.

What, therefore, if Betty and I were poisoned in October 1950, was the causative agent of our poisoning? In what context did it take place? In the absence of thorough and authoritative investigation we can at least indulge in enlightened and perhaps entertaining speculation.

I have developed previously the most obvious theory that occurred to me, namely that I was poisoned in a deliberate attempt to render me insane by a mixture of indian hemp, datura and opium—not quite the mixture you would expect to find in the centre of England but, on the other hand, you never know at a time when the indian hemp traffic thrives apace. Even a play (*Poison Unsuspect* by Ivan Butler) has been written round this thesis.

It was only at the end of seven years that an alternative theory saw the light of day. In the interval between the writing of his *Twentieth Century* account and its appearance in print, in August 1957, Dr. Osmond and his colleague, Dr. Abram Hoffer, Director of Psychiatric Services for the Province of Saskatchewan, during a visit to England, called at our Sutton home to spend an evening with Betty and myself.

After these many years of neglect it was flattering indeed to us to be the subject of interest and enquiry on the part of these two wise men from afar.

As we sat and talked in our upstairs flat, we amplified our evidence in the way desired, while Humphry Osmond, with his almost uncanny resemblance in appearance, manner and voice to Lord Hailsham, and Abram Hoffer, a spare and lanky son of the prairie Province, expatiated on the remarkable progress they had made in the exciting branch of knowledge they had made their own—with the object, no less, of ultimately finding a biochemical cause to schizophrenia.

It was with some pride we found ourselves categoried amongst their constellation of cases for special study—a study that still proceeds. At last we were famous cases, as these many years ago my doctor friend Herbert, who had shown us so much kindness in our early days of bewilderment, had prophesied we would be!

One of our mysteries, one of the pieces of the jig-saw that had not fitted, had been the fact that, though the incident with the glass of sherry, the glass intended wholly for me, but of which Betty had also accidentally taken two or three sips, had occurred on the Tuesday, our abnormal mental symptoms had not ensued until the Friday and Saturday. It was explained to us how the class of substances which they were investigating—adrenochrome, for instance (and Abram Hoffer took a small tube of red crystals from his pocket as he spoke and proudly displayed them, telling us that it was the first time they had been isolated chemically)—had the curious property of being taken up by the corpuscles of the blood stream and then gradually being released into the system over a period, some days later. An ideal substance for delayed poisoning! Though, of course, the sherry was a pure guess on our part: any chance of proving it was the sherry is long past and it is just one of many possible vehicles for the poison that might have been used.

But what connection had these substances, and these experiments, to do with us, poisoned at a hotel in a small country town?

"Possibly an agricultural insecticide?" said Abram Hoffer. "Have you thought of these? There have been some pretty complex substances put out in recent years."

"And pretty deadly ones," rejoined Humphry Osmond. "You have not considered, I suppose, that you might have been the victims of an attempt at murder, from the full effects of which you would have been saved, partly by your wife taking, by accident, some of the dose intended for you, and partly through your excess body-weight, through which you would need a larger dose than the average for it to be effective. It's rather more straightforward than an insanity-producing trick, you know."

Agricultural insecticide! I had certainly not thought of this. Careless of me! For there is every reason why I should have done. Here was something very much more near-at-home than an exotic plot by an Eastern drug.

Of course, I should have thought of agricultural insecticides many years previously when I investigated the curious epidemic of madness that occurred at the town of Pont Saint Esprit ('the mad village') in the south of France in August 1951, when some thirty people went mad after eating bread from the same baker. I have told in *Bars and Barricades* how I had discovered the extraordinary similarity between the symptoms of the poisoned people of Pont Saint Esprit and those shown by Betty and myself during our illness. Then, since this was my theory and I meant to stick to it, I represented in that book, and continued to represent with some obstinacy in other books, that the cause of this epidemic was indian hemp and similar vegetable substances. The official verdict, on the other hand, sanctioned by highly expert opinion was that the cause was a poisonous chemical weedkiller which had found its way into the bread.

It is now my duty to give way to this official verdict and, since my talk with Drs. Osmond and Hoffer a year ago, I have bent my curiosity towards digging out knowledge concerning the highly complex chemical substances which are used as insecticides and weedkillers by means of spraying on crops. ("Is the Minister aware that potatoes are tasting like mothballs?" asked Norman Dodds recently.) Developed since the War, so toxic to man have these proved that in 1951 a Working Party composed of Professor Solly Zuckermann and other highly respected members of the Agricultural Establishment reported with a view "to making recommendations for the promotion of the safety of workers in the agricultural use of substances which are toxic or harmful to human beings". In the report of this Working

Party, there is instanced the substance D.N.C. or dinitro-ortho-cresol, a weedkiller with which no less than 300,000 acres were sprayed in 1950. "It is known," says the Report of the Working Party, "that seven agricultural workers have died as a result of D.N.C. poisoning in Great Britain since 1946."

Dangerous stuff! However I cannot expand this book to cover every aspect of the toxicity of chemical fertilizers as they affect our food, or our wild life. The concern caused by this is ably put forward by other authors.

Nor have I space to reproduce the complex chemical formulas revealed when I asked the Minister of Agriculture a question as to what were the composition of the principal substances used in this way.

It is also known, however, that on the 2nd and 3rd May, 1956, there was another epidemic of poisoning at Pontardawe, South Wales, attributable to the eating of bread from contaminated flour. No less than 59 cases of poisoning were notified, the symptoms varying with the amount of bread consumed. Half of these people became unconscious and developed sudden fits lasting several minutes, with recovery of consciousness in a quarter to half an hour. Less acute cases suffered from dizziness, weakness, abdominal discomfort and nausea. The contaminant was identified as endrine, a weedkiller.

But let me return to the evening of the visit of the two Saskatchewan doctors to our home in Sutton in September of 1957. As, at the end of this, I talked with Humphry Osmond on our walk down to the station together (Hoffer had gone back to London earlier in the evening), I recounted once more how, in my search for parallel cases to my own, in investigating unusual cases of insanity—certification throughout the country, I had virtually drawn a blank.

"Maybe," suggested my mentor, "we have been looking for insane people, when we should be looking for dead people in graveyards throughout the countryside."

Maybe so!

s

"This is a complex business," writes Humphry Osmond at a later date, "but it is extremely unlikely, to my way of thinking, that potent chemicals exist without someone using them feloniously. If there was no record of this happening one would begin to suspect that, for one reason or other, they were being overlooked."

I agree with Humphry Osmond. Even poisons which produce such obvious symptoms as arsenic and strychnine are not only used, but even used repetitiously by the same person, in this country.

A better example comes, however, from Australia, a country of equal civilization to our own.

Until quite recently it was possible in Australia to buy without difficulty a rat poison known as Thall-rat whose active principle is the metal, thallium. Thallium is also a poison to the human frame. It acts in shocking and terrible ways, rotting the fibres of the nervous system so that the victim becomes blind and paralysed before death finally occurs. Despite this, little general attention was given to the possibilities of Thall-rat as a poisoning agent, until a number of fatal poisonings had taken place.

The first poisoning which came to light was on 23rd March, 1952, when a male person (married) died at the Royal Prince Alfred Hospital, Sydney, aged 27 years. A post mortem examination was conducted and organs from the body were submitted to the Government Analyst who received information that the victim may have been partaking of food which contained rat poison. A further examination then revealed the presence of thallium in the organs.

The wife of the deceased was subsequently charged with the murder, not only of this husband but also of her first husband who died with similar symptoms on the 29th July, 1948. On the 21st April, 1952, the coffin containing the remains of her first husband was exhumed and again thallium was detected in the remains.

This case naturally received wide publicity following the arrest, the committal and the death sentence being recorded against the woman poisoner. The publicity caused further police investigations which revealed that five other persons had also met their deaths by the felonious administration of thallium prior to the above-mentioned case being discovered.

There were, in all, no less than nine cases of fatal poisoning by Thall-rat known in the State of New South Wales. They were of widespread location and the victims were mainly inconvenient relatives.

In one instance the perpetrator was a middle-aged woman who was always regarded as a kindly person, ever ready to assist any relatives or friends. She is known to have poisoned four persons and attempted to poison another with thallium. Her victims were relatives and friends and for what purposes she poisoned them was never definitely established. She was not mentally disordered, did not appear to be vindictive, and her slight monetary gain was practically of no consequence.

There is, after all, nothing like police investigations—if you can get them started, that is. Obviously any case of poisoning can only be enquired into, consequent on complaints of friends and relatives in the first place.

As this book is published, Humphry Osmond continues his report for submission in due course to a psychiatric journal of high repute. He writes in his last letter to me: "Few would quarrel with the point of view that, if two people simultaneously develop florid psychotic symptoms, and if their friends deny (as yours do!) that they are regular and determined drunks or druggers, then the very least that one should ask is a rigorous, determined and persistent public health enquiry."

I shall look forward therefore, when it appears, to sending Humphry Osmond's report to the Minister of Health, who at last, I should add, in the person of Mr. Derek Walker-Smith, has been kind enough to release my notes for the confidential inspection of Dr. Osmond for the purpose of his studies.

IS THERE A GIANT SLAYER IN THE HOUSE?

M Y story, as far as it concerns the general political and parliamentary scene, stopped at the Suez crisis at the end of my tenth chapter.

What has happened since then?

Many of the problems of which I have written are less accentuated today: generally, our affairs are being conducted with greater wisdom. The blaze of discontent against the Government in the country has subsided, though it cannot yet be said whether the revival of fortunes is temporary or permanent.

Whichever it may be, a big factor in the recent increase in Government support has been its new firmness in the face of Trade Union demands. Simultaneously with this, my firm published *A Giant's Strength*, written by a group of Conservative lawyers. The Giant is the Trade Union Movement and, according to this booklet, the Trade Unions constitute a new estate of the realm whose powers have grown to the extent which calls for them to be checked, as in their day did the powers of the kings, the barons, the great landowners and the capitalists.

Have we, however, another giant to slay?

It is the argument of my own book that we have.

This is the bureaucracy which has expanded under the aegis of the welfare state so that it infiltrates all aspects of our national life with the power of the Establishment—which will, moreover, if it continues unchecked, grow further until, as in Soviet Russia, none will be able to go anywhere or to do anything unless sponsored by some form of Establishment organization.

Meanwhile, with the shift of power to Government offices, Parliament will degenerate in the manner predicted by its critics, prominent amongst whom are former M.P.s who have retired. Thus, Christopher Hollis, writing in the *Spectator* in his article 'The Sickness of Parliament' and commenting upon the two Party machines, talks of the "unreal issues of a dead past", and alleges that "never have men differed more and more about less and less", while Sir Hartley Shawcross simultaneously declares that there is "far too much sham fighting about irrelevant trivialities".

Like many arresting political commentaries, these perhaps need qualifying. Despite our social changes, one glance at the House of Commons will still show the 'two nations' of Disraeli on either side, though the outlines are becoming blurred. Yet even in the House of Commons we now and then glimpse two other nations showing themselves, those of the Established and the Un-established—those who have come to terms with the new dispensation of the Planned Society, and those who, for one reason or the other, have not. Did we do so, for instance, in the debate on the Report of the Royal Commission on the Law relating to Mental Illness in July 1957? This was not, in the nature of things, a Party debate. Yet an even stanger difference of opinion occurred in which we conspicuously saw the two opposite front benches combining in support of the Establishment against critical backbenchers on either side such as Norman Dodds and myself. Hansard quotes me as follows:

"When one tries to look at the Report from a detached point of view, what inevitably strikes one is the revolutionary nature of the recommendations as compared with the general mildness of its criticism of the existing system. I think any newcomer to this House listening to the opening speeches of this debate, would wonder whether there was any necessity to make changes at all."

I referred to the speeches made by Mr. John Vaughan-Morgan on the one side of the House speaking for the Government and Dr. Edith Summerskill speaking for the Opposition on the other, both of identical tone. Indeed, the extraordinary 'Establishment' speech of Dr. Edith Summerskill on this occasion ("I agree with the Parliamentary Secretary about sensational publicity. I deplore it," said Dr. Summerskill) led to the resignation from the Labour Party of that old-timer, Mr. Hannen Swaffer, by way of protest. I have allowed Mr. Kenneth Robinson, also a member of the Opposition, to speak for himself during the course of this book.

*   *   *

What can a Conservative Government do to counter such criticisms as I have quoted?

First the nature of the problem must be appreciated. Just as generals fight a war in terms of the previous one, so does a community tend to solve its social problems in the terms of a previous generation. In our case these terms were those of an upper and middle class of substantial wealth on one side contrasted with a class of low-paid slum dwellers on the other. The immediate injustices have been corrected by remedial Welfare State legislation: but this legislation has shown an inability to adjust itself to the social changes that have simultaneously taken place. Thus we have, bespattered throughout council estates, people whose earnings are at super-tax level enjoying the advantage of housing subsidies, based on legislation for the housing of the poor: just as we have earnest people plying well-fed mothers and children with orange juice and cod-liver oil, originally intended as a corrective for the low vitamin diet of a partially starved and poverty-stricken population— and so endangering them with the condition of hyper vitaminosis, or excess of vitamin intake, rather than the reverse.

In parallel with this, just as we have originally needed the authority of the Welfare State as our ally, so do we now suffer from a hypervitaminosis of authority, in regard to which the need is now for a fresh and different view. In the contest to maintain the balance between the State (or at least the government machine, be it central or local) and the individual, whereas the task of the first part of the twentieth century was to curb the excesses of rugged individualism bred by the capitalist system, that of the second part is equally to curb the excess of governmental power and to inculcate the principles and the ways of a liberal society into a newly prosperous population.

With this thesis there is perhaps general agreement. But who, as Mr. Hugh Fraser said in the Suez Debate, who is going to bell the cat? If the Conservative Party cannot do this in Government, who is going to do it?

It is the feeling that Parliament is not working as it might do, that exists even amongst M.P.s, which has led to the appointment of a Committee to consider Parliamentary Procedure. Many beneficial suggestions will be put up to this Committee, which, if implemented, will alleviate some of the major inconveniences that afflict us. But I personally am doubtful whether it is parliamentary procedure that is at fault: indeed it is the one remaining thing that protects the individual member.

The essential need is not so much for a review of parliamentary procedure, as for a review of the exercise of authority as a whole in the light of its vast extension in a changing age.

Starting with Parliament, to what extent is the accusation justified that too much happens behind the scenes, not only in Party committees (which is inevitable and which is no longer always secret anyway), but also in Government departments?

To what extent is it desirable that Departmental Committees should exercise an over-riding influence in the framing of governmental policy, to the exclusion of those who are presumably elected for that purpose, so that in respect of legislation

Parliament tends to be presented with *faits accomplis*, which then become law by the automatic action of the Party majorities? Even though the apparent secrecy of this process is attributable rather to the complexity and the devious nature of its working than anything else: and this book may have shown that many of these secrets are capable of being unravelled by those who delve into them.

To maintain the calibre of M.P.s it is important that back-benchers, particularly Government backbenchers, should be given the opportunity of constructive work. Therefore, finally and most importantly, to what extent is the system of depart-mental and bureaucratic power aided and abetted by the custom of regarding every phrase and every comma of a Bill as a vote of confidence in the Government as a whole? For, as I have endeavoured to indicate, there is probably nothing that stultifies us in Parliament more than this.

In my introductory remarks I contrasted the Parliament in which I found myself in and Parliament as I had imagined it to be in the days of my youth. I speculated whether or not the imaginations of my youth were correct. I have now to report that, though this was unbeknown to me when I wrote, my impressions were not erroneous. Whatever may be the differ-ences otherwise between the Parliaments of forty years ago and the Parliaments of today, certainly a greater elasticity of voting was one of them.

An examination of the working of the House forty years ago shows, most surprisingly, the comparatively small number of occasions on which the House divided at all as compared with today. It also reveals that considerable cross-voting took place and that individual M.P.s could vote against their own Parties on issues of major importance without being disciplined or even without very much comment being elicited by their doing so. A few of these instances are reproduced in Appendix II. There are many more and, though these refer to an era of Liberal Government, they must be regarded more as a 'period piece' than the prerogative of any one Party or Government—the cross-voting was as common amongst Unionists as amongst Liberals, and doubtless took place under the preceding Unionist Government.

An incident that invites comparison in particular was when, on Monday, 20th July, 1908, there was an uproar in the House when Mr. H. C. Lea (Liberal) disclosed that he had been asked to refrain from speaking by the Liberal Whip in order to expedite proceedings in the Government for the day. Back-benchers were, indeed, made of sterner stuff in those days!

These were, of course, the days before the complexities of the Welfare State, before, too, the way of life of our whole society was in dispute owing to the rise of socialism. None the less, one cannot help wondering whether, now that the issues between the Parties are narrowing, we might revert with benefit to the customs of a more leisurely age.

From here we must proceed to consider the actual exercise of authority. With perhaps good reason, an excess of centralized authority has been the 'bogey' as it were of the liberal tradition. Yet the danger to liberty today is less from centralism than it is from the capricious exercise of authority by those to whom the power on the spot has been delegated without proper control. It is this last that should be our concern. Whether it be administrative authority from the Town Hall, or executive authority by police officers, we have too many people in our community who are a 'law unto themselves' as a consequence of the individual citizen having inadequate protection against powers that have been over-confidently delegated. Legislation based on the Franks Report on Tribunals is being introduced as these words are written. But we need to go further—the need is for a meticulous review of the whole structure of the Welfare State to discover where the powers of local officials impinge on the individual and to find the appropriate remedy.

The few cases quoted in this book are only examples of the

many that clutter my files, which in turn take up every bit of shelf room in my private office.

One of the more enlightened spirits in the House of Commons is that of young Mr. Anthony Wedgwood Benn. (Mr. Benn, incidentally, has promoted a debate on the problem of the public relations of authority that has dealt, albeit superficially, with the problem I have posed.) A brain child of Mr. Wedgwood Benn's during the present term of Parliament has been the Human Rights Bill which lies in its present state in print as one of these worthy Bills awaiting adoption by some Member who has been fortunate enough to secure a place in the Ballot—or alternatively perhaps by a sufficiently enlightened Government. It is also sponsored, as one might expect, by Mr. Fenner Brockway and Mrs. Barbara Castle.

This excellent Bill represents itself as an enabling bill conferring power to establish Human Rights Commissions throughout territories under British control. A schedule to the Bill proclaims amongst other things:

All are equal before the law and are entitled without any discrimination to equal protection of the law. All are entitled to equal protection against any discrimination in violation of this Declaration and against any incitement to such discrimination.

No one shall be subjected to arbitrary interference with his privacy, family, home or correspondence, nor to attacks upon his honour and reputation. Everyone has the right to the protection of the law against such interference or attacks.

A Second Schedule gives a list of the territories to which the Act should apply. This is an imposing list of territories. There is only one curious omission—namely the United Kingdom of Great Britain and Northern Ireland. In the meantime, even this short book contains instances of violation of the two articles which I have quoted, occurring, not amongst black or brown people, in Asia or in Africa, but amongst white people in provincial England.

As this book goes to press in the middle of July, 1958, once again the lobbies of Westminster are electrified with startling news from the Middle East.

"Another Suez?" runs the query from mouth to mouth amongst Members of both sides of the House of Commons as the possibility of intervention in Middle East affairs is discussed.

In some ways, indeed, it is another Suez, but a more subdued Suez, a more sensible Suez, indicating that lessons have been learned, perhaps on both sides of the House—that, on the Labour side, amongst a large number anyway, it has been learned that policies of Appeasement alone will get us nowhere, while on our Conservative side it has been learned that we need a policy of equal dynamism to compete with the forces of Nasser's so-called 'Arab nationalism' on the one hand and Russian Communism on the other.

Need it be said that such a policy should be one of freedom, liberal democracy and Rule of Law, based of course on economic welfare. Such a formula as this has been intoned many thousands of times. Yet, despite our protestations, it would seem as if we had largely failed and it is proper to ask if we have not failed abroad in upholding the tenets of a free society because we have failed at home.

I again refer to our satirists, that amusing and recently published book *The Barford Cat Affair*, by P. H. H. Bryan:

"In Barford," says Mr. Bryan, or at least one of Mr. Bryan's cats, "the Local Government Official is the nearest thing to God, perhaps even a shade above in Housing and Education, and a citizen who addresses one without suitable deference is apt to have his daughter whisked away to a mental defective home before the echo of his disrespectful words has died away."

While such words can be written, even in jest, about our home affairs, we can scarcely call ourselves free. Should we not, therefore, after the Stalinist precedent, 'build Freedom in a single country' before we start to attempt to export it: should we not have a Human Rights Bill to ensure that liberty is the same for all, in Burnley as well as Basutoland, in Oxfordshire as well as Uganda?

Whether, of course, I shall still myself be a Doctor in Parliament to see any part of this is, in the nature of things, still a matter for further speculation. I cannot say more than that it will be my continuing endeavour so to be.

APPENDIX I

Written Answer, Col. 32 Hansard Report, 4th June, 1954

N.H.S. (Working Parties and Committees)

Dr. D. Johnson asked the Minister of Health to give the names of the members of the eleven working parties and committees who are due to report on different aspects of the National Health Service.

Mr. Turton : Following is the information:

Mileage Committee

E. Cassleton Elliott, Esq., C.B.E., F.S.A.A. (Chairman).
S. H. Bennett, Esq., A.C.I.I.
A. Brown, Esq., M.B., Ch.B.
R. J. Buckland, Esq.
A. J. F. Danielli, Esq., C.B.E., M.C.
C. F. R. Killick, Esq., M.B., Ch.B
W. S. MacDonald, Esq., M.C., M.B., B.Ch.
W. J. Mottram, Esq.
E. J. Rees, Esq., M.R.C.S., L.R.C.P.
J. A. Speed, Esq., O.B.E.
T. Williams, Esq., F.C.I.I.

Committee of Inquiry on the Rehabilitation of Disabled Persons

The Rt. Hon. Lord Piercy, C.B.E. (Chairman).
Brigadier J. A. Barraclough, C.M.G., D.S.O., O.B.E., M.C.
R. Bray, Esq., C.B.
Sir Claude Frankau, C.B.E., D.S.O., M.S., F.R.C.S.
Anthony Greenwood, Esq. M.P.
Dame Florence Hancock, D.B.E.
H. L. Ludgate, Esq., C.B.E.
Dr. C. G. Magee, C.B.E., F.R.C.P.
E. Pater, Esq., C.B.
A. B. Taylor, Esq.
Miss J. Hope Wallace.
H. St. John Wilson, Esq., C.B.E.

Working Party on the Recruitment and Training of Health Visitors

Sir Wilson Jameson, G.B.E., K.C.B., M.D., F.R.C.P. (Chairman).
A. Beauchamp, Esq., O.B.E., M.B., Ch.B., M.R.C.S., L.R.C.P.
Alderman Mrs. K. Chambers, C.B.E., LL.D., J.P.
Miss E. W. Himsworth, R.C.N., S.C.M., Q.N., H.V.
Miss E. Stephenson, S.R.N., R.F.N., S.C.M., H.V.
F. Warin, Esq., M.D., D.P.H.

Committee on Hospital Supplies

Sir Frederick Messer, C.B.E., J.P., M.P. (Chairman).
Alderman A. F. Bradbeer, J.P.
Professor Sir Henry Cohen, J.P., M.D., D.Sc., LL.D., F.R.C.P., F.F.R.
P. H. Constable, Esq., M.A.
Sir Basil Gibson, C.B.E., J.P.
The Hon. Sir Arthur Howard, K.B.E., C.V.O.
H. Lesser, Esq., C.B.E.
Sir George Martin, K.B.E., LL.D., J.P.
T. E. Parker, Esq.
F. S. Stancliffe, Esq.
Captain J. E. Stone, C.B.E., M.C., F.S.A.A.

Joint Sub-Committee on the Control of Dangerous Drugs and Poisons in Hospitals

Miss J. Aitken, C.B.E., M.D., F.R.C.P. (Chairman).
Sir Ernest Rock Carling, M.B., F.R.C.S., F.R.C.P., LL.D., F.F.R.
Miss K. G. Douglas, S.R.N., S.C.M.
Miss B. N. Fawkes, S.R.N., S.C.M
C. R. Jolly, Esq., F.H.A., A.R.San.I.
J. B. Lloyd, Esq., M.P.S.
W. G. Masefield, Esq., C.B.E., M.R.C.S., L.R.C.P., D.P.M.
S. C. Merivale, Esq., M.A., F.H.A.
Miss A. E. A. Squibbs, S.R.N.
W. Trillwood, Esq., M.P.S.
J. H. Wood, Esq., M.P.S.

Study Group on Maintenance of Building Plant and Grounds

A. R. W. Bavin, Esq. (Chairman).
L. T. Davis, Esq., A.M.I.E.E., A.M.I.Mech.E.
A. Roberts, Esq., A.R.I.B.A.
W. H. Evans, Esq., A.M.I.Mech.E.
C. M. Ker, Esq., O.B.E.
C. F. Scott, Esq., A.R.I.B.A.
A. L. A. West, Esq., F.I.M.T.A., F.H.A.

Committee on Medical Manpower

Rt. Hon. Henry Willink, M.C., Q.C. (Chairman).
J. T. Baldwin, Esq., M.B., Ch.B.
Sir Harold Boldero, D.M., F.R.C.P.
Sir John Charles, M.D., F.R.C.P., D.P.H.
Professor Sir Henry Cohen, M.D., F.R.C.P., J.P.
Sir Andrew Davidson, M.D., F.R.C.P.Ed., D.P.H.
A. B. Davies, Esq., M.B., Ch.B.
J. P. Dodds, Esq., C.B.
Professor Sir Geoffrey Jefferson, C.B.E., M.S., F.R.C.P., F.R.C.S., F.R.S.
L. G. K. Starke, Esq., C.B.E., F.I.A.
A. B. Taylor, Esq., D.Litt.

285

Committee on Recruitment to the Dental Profession

The Rt. Hon. Lord McNair, C.B.E., Q.C., F.B.A., LL.D. (Chairman).
J. E. H. Duckworth, Esq., M.C., L.D.S., R.C.S.(Eng.).
Sir Wilfred Fish, C.B.E., M.D., Ch.B., F.D.S.R.C.S.(Eng.), D.D.Sc., D.Sc.
C. E. Gittins, Esq., M.A.
I. D. McIntosh, Esq., M.A.
G. R. Moxon, Esq.
Mrs. Mary Stocks, B.Sc.
A. P. Thomson, Esq., M.C., M.D., F.R.C.P.
J. L. Trainer, Esq., L.D.S.R.C.S.(Edin), L.R.C.P.(Edin.), L.R.C.S.(Edin.), L.R.F.P. and S.(Glas.).
R. O. Walker, Esq., L.D.S., H.D.D.(Edin.), F.D.S.R.C.S.(Eng.), L.R.C.P.(Edin.), L.R.C.S.(Edin.), L.R.F.P. and S.(Glas.).
F. C. Wilkinson, Esq., M.D., Ch.B., B.D.S., D.D.Sc., M.Sc., F.D.S.R.C.S.(Eng.).

Working Party on Social Workers

Dr. Eileen Younghusband, C.B.E., LL.D., J.P., (Chairman).
R. Huws Jones, Esq., M.A., B.Sc. (Econ.).
Miss Robina Addis.
Mr. C. G. T. Berridge.
Dr. Peter Crawford McKinlay, M.D. (Edin.).
Professor A. B. Semple, V.R.D., M.D., D.P.H.
Mrs. P. E. Steed.
Miss E. Swallow.
P. S. Taylor, Esq., M.A.
Mr. T. Tinto.

Study Group on Application of Electronic Devices to Hospital Accounts and Costing

W. O. Chatterton, Esq., C.B.E. (Chairman).
N. Hollens, Esq.
J. Wrigley, Esq.
F. S. Adams, Esq., A.I.M.T.A., A.S.A.A.
S. F. King, Esq.
G. McLachlan, Esq.
C. Montacute, Esq., LL.B., D.P.A. (Lond), F.I.M.T.A., F.H.A.
J. W. D. Rowlandson, Esq., A.C.A.
R. Stacey, Esq., M.B.E., F.I.M.T.A., A.A.C.C.A.
Captain J. E. Stone, C.B.E., M.C., F.S.A.A.
H. W. White, Esq., A.H.A., F.C.C.S., A.I.C.A., F.S.A.A.

Committee on Maternity Services

The Earl of Cranbrook, C.B.E. (Chairman).
Dr. A. Beauchamp, O.B.E., M.B., Ch.B, M.R.C.S., L.R.C.P.
Mr. G. F. Gibberd, M.S., F.R.C.S., L.R.C.P., F.R.C.O.G.
Sir Basil Gibson, C.B.E., J.P.
Dr. W. V. Howells, O.B.E., M.B., B.Ch, M.R.C.S., L.R.C.P.
Dr. Jean Mackintosh, M.D., Ch.B., D.P.H, D.P.A.
Mr. H. J. Malkin, M.D., F.R.C.S. (Ed.), F.R.C.O.G.
Lady Pakenham.
Miss V. Shand, S.R.N., S.C.M., M.T.D.
Dr. J. Forest Smith, F.R.C.P., M.R.C.S.
Miss M. Williams, S.R.N., S.C.M., M.T.D.
Mrs. Geoffrey Wilson.

APPENDIX II

*Examples of cross-voting in Parliamentary divisions
during the years 1907–12*

1907. June. 20 Liberals voted for the Conservative amendment
to Asquith's resolution proposing a reduction in the power of
the House of Lords.

1907. July. 4 Liberals voted with the Unionists against the
provision in the Budget continuing the duty on sugar.

1907. On the Unionist *motion of censure* on the Government
for failing to give Imperial Preference—1 Unionist voted with
the Liberals and 10 abstained.

1908. May. At the end of the four-day debate on the Government's Licensing Bill Second Reading—5 Liberals voted with
the Unionists against the Bill. Every Unionist representative
for an Irish constituency voted with the Liberals.

1908. June. On the Second Reading of the Government
Education Bill—3 Liberals voted with the Unionists.

1908. June. 12 Liberals voted against the Foreign Office vote.

On the Budget that year, several Unionists consistently voted
against their Party's amendments to the Finance Bill.

1909. February. Several Unionists voted against their own
amendment to the King's Speech on tariffs.

1909. Two Liberals voted for a motion of no confidence in
their own Government.

1909. Mr. John Ellis (Liberal) moved an amendment to reduce
the Navy Estimates by £100. 41 Liberals voted for this amendment (many abstained): 11 Labour men voted for the amendment and 5 against it. All Unionists voted for the Government.

1909. On the Third Reading of the Finance Bill, Austen Chamberlain moved rejection. He was supported in the lobbies by 2 Liberals and one Irish Nationalist and 4 Liberals and 10 Irish Nationalists abstained.

1910. We find two Liberals opposing their own Chief Whip when he moved the writ for a by-election in East Dorset, on the grounds that the Liberal candidature had been so corrupt at the General Election that the election of a new Member should wait until the new session! 22 other Liberals voted for this suggestion.

On a vote on women's suffrage the parties divided as follows:

	for	*against*
Liberal	161	60
Labour	31	2
Unionist	87	113
Irish Nationalist	20	14

1912. On the Third Reading of the Welsh Disestablishment Bill, two Liberals voted against the Government and many abstained.

1912. On the Irish Home Rule Bill Second Reading, one Liberal voted against and one abstained.

1912. Mr. Agar-Robartes, a Liberal, took four other Liberals and the whole of the Unionist Party with him into the lobby to vote for his amendment to exclude four counties from the provisions of the Home Rule Bill.

1911. Throughout the Committee Stage of the controverial Insurance Bill to set up the medical panel system, Liberal M.P.s were voting for Conservative amendments, while many Unionists were supporting the Government against their own Party.

On the Third Reading of the Insurance Bill, 11 Unionists defied Mr. Bonar Law and voted with the Government.